Functioning of Administrative Judiciary in the Context of Economic Changes

Ius, Lex et Res Publica
Studies in Law, Philosophy and Political Cultures

Edited by Barbara Janusz-Pohl and Anna Jaron

Volume 34

Dominik J. Gajewski (ed.)

Functioning of Administrative Judiciary in the Context of Economic Changes

PETER LANG

Berlin - Bruxelles - Chennai - Lausanne - New York - Oxford

Bibliographic Information published by the Deutsche Nationalbibliothek
The Deutsche Nationalbibliothek lists this publication in the Deutsche Nationalbibliografie; detailed bibliographic data is available in the internet at http://dnb.d-nb.de.

Library of Congress Cataloging-in-Publication Data
A CIP catalog record for this book has been applied for at the Library of Congress.

This monography is the result of scientific research carried out as part of the grant from the National Science Centre Poland on "Tax authorities and administrative courts during the business cycle - Law&Economics perspective" – OPUS 15 (No. 2018/29/B/HS5/00260).

Cover illustration: Courtesy of Benjamin Ben Chaim.

ISSN 2191-3250
ISBN 978-3-631-91911-8 (Print)
E-ISBN 978-3-631-92308-5 (E-Book)
E-ISBN 978-3-631-92309-2 (E-PUB)
DOI 10.3726/b22076

Published by Peter Lang GmbH, Berlin, Deutschland

info@peterlang.com - www.peterlang.com

This publication has been peer reviewed.
www.peterlang.com

Table of Contents

List of Abbreviations

CBOIS	Centralna Baza Orteza i Informacji o Sprawach – Central Database of Case Law and Case Information in an anonymised version available at https://orzeczenia.nsa.gov.pl
FC	the Financial Chamber of the SAC
EC	the Economic Chamber of the SAC
GAC	the General Administrative Chamber of the SAC
SAC	the Supreme Administrative Court
TO	Act of 29 August 1997 on the Tax Ordinance (Journal of Laws of 1997 No. 137, item 926, as amended)
RIA	Regulatory Impact Assessment
PbAC	Act of 30 August 2002 on Law on Proceedings before Administrative Courts (Journal of Laws of 2002 No. 153, item 1270, as amended)
SoAC	Act of 25 July 2002 on the System of Administrative Courts (Journal of Laws of 2002 No. 153, item 1269, as amended)
FIAC	First Instance Administrative Court

Dominik J. Gajewski (SGH Warsaw School of Economics)

Introduction

The claim about the key importance of the so-called institutional environment for the economic development of a state falls within the canons of modern economics.

On the theoretical level, the achievements of such trends as the new institutional economics or the economic analysis of law have contributed to the above; while their representatives – G. Becker, R.H. Coase, D.C. North, G.A. Akerlof, O.E. Williamson, O. Hart, and B. Holmström – have been awarded the Sveriges Riksbank Prizes in Economic Sciences in Memory of Alfred Nobel in economic sciences.

At the practical level, this consensus is reflected in the activity of international organisations, e.g., the World Bank, aimed at advancing institutional reforms in areas such as good governance and the rule of law.

However, the fact that the economics appreciated the importance of legal institutions in such a way and the jurisprudence developed the postulate of "external integration of legal sciences" has not eliminated the problems faced by multidisciplinary research projects at the interface of law and economics. In particular, the crucial issues are the level of detail of analyses and the preferred tools (i.e., qualitative versus quantitative).

In the approach characteristic of the economics, analyses are carried out from a bird's eye view, on a significantly general level with attempts to quantify complex legal concepts (or, in fact, ideas drawn from the philosophy of law, such as the "rule of law" or "judicial independence") in the form of indices. The key category seems to be the "typical" state that under given circumstances of time and place can be considered the norm.

On the other hand, the approach traditionally attributed to lawyers is dominated by focus on detail, e.g., on a specific legal institution functioning in a given branch of law. Qualitative tools are preferred, if the research problem defined in a such a way, including in empirical studies (e.g., case law analyses indented to answer the question of how a given institution functions in judicial practice). Exception becomes of immense significance in such an approach as even a single judgement deviating from the established line of case law calls for analysis precisely because it opens up previously undiscovered horizons of interpretation.

This study is a summary of a research project that was intended to overcome this type of "particularities" of both of these disciplines. At the heart of the project, there is an institution of great importance for both the citizens and the enterprises – and thus an important component of the institutional environment of the economy – namely, the administrative judiciary.[1]

The history of the Polish administrative judiciary dates back to the times of the Congress Kingdom of Poland and 2022 marks the 100th anniversary of the establishment of the Supreme Administrative Tribunal (SAT) in the Second Polish Republic (SPR). The administrative judiciary has functioned within the framework of its modern system composed of sixteen Regional Administrative Courts (RACs) and the Supreme Administrative Court (SAC) for 18 years.

During this period, the administrative courts, which were exercising control over the legitimacy of public administration activities, including as regards collection of public levies, faced numerous challenges. Poland's accession to the European Union (EU) and advancement of convergence processes have altered the Polish economy, which also affected the entities that were parties to court and administrative cases. The economy was subject to cyclical fluctuations as well. Public administration, including tax administration, underwent reforms in an attempt to solve problems such as the so-called VAT gap. Finally, the administrative judiciary itself has developed, for example as a result of computerisation.

This study attempts to analyse these processes from an interdisciplinary perspective. Its purpose is to present the administrative court system as a public institution in a specific economic context. Namely, the analysis is performed against the background of the economy, which serves as an environment for the entities interacting with administrative bodies to operate in (while the interactions sometimes take the form of disputes settled by the courts).

The starting point is inquiry into the history and reforms of administrative courts. It presents the administrative judiciary in terms of its dynamics and evolution as an institution created and transformed under specific social and political conditions, which was charged with particular tasks and designed in accordance with the current scientific trends.

---

1 The project carried out under the direction of Professor D.J. Gajewski, which is entitled "Organy podatkowe i sądy administracyjne a zmiany koniunktury gospodarczej – perspektywa ekonomicznej analizy prawa" [Tax Authorities and Administrative Courts versus Economic Changes – the Perspective of Economic Analysis of Law], was financed with the funds provided by the National Science Centre, grant No. 2018/29/B/HS5/00260.

In this context, the publication provides a statistical picture of the operation of administrative courts, which is organised around two categories that can be equated with the economic categories of "supply" of and "demand" for judicial settlement of disputes with public administration. The measure of "demand" is, obviously, the number of cases brought before administrative courts, which fall within different categories. The measure of "supply" – or rather the administrative judiciary's organisational capacity to exercise the right to trial expressed in Article 45 of the Constitution of the Republic of Poland of 1997 – is the effectiveness of the courts. The study uses aggregated statistical data from the period 2004 to 2021. Therefore, it presents findings affected by the first period of the COVID-19 pandemic and its impact on the functioning of administrative courts.

The next chapter analyses selected tax cases[2] based on individual data: details collected at the level of individual court judgements. The aim is to outline the course of an administrative court dispute starting from the strictly economic domain (i.e., an event that has occurred within the framework of economic trade) through interaction with public administration (i.e., issuing a tax decision) to the stage of a court dispute. Thus, the functioning of administrative courts as a component of the institutional environment of the economy is illustrated. The analysis is complemented by another chapter that attempts to move from the level of the number of cases on to their monetary "value" (i.e., the amount of the challenged claim) based on the example of VAT cases.

The study ends with three chapters devoted to the administrative courts' interpretation of the law. The first one analyses interpretative strategies adopted in the so-called difficult cases. Based on the selected examples, the chapter shows how the dialogue between the SAC and the Constitutional Court shapes resolution of complex tax law issues. The second chapter describes the use of information available in the so-called Regulatory Impact Assessments (RIAs) – which have been introduced into the Polish law-making process in order to improve its rationality (among others, with economic tools) in accordance with the paradigm of evidence-based public policymaking – in the process of purposeful and functional interpretation of the law. The next and final chapter contains an analysis of the impact of the preliminary ruling procedure applied by administrative courts on the consideration of economic reality in the process of interpreting tax law. It made it possible to answer whether and how the dialogue with the CJEU shapes the jurisprudence of administrative courts in relation to changing economic realities.

---

2 They are concerned with excise duty and VAT due to the number of cases and its fluctuations over the period under examination.

Roman Hauser (Adam Mickiewicz University, Poznan)

Marta Szustkiewicz

1. Judicial Control of Public Administration as a Component of the Institutional Environment of the Economy

Abstract: Independent administrative courts control the public administration and assess lawfulness of operation of the authorities responsible for i.a. crucial issues concerning the economy (fiscal policy, economic activity, and customs control). In Poland, the administrative judiciary has undergone transformations which is a consequence of historical conditions. After World War II, the administrative judiciary did not exist. In the 1970s, due to an increasingly difficult economic climate, the preparation of regulations establishing judicial review of administrative decisions has started. It resulted in the adoption of the Act of 31 January 1980 on the Supreme Administrative Court and Amendments to the Act on Code of Administrative Procedure. This law led to the establishment of the Supreme Administrative Court. Another turning point for defining the role of the administrative judiciary was year 1997, which is the year of adoption of the Constitution. As a result of implementation of the constitutional provisions, Regional Administrative Courts were established (as first-instance courts) as well as the Supreme Administrative Court.

Keywords: Supreme Administrative Court, voivodeship administrative courts, Constitution, cassation appeal, resolution of the Supreme Administrative Court, computerisation

> *(...) A State governed by the rule of law is inextricably welded with the institution of the administrative judiciary as there is no rule of law without administrative judiciary just as there is no administrative judiciary without the rule of law, therefore, it is in the most vital interest of the science of both political and administrative law to instil this awareness into the society for what follows from it – what has to follow – is not just knowledge, but also understanding of the law.*[1]
>
> *J. Langrod*

1 J. Langrod, *Zarys sądownictwa administracyjnego ze szczególnym uwzględnieniem sądownictwa administracyjnego w Polsce*, Warszawa 1925, p. 6.

Introduction

The activities of public authorities and administrative bodies exert a significant impact on the condition of the economy. Among other things, the way public institutions exercise their competences defined in the law influences economic outcomes. Within the limits of their statutory powers, institutions may establish specific regulations, impose obligations, and set out procedural rules allowing the exercise of these powers and restrictions. It is thus of paramount importance to have an effective and impartial system of law in place as well as independent courts, including administrative courts, which are capable of enforcing the regulations that are laid down.[2]

Administrative courts are authorised to assess the legitimacy of the activities carried out by the authorities that are responsible, among other things, for the tax policy, operation of business entities, and other such vital matters for the state. Therefore, when assessing the actions of the administration, the administrative courts must properly balance the private interest of the citizen (including, e.g., the taxpayer) against the public interest represented by the authorities. In this context, immense significance is assumed by the fundamental principle that administrative courts must be independent of the executive authority that they control. Otherwise, they would be unable to reliably assess whether an authority's action falls within the law. Resolving conflicts between state interest and fiscal interest can be assessed as a component of the policy on the entrepreneurs. One should also bear in mind that administrative courts shape the way the law is interpreted and applied by public authorities (and in this respect, the resolutions of the SAC explaining complex and ambiguous legal issues are paramount. The resolutions of the SAC harmonise court case law, put views on cases with disparate judgements in order or guide decisions in important and complicated cases). Due to the high rank of administrative courts, their judgements are crucial not only for the parties to the proceedings, but also for all the participants in legal transactions. Administrative courts consider cases of considerable importance and complexity; the regional administrative court is, in principle, the third and the Supreme Administrative Court is the fourth state authority that decides a specific case (after the first and second instance administrative bodies). This may suggest that administrative courts are expected to handle the most complicated cases. In such cases, the discretionary power of an independent

2 D.C. North, *Instytucje, ideologia a wyniki gospodarcze*, Forum Obywatelskiego Rozwoju, Warszawa 2007, https://for.org.pl/upload/File/Instytucje_%20ideologia_%20i_%20wyniki_%20gospodarcze1.pdf (accessed on: 5.11.2022).

judge manifested as arrival at an appropriate decision plays a particular role.[3] It is also worth emphasising that besides significantly affecting the business practice, the case law of administrative courts is binding on tax authorities and taxpayers in individual cases. In addition, the judgements issued often lead to legislative changes, which may clarify vague provisions of the law. The views expressed in the judgements or resolutions of the SAC are not sources of the law, but due to the authority of the Supreme Administrative Court, the textual, systemic, and functional interpretation contained therein may prove useful when it comes to interpreting the provisions of tax law.[4]

While controlling the activities of administrative bodies, administrative courts often stress that effective administration should successfully respond to the emerging social and economic challenges as well as skilfully use the available knowledge and experience to improve the quality of its operation.

As far as the citizens and other legal entities are concerned, effective administration means, among other things, simplifying procedures and improving quality of service. From the point of view of the citizen, effective public administration is one that does what is expected of good governance. The Preamble to the Constitution of the Republic of Poland indicates that the purpose of its establishment is to "guarantee civil rights and ensure the reliability and efficiency of public institutions." The Constitution, therefore, obliges the authorities to act efficiently and the citizens have the right to demand that this obligation be fulfilled.[5]

1.1. Nature of Administrative Judiciary

Administrative law is a vast, dynamic, and multi-level branch of the law. The norms of administrative law are largely influenced by the structure of the ministries. In addition, owing to the significant legislative competences of the local government, there are also local particularities in effect apart from the ministerial ones. The very essence of the administrative-legal relationship

3 See more in: D. Galligan, M. Matczak, *Strategie orzekania sądowego. Raport opracowany w ramach programu Sprawne Państwo*, Ernst &Young, Warszawa 2005.

4 A. Mudrecki, *Główne problemy występujące w podatkach dochodowych na tle orzecznictwa sądów administracyjnych*, „Annales Universitatis Mariae Curie-Skłodowska" 2016, sectio H, vol. L 1.

5 A. Gołębiowska, B. Zientarski, *Efektywność działania administracji publicznej w Polsce*, w: *Prawo do dobrej administracji jako prawo podstawowe o randze konstytucyjnej*, Warszawa 2016, s. 11.

poses the risk of subjectivity in applying the law as the authority is not only a party to the proceedings, but it is itself also entitled to imperiously shape the position of the other party. Thus, the administrative judiciary serves an important function in the system of the authorities of a state ruled by law. Its operation is fuelled by the conviction that the rights *ratione personae* of the individual in the sphere of public law need to be protected. This necessity mainly arises from the ubiquity of the administration in social life and the risk that its bodies might dominate over the citizen. When dealing with specific administrative cases, the authority manifests the characteristics of both a party to the proceedings and an arbitrator deciding about the rights and obligations of the individual on behalf of the state. When passing judgement on the legal situation of an individual, the authority always occupies a dominant position. This violation of the equality of parties' rights disappears, however, at the stage of court proceedings where an independent court decides a dispute between an individual and an authority. Control exercised by the administrative courts covers issues related to the process of applying the law, that is, whether the administrative authority has made accurate findings as to the validity of the applicable legal norm; whether it has correctly interpreted that norm; whether it has not breached the principles for proving certain facts; and whether it has caused appropriate consequences to follow from the established facts.[6]

The very principle of the rule of law requires that the administrative judiciary exist and exercise justice. The apex of the rule of law in a state is the existence of administrative judiciary as only the latter can guarantee that the administration comply with the law.[7] It is also important to create appropriate conditions that arise from the provisions of the law, which a party may use to defend itself against interference from public administration. Such interference of public administration bodies may be within their competence and thus might *ex officio* impose obligations on the individual. Therefore, everyone enjoys the right to demand that an administrative case be examined and finally resolved by a court independent of other state bodies and political parties and which is subject only to the Constitution and an act of law.[8]

---

6 J. Borkowski, J. Jendrośka, R. Orzechowski, A. Zieliński, *Kodeks postępowania administracyjnego. Komentarz*, Warszawa 1985, p. 281.

7 J. Borkowski, *Kodyfikacja postępowania administracyjnego w Polsce*, „Studia Prawno-Ekonomiczne" 1983, Vol. XXX, p. 40.

8 L. Wiśniewski, *Gwarancje praw i wolności człowieka i obywatela w przyszłej konstytucji*, w: *Prawa, wolności i obowiązki człowieka i obywatela w nowej polskiej konstytucji*, Poznań 1990, pp. 72–73.

The administrative judiciary has undergone a fundamental evolution since its reactivation in 1980. In the very first judgements, the judges pointed out that within the structure of the state bodies (even in a non-democratic state), the court protects the citizen from the authority of public administration. The views presented in the case law, and in particular the principle that only a generally applicable legal norm may be the basis for judgements interfering with the civil rights and freedoms, have paved the way to the formation of the current model of administrative judiciary whose status is derived from the Constitution.

The main intention behind the establishment of administrative courts was to create such state bodies that would primarily take care of safeguarding the rights *ratione personae* of the individual and only secondarily protect the objective legal order. The scope of activity of public administration is very broad and covers a significant portion of social and economic life.[9] Performance of administrative functions is the basic method of managing a modern state. In this context, the administrative judiciary plays an essential role in protecting the rights and freedoms of the individual as well as securing the rule of law and shaping the standards of legal culture.

The above-mentioned protection is particularly important in the sphere of public law as far as the relationship between the individual and state bodies is concerned, which by its very nature is characterized by the state bodies holding the position of power.[10] The operation of administrative judiciary in modern democratic countries is a legal standard adopted by civilised nations. The addressee of a given administrative act (or the complainant challenging failure to act or lengthy proceedings) has the option of asking an independent court to check the action (or failure to act and length of the proceedings) of the administration according to the standard of compliance with the law. A dispute over the legitimacy of an act is settled in court proceedings built on the principle of equality of the parties (i.e., the addressee of the act and the administrative authority) and the principle of having instance-based court proceedings.[11]

The basic function (or nature) of judicial control of administration should be associated with the defects in the legal forms of operation of the administration.

---

9 R. Hauser, *Dziesięciolecie przekształceń ustrojowych Naczelnego Sądu Administracyjnego i jego orzecznictwa*, „Samorząd Terytorialny" 2000, No. 1–2, p. 30.

10 J. Trzciński, *Sądownictwo administracyjne jako gwarant ochrony wolności i praw jednostki*, w:] A. Szmyt (ed.), *Trzecia władza, sądy i trybunały w Polsce*, Gdańsk 2008, p. 129.

11 R. Hauser, *Sądownictwo administracyjne w przyszłej konstytucji*, „RPEiS" 1995, No. 2, p. 59.

The authorities applying the law within the framework of the administrative relationship implement the rule of law while weighing the interests of the general public against the interests of the individual, so the authorities' actions must be effectively controlled by the administrative court. Entities involved in legal transactions should be guaranteed an effective mechanism protecting their rights and freedoms in disputes with state administration.[12] The nature of the functioning of the administrative judiciary should be inferred from the relevant constitutional regulations. Pursuant to Article 2 of the Constitution of the Republic of Poland, the Republic of Poland is a democratic legal state adhering to the principles of social justice. This provision of the law establishes a formal relationship between the state and the law and indicates that the state and its bodies are subject to relevant legal regulations; in accordance with Article 7 of the Constitution of the Republic of Poland, public authorities operate on the basis and within the limits of the law. Compliance of administrative authorities and other entities performing public functions with the rule of law is primarily ensured by administrative courts.[13]

The existence of judicial control of administration also results from international regulations, that is, Article 14 of the International Covenant on Civil and Political Rights (ICCPR)[14] and Article 41(1) and (2) of the Charter of Fundamental Rights of the European Union, which imposes an obligation on EU bodies and institutions to ensure that citizens are heard before any action that might have a negative impact on their situation is taken, have access to case files, and may learn the reasons behind a decision.

The Polish system of judicial control over the administration is also in line with the recommendations arising from the "soft law," that is, the recommendations of the Committee of Ministers of the Council of Europe. First and foremost, Recommendation No. 20 of 2004 on Judicial Review of Administrative Acts[15] is important in this respect, because it provides for certain standards arising, in particular, from Article 6 of the European Convention on Human Rights

12 B. Adamiak, *Model sądownictwa administracyjnego a funkcje sądownictwa administracyjnego*, in: J. Stelmasiak, J. Niczyporuk, S. Fundowicz (ed.), *Polski model sądownictwa administracyjnego*, Lublin 2003, p. 16.

13 L. Garlicki, *Polskie prawo konstytucyjne. Zarys wykładu*, Warszawa 2009, p. 58.

14 All men are equal before courts and tribunals. Everyone has the right to a fair and public trial before an independent and impartial court.

15 Recommendation Rec(2004)20 of the Committee of Ministers to member states on judicial review of administrative acts, https://rm.coe.int/09000016805db3f4 (accessed on: 5/11/2022).

(ECHR) and the case law of the European Court of Human Rights (ECtHR) regarding administrative disputes.[16]

1.2. Development of Administrative Judiciary

According to J. Starościak, the point of departure for the institution of judicial control of administration was the desire to establish a special institution ensuring protection of the rights *ratione personae* of the individual. Later, this institution also started to be seen as a form of securing the objective legal order.[17] However, J. Borkowski emphasises that the tradition of judicial control of administration in Poland is long, but "continuity and uniformity of legislative solutions were lacking, which neither contributed to the consolidation of the model of judicial control of administration in legislative practice and public awareness nor helped assign it a permanent value in terms of control of compliance of public administration with the law."[18] The Polish administrative judiciary has undergone numerous transformations; it has been reformed, dissolved or reconfigured, which resulted from complicated historical conditions (such as the need to unify the legal systems after the partitions, the war, reactivation attempts after World War II, the period of the Polish People's Republic, the beginnings of court activity under the socialist regime or adjustment of court organisation to constitutional requirements).

After World War II, despite what the provisions of the Small Constitution of 1992[19] initially foreshadowed, the administrative judiciary existing during the Second Polish Republic has not been reactivated. Although Article 26 of the Small Constitution stipulated that "A separate act of law shall establish the scope and mode of operation of the authorities competent to decide on the legitimacy of administrative acts in the sphere of public administration" – this provision has not been implemented. It was not until after 1956 (after the October Thaw of 1956) that the initiative to restore the administrative judiciary was born; to this end, a team was organised within the Codification Commission at the Ministry of Justice to draft the relevant act of law. The team chaired by Prof.

---

16 H. Izdebski, *Sądownictwo administracyjne w Europie*, „ZNSA" 2007, No. 4.

17 E. Iserzon, J. Starościak, *Prawo administracyjne w zarysie*, Warszawa 1959, p. 225.

18 J. Borkowski, *Reforma polskiego sądownictwa administracyjnego*, „Państwo i Prawo" 2002, No. 5.

19 Constitutional Act of 19 February 1947 on the Regime and Scope of Operation of the Supreme Authorities of the Republic of Poland (Journal of Laws No. 18, item 71, as amended).

S. Rozmaryn was put together on 17 December 1956. Prof. M. Zimmermann was the main policy officer for the draft and Prof. J. Litwin was the policy co-officer. The team created the final version of the draft on 31 December 1957, however, as a result of the decision of the authorities of the Polish People's Republic, further work on the project was discontinued. Resumption of the administrative courts' operation was only made possible in 1980 due to the partial support of the political establishment that saw administrative judiciary as a chance to defuse social tensions between the authorities and the citizens and streamline the operation of state administration.[20] Owing to the pressure of the festering socio-political situation and the economic crisis, legislative work was launched in 1977 on a new draft providing for the establishment of administrative courts.[21] The draft law was prepared by a team of experts at the Chancellery of the Sejm as well as a Subcommittee on the Code of Administrative Procedure chaired by the member of parliament Prof. S. Zawadzki. The team chaired by the Head of the Chancellery of the Sejm consisted of, among others, Prof. J. Borkowski, Prof. W. Dawidowicz, Z. Janowicz, PhD, Prof. J. Jendrośka, and M. Wyrzykowski, PhD. During the lengthy legislative work[22], the main goal of the reformers was being "masked" in order to hide it from the opponents of the establishment of administrative judiciary. Officially, the work was concerned with the amendment to the Code of Administrative Procedure in connection with the approaching 20th anniversary of its adoption.[23] Therefore, a very general topic was formulated in the course of preparing the working plan of the Sejm committees, that is: Monitoring the Implementation of the Administrative Procedure Code. Such an "uncontested" formulation of the topic made it possible to include it in the working plan of the Commission on Administration, Spatial Development, and Environmental Protection as well as the Committee on Legislative Work. On the basis of information obtained from the authorities, the committees came to

---

20 J. Zimmermann, *Z podstawowych zagadnień sądownictwa administracyjnego*, w: *Sądownictwo administracyjne gwarantem wolności i praw obywatelskich 1980–2005*, J. Góral, R. Hauser, J. Trzciński (eds.), Warszawa 2005, p. 490.

21 J. Świątkiewicz, *Jak kształtowało się orzecznictwo Naczelnego Sądu Administracyjnego*, w: *Sądownictwo administracyjne gwarantem wolności i praw obywatelskich 1980–2005*, *op. cit.*, p. 436.

22 About the work on the project, see S. Zawadzki, *Mój życiowy sukces: NSA*, w: *XX lat Naczelnego Sądu Administracyjnego*, Warszawa 2000, s. 102.

23 W. Piątek, A. Skoczylas, *Sądownictwo administracyjne po II wojnie światowej*, w: *Sądowa kontrola administracji publicznej*, t. 10, System Prawa Administracyjnego, R. Hauser, Z. Niewiadomski, A. Wróbel (eds.), p. 32.

a conclusion that there was a need to introduce a principle of judicial review of administrative acts in terms of their legitimacy.

The Act of 31 January 1980 on the Supreme Administrative Court (SAC) and amending the Act – Code of Administrative Procedure (CAP)[24] regulated systemic issues, whereas procedural issues were introduced by way of amendment to the CAP. The Act presented the SAC as a special, one-instance court whose case law was judicially supervised by the Supreme Court. Concerns over the judicial control of the administration caused the position of the court, its jurisdiction, and place within the justice system to be designed in a way that these times had allowed. The following should be pointed out in particular: systemic provisions regarding the Supreme Court were limited in terms of their content; court proceedings were included under the CAP; there was positive enumeration when it comes to matters covered by court jurisdiction; and there was judicial supervision exercised by the Supreme Court. The above mentioned supervision was intended to provide some sense of security that could be threatened with too far-reaching judgements of the SAC.[25] It should be highlighted that under this act of law, the following decisions, among others, could be challenged at the administrative court: decisions regarding tax obligations, prices, fees, and tariff rates – so evidently ones made in cases that directly affected the condition of the public finances. The SAC's case law of the 80s of the 20th century was based on widely recognised values (such as the principle *nulla poena sine lege certa*, the principle of trust placed by the citizen in the state, and protection of vested rights).[26] The judgements were fully approved by the society of that time and

---

24 Journal of Laws No. 4, item 8.

25 R. Hauser, *Sądownictwo administracyjne w przyszłej konstytucji*, „Ruch Prawniczy Ekonomiczny i Socjologiczny" 1995, No. 2, p. 59.

26 For example, in the Judgement of 13 January 1984, SA/Wr 701/83 (CBOSA – Central Database of Administrative Courts' Case Law), the court set aside the decisions of the authorities of both instances and found the interpretation of Article 7 of the Act of 26 October 1982 on Proceedings against Persons Absconding from Work (Journal of Laws No. 35, item 229) – claiming that since the Jehovah's Witnesses denomination is not a state-recognised religious association, if the preacher of that faith refuses to work, they will be put on the list of people persistently absconding from work – to be incorrect. In the Judgement of 6 February 1981, SA 819/81 (CBOSA), the court upheld that the so-called independent resolution of the Council of Ministers cannot serve as legal basis for imposing obligations on the citizens. In the Judgement of 26 October 1984, II SA 1161/84 (ONSA 1884, No. 2, item 97), the court set aside the decisions of authorities of both instances and ruled that although the principle of equality before the law had not been explicitly formulated in administrative law, it arises from Article

perceived as intended to limit the arbitrariness of the authorities. In the course of the proceedings before the court, the administrative authority held a position equal to the party and sought settlement of a dispute with the party from a judicial authority that was uninterested in the result, independent of the executive authority, and whose judges were autonomous. At the very commencement of its activity, the SAC heavily stressed that it would solely follow the principles of the law in its case law.[27] The list of cases falling within the jurisdiction of the SAC was exhaustive so a complaint on a decision that was not mentioned in Article 196 of the CAP would be rejected by the court.

The previous model of the SAC's jurisdiction was significantly modified after entry into force of the Act of 8 March 1990 on Local Self-Government[28], the Act of 22 March 1990 on Self-Government Officers[29], and the Act of 17 May 1990 on Division of Tasks and Jurisdiction Specified in Special Acts among the Bodies of Gmina (i.e., a municipality) and Government Administration and on the Amendments to Some Acts.[30] The outcome produced by the Commission on Preparation of a Draft Law on the SAC, which was appointed in July 1988 by the President of the SAC of the time, Prof. A. Zieliński, was also significant for the expansion of the SAC's cognition. The input materials were an original preliminary draft law on the SAC compiled by Prof. J. Borkowski as well as the view expressed by the Legislative Council on 22 June 1988 on new solutions in the field of judicial review of administrative decisions. The Commission's draft reinforced the position of the SAC as a court appointed to exercise justice by way of verifying compliance with the law of administrative decisions as well as other forms of activity of the administration. The changes that were prepared primarily consisted in the introduction of a general clause subjecting all administrative decisions to the SAC's control except for a few ones that were explicitly excluded (based on Article 196(4) of the CAP).

After the adoption of the Constitutional Act of 23 April 1992 on the Procedure for Preparing and Adopting the Constitution of the Republic of Poland[31],

---

67(2) of the Constitution of the Polish People's Republic of 1952 and must be respected in all areas of Polish law like any other constitutional principle.

27 R. Hauser, *Kształtowanie się pozycji i ustroju Naczelnego Sądu Administracyjnego*, „Zeszyty Naukowe Sądownictwa Administracyjnego" 2010, wydanie jubileuszowe z okazji 30-lecia NSA 1980–2010, No. 5–6, p. 157 et seq.

28 Journal of Laws No. 16, item 95.

29 Journal of Laws No. 21, item 123.

30 Journal of Laws No. 34, item 198.

31 Journal of Laws No. 67, item 336.

discussion on the model of administrative judiciary resumed. In 1992, preparation of a preliminary draft law on the Supreme Administrative Court commenced at the SAC. The draft law compiled by a team of judges of the SAC under the direction of the President of the SAC of the time, Prof. R. Hauser, was handed over to the Chancellery of the President in the second half of 1993. Following discussions within the environment, the draft was submitted as a President's initiative and then subjected to the legislative process. The Act of 11 May 1995 on the Supreme Administrative Court[32] entered into force on 1 October 1995. The Act kept the model of the SAC as a single-instance court with remote branch offices. The Act subjected to court review not only the decisions, but also acts and activities performed within the framework of public administration. The SAC's cognition covered the administration's activities capable of shaping the legal situation of a citizen, even if devoid of the form of a formal decision.

The Act included the entirety of the provisions and so it determined the Court's organisation, its scope of activity as well as administrative court proceedings. A separate chamber for dealing with financial matters was singled out within the organisational structure of the Court based on the Act; and the Act authorised the President to determine the bylaws and organisational structure of the Court based on Article 3(1). The President of the Republic of Poland divided the Court into the Financial Chamber and the General Administrative Chamber by way of the Implementing Regulation of 28 September 1995 on the Establishment of the Bylaws and the Organisational Structure of the Supreme Administrative Court.[33] In accordance with Article 11(1) of the Regulation, the jurisdiction of the Financial Chamber covered cases concerned with custom duties, tax liabilities, and other monetary benefits that tax regulations apply to, prices, fees, tariff rates, the budget, foreign exchange law, securities, banking and insurance institutions, and administration of monetary benefits.

Another crucial moment for the development of the model of administrative judiciary was the process of drawing up the Constitution of the Republic of Poland. Within the framework of works on the Constitution, the issue of the judiciary was dealt with by a Subcommittee on Law Protection Institutions and Judicial Authorities chaired by a member of parliament A. Bentkowski. In the discussion on administrative judiciary, the key issues were the nature of the SAC's control, the relationship between the Supreme Court and the SAC, and the manner of appointing the President of the SAC. In January 1997, following

32 Journal of Laws No. 74, item 368.
33 Journal of Laws No. 112, item 540.

completion of the editing of the text, the Constitutional Committee adopted a report on the draft Constitution.[34] The solutions adopted in the Constitution, in particular the ones concerning operation of the judiciary within a two-instance structure, necessitated undertaking legislative work aimed at implementing the provisions of the Constitution since Article 236(2) thereof stipulated that the acts of law implementing Article 176(1) as regards proceedings before administrative courts would be passed within five years from the date of entry into force of the Constitution. In 1998, in order to implement the above provisions of the Constitution of the Republic of Poland, Prof. R. Hauser, the President of the SAC, put together a team under his own leadership, which was composed of: J. Borkowski, A. Kabat, J. Kacprzak, E. Mzyk, W. Ryms, J. Świątkiewicz, J. Trzciński, T. Woś, and A. Wróbel and drafted the relevant laws. Following a far-reaching discussion with the environment, the resultant drafts were handed over to the Chancellery of the President of the Republic of Poland. On 22 October 2001, the President of the Republic of Poland presented three draft laws to the Sejm of the Republic of Poland: Law on the System of Administrative Courts,

Law on Proceedings before Administrative Courts, and the provisions introducing the Act on the System of Administrative Courts and the Act on Proceedings before Administrative Courts.[35] Whereas in November, a parliamentary package of acts of laws regarding the reform of the administrative judiciary[36] was submitted and the representative of the proposers was a member of the parliament J. Rokita. The draft provided for the abolition of the second instance in administrative proceedings and adoption of a structure where decisions taken at the level of the first instance would be subject to judicial review. In accordance with the parliamentary draft, administrative courts were supposed to be the Supreme Administrative Court, Regional Administrative Courts, and District Administrative Courts.[37] After the first reading, the drafts

34 R. Chruściak, *Prace parlamentarne nad konstytucyjnym i ustawowym uregulowaniem Naczelnego Sądu Admi-nistracyjnego*, w: *Sądownictwo administracyjne gwarantem wolności i praw obywatelskich 1980–2005*, J. Góral, R. Hauser, J. Trzciński (eds.), Warszawa 2005, p. 90 et seq.

35 Sejm prints No. 18, 19, 20.

36 These were draft laws: on the System of Administrative Courts (print 77), on Proceedings before Administrative Courts (print 78), and provisions introducing the Act on the System of Administrative Courts and the Act on Proceedings before Administrative Courts (print 79).

37 Zob. D. Kijowski, J. Płoskonka, S. Prutis, S. Srocki, *Model ustrojowy sądownictwa administracyjnego. Raport Programu Reformy Administracji Publicznej*, Warszawa 1999.

were handed over to the Committee on Justice and Human Rights and the Legislative Committee. The Sejm passed Acts of law based on the presidential drafts. The Senate did not move amendments, which the senator Prof. T. Liszcz explained as follows when she recommended the adoption of the draft without amendments: "My satisfaction primarily arises from the fact that we are not only dealing with a very important systemic law, but a well-prepared one too. As I said at the beginning, this is a highly uniform and really coherent package of laws that together meet the obligations laid down in Article 236(2) of the Constitution, that is, the obligation to adapt the administrative judiciary, and in particular the proceedings before administrative courts, to the requirement contained in Article 176 of the Constitution calling for two-instance judicial proceedings in all cases."[38] As a watcher of and participant in the works on legislative reforms of the administrative judiciary, Prof. R. Hauser believed that the Sejm committees had worked smoothly and without major disputes. As far as procedural law is concerned, this was no surprise since the procedural regulations were based on the provisions of the Civil Procedure Code (CPC). One should bear in mind that since the beginning of the reactivation of administrative judiciary, the relevant provisions on proceedings before the SAC had been the provisions of the CPC, hence it was rational to use the adjudicating experience developed over those years for the establishment of the new regulations. Mediation and summary proceedings were introduced as novelties. However, these forms of decision-making had not met with vivid interest.

Some broader discussions were triggered by the possible conflicts of competence among the Supreme Court, the Supreme Administrative Court, common courts, and administrative courts. This was caused by the lack of constitutional solutions similar to those in force at the time of the Second Polish Republic (such as the Court of Competence) as well as incomplete separation of administrative judiciary and the absence of justification for further operation of the College of Competence at the Supreme Court.

The amendment to the CPC and the solutions proposed in the PbAC have led to the adoption of the solution currently in place (i.e., if the administrative court rejects a complaint, the common court cannot reject a claim and vice versa). This solution has been in operation for years, which confirms the validity of the adopted regulations. There have also been no major disputes regarding the system of administrative courts. The view that it is valid for the general administrative

38 Stenographic report from the 23rd session of the Senate on 6, 7 and 8 of August 2002, http://ww2.senat.pl/K5/DOK/STEN/023/21.HTM#A00174 (accessed on: 5/11/2022).

procedure to continue to be based on two instances prevailed in the discussions and thus the parliamentary proposals for having a three-level structure of administrative courts turned out to be insubstantial. In addition, in the course of discussion, it was pointed out that the possible elimination of the second instance in administrative proceedings would require a huge expansion of the network of administrative courts, which would significantly increase the costs of the reform of administrative judiciary and, on top of that, if administrative courts were to make fully substantial judgements at the first instance, it would be necessary to introduce an extensive evidentiary hearing, which would immediately slowdown administrative court proceedings. It was also voiced that, in practice, such a solution would limit the possibility of carrying out a specific administrative policy of the executive authority. In the course of parliamentary work, the status of judges of the Regional Administrative Courts has changed significantly.

In line with the draft statutory law, the status of these judges was supposed to be the same as that of the judges of District Courts within the system of common courts. The change that has been introduced equated the status of the judges of Regional Administrative Courts with the status of the judges of Appeal Courts. The main argument was that since a complaint against the judgements of Regional Administrative Courts is considered by the Supreme Administrative Court, the position of the judges of Regional Administrative Courts should correspond to the position of judges of Appeal Courts within the system of common courts. The regulations adopted at that time have proved their worth, and the administrative judiciary is one of the leaders in Europe in terms of efficiency of adjudication.

The Act of 25 July 2002 on the System of Administrative Courts[39] stipulates that courts of the first instance consider all judicial administrative cases, except for the ones reserved for the SAC.

The organisational structure of administrative courts adopted in the Act includes the existing Supreme Administrative Court and the newly created Regional Administrative Courts. The SAC supervises the adjudicating activity of administrative courts of the first instance, in particular, it considers appeals against the judgements of these courts and adopts resolutions clarifying legal issues.

In the meantime, between the adoption of the laws reforming the administrative judiciary and their entry into force (on 1 January 2004), organisational and technical activities were undertaken to ensure that adjudicating activities would be performed. During this period, the facilities of Regional Administrative

39 Journal of Laws No. 153, item 1269.

Courts were prepared and judges as well as the administrative staff were employed. In 2013, the President of the SAC initiated work at the Court with an objective to streamline adjudication and broaden the possibility of substantive adjudication. The Act of 9 April 2015 amending the Act on Law on Proceedings Before Administrative Courts equips judges with instruments allowing for more efficient adjudication as it gives them the possibility to oblige an authority to issue – where possible – a specific decision. The current trends and relevant legislative changes suggest a clear shift of the administrative court's competences toward increased reformatory powers.

The second important tendency that can be noticed in administrative case law is a gradual departure from the formalistic model of adjudication and emergence of the elements of the argumentative method of adjudication intended to solve a particular legal problem.

1.3. Models of Adjudication in Administrative Judiciary

As far as judicial review of administration is concerned, there are two fundamental models of adjudication in administrative judiciary. Administrative Courts may issue judgements whose character is that of a verification (cassation) or judgements reformatory (substantive) in nature, which is the so-called full ruling and can be seen – in some respects – as settlement of an administrative matter. In Poland, there is a cassatory (verifying) model of adjudication in place. The model provides for a passive protection of the addressee of an administrative act. It is passive in a sense that the Administrative Court has a clearly limited right to substantively settle the case as regards its substance. Under the adopted model of adjudication, control of public administration (i.e., settlement of an administrative court case) is, therefore, separated from exercising public administration (i.e., settlement of an administrative matter).

In principle, the administrative court does not have the competence to take over an administrative matter and settle it ultimately (i.e., decide on its substance). The role of the court adjudicating within the limits of the case and on the basis of the facts established by the administrative authority is to review and assess the actions of the authority from the point of view of compliance. Thus, the subject matter of the proceedings before an administrative court is not an administrative matter *per se* but verification whether the contested act or action was compliant with the law.[40] Therefore, a judgement of an administrative

40 R. Hauser, *Dziesięciolecie przekształceń ustrojowych Naczelnego Sądu Administracyjnego i jego orzecznictwa*, „Samorząd Terytorialny" 2000, No. 1–2, p. 30 et seq.

court leads either to confirmation of the legal status of an administrative act or its removal from the pool of legal transactions. The subject matter of the court's judgement itself is not, in principle, specific application of a legal norm but review of the application exercised by the administrative authority from the point of view of compliance with the law.[41] Pursuant to Art. 145 of the PbAC, if the Regional Administrative Court considers a complaint against a decision and finds that it violates substantive law, which has affected the outcome of the case, or that a revealed volition substantiates resumption of administrative proceedings or if the Court discovers a different breach of procedural regulations that could have significantly affected the outcome of the case, it repeals the decision in whole or in part. The administrative court is also entitled to declare a decision invalid in whole or in part due to reasons specified in Article 156 of the CAP or in other provisions of the law. Moreover, on the basis of considerations specified in the CAP or in other provisions, the court may find that a decision has been issued as a result of violation of the law. Therefore, the PbAC provides for a cassatory model and – in principle – gives the court no possibility to issue judgements reformatory in nature. Following removal of a decision on a case from the pool of legal transactions as a result of a final and binding ruling of an administrative court, the case returns to the authority that – despite being bound by the indications contained in the justification to the ruling – carries out the proceedings again and issues a substantive judgement on the administrative matter in question. However, the principle of the cassatory (verifying) model of adjudication in the Polish model of judicial control of administration is not absolute in character.

In Europe, there is a tendency to alter the competence of the administrative court towards greater authority to adjudicate substantially. The amendment of 2015 to the PbAC[42] takes these trends into account and highlights, first and foremost, the influence of substantial adjudication on improved effectiveness of administrative judiciary in Poland.

The intention is to broaden the scope of substantive adjudication by administrative courts as part of control of the activity of public administration, which the courts exercise. Based on Article 145a added to the amended PbAC, the court may oblige an authority to issue a decision within a specified time limit

41 Judgement of the Supreme Administrative Court of 4 November 2013, ref. No. II GSK 930/12, CBOSA.

42 Act of 9 July 2015 amending the Act on Law on Proceedings before Administrative Courts (Journal of Laws, item 1191).

and indicate the way a matter should be settled or resolved, if justified by the circumstances surrounding the case and if the decision is not left to the discretion of the authority. In the event of failure to issue a decision within the time limit set by the court, the party may lodge a complaint and request a judgement to be issued, which states the existence or non-existence of a right or obligation.[43] Within the framework of efforts aimed at broadening the competence of administrative courts in order to include reformatory adjudication, it was pointed out that this does not violate any constitutional principles, in particular the principle of division and balance of power. Evidently, complete separation of the authorities in line with the principle of separation of powers expressed in Article 10 of the Constitution of the Republic of Poland is not possible, and deviations based on strictly defined exceptions are permissible. Justification to these draft changes stressed that greater reformatory competence comes down to resolving disputes about violation or exercise of the rights *ratione personae* of the individual. When ruling in adversarial litigation, administrative courts will not substitute for the executive authority in shaping and implementing the administrative policy but will apply justice acting as the guarantor of protection and exercise of the rights and freedoms of the individual within the framework of performing administrative tasks, thus ensuring the constitutional right to actually pursue the infringed rights by judicial measures.[44]

Introduction of the elements of "full" adjudication contributes to a gradual departure from the strictly formalistic model of adjudication and emergence of the elements of the so-called argumentative method of adjudication aimed at solving a specific legal problem. The legalistic approach to the judicial process of application of the law is coming under growing criticism. Social expectations as well as efforts of the judiciary itself strive for the reinforcement of the position of the judge at the administrative court. This process unfolds not by way of introducing specific systemic and organisational changes but above all by means of changing the way judicial application of the law is perceived.[45]

---

43 M. Kamiński, *Orzekanie merytoryczne sądów administracyjnych. Uwagi na tle szwajcarskiego, austriackiego i niemieckiego systemu prawnego*, w: *Przyszłość sądownictwa administracyjnego w Polsce z uwzględnieniem tendencji europejskich*, Biul. RPO 2012 No. 75, p. 120.

44 Justification to the draft Act of 9 July 2015 amending the Act on Law on Proceedings before Administrative Courts (Journal of Laws, item 1191), print of the Sejm of the 7th term of office, No. 1633.

45 M. Kowalski, *Prawo pomocy w systemie ochrony praw człowieka*, Warszawa 2013, p. 64.

1.4. Proceedings before an Administrative Court

Administrative law is a branch of the law that is the most dynamically and the most closely related to social life. The number of cases handled by administrative courts is regularly increasing. In 1980, there were 2,470 cases submitted to the SAC; in 1981 there were 6,594; in 1982 – 8,829; in 1983 – 9,582; in 1990 – 12,218; in 1995 – 39,741; in 2000 – 65,054; in 2003 – 69,011; in 2004 – 58,815 (to the RAC) and 6,167 (to the SAC); in 2005 – 62,909 (to the RAC) and 9,549 (to the SAC).[46] Procedural laws are instrumental in relation to the substantive law as they are essential for shaping legal and administrative relations by the public administration. Their proper application decides the quality of operation of state administration and, consequently, of the entire state.[47] The proceedings should be conducted in a way that allows them to end with a decision resolving the substance of the matter, that is, with a substantive decision, as quickly as possible. Such a result is expected by a party submitting an application within the framework of an individual case. And so, the authority initiating the procedure should be guided by such an objective. This arises directly from the general principle of having speedy and simple proceedings pursuant to Article 12 of the CPC. It obliges the authorities to act diligently and promptly using the simplest possible means to resolve the matter under examination.[48]

Judicial control is exercised over cases that were earlier dealt with in the course of administrative proceedings where the position of the individual was not equal to the position of the public administration authority. The grounds for the admissibility of proceedings before an administrative court are the existence of a challenged claim and the submission of an appropriate letter initiating the proceedings. Proceedings before the Regional Administrative Court are initiated as a result of filing a complaint (based on Article 50 of the PbAC) or filing an application (based on Article 63 of the PbAC); only in cases of loss or destruction of files proceedings may be initiated *ex officio* (based on Article 281(1) of the PbAC). This is because the proceedings before the RAC are carried out on complaint-basis and can only be initiated, if a complaint or an application

---

46 www.nsa.gov.pl (accessed on: 5/11/2022).

47 R. Hauser, *Rola przepisów procesowych w realizacji materialnego prawa administracyjnego*, w: *Rola materialnego prawa administracyjnego a ochrona praw jednostki*, Z. Leoński (ed.), Poznań 1998, p. 26.

48 R. Kusiak-Winter, *Wartości i antywartości w prawie administracyjnym z perspektywy nauki administracji*, in: *Anty-wartości w prawie administracyjnym*, A. Błaś (ed.), Warszawa 2016, p. 49.

is submitted.[49] Owing to the principle stating that administrative judiciary is complaint-based, in order to initiate administrative court proceedings, an entity entitled to do so is required to file an appropriate request.

Filing a complaint with the court is the first action of a complainant, which is an expression of their will to seek protection of their rights in the course of administrative court proceedings. If a complaint is submitted, proceedings before the court are initiated, the case under the jurisdiction of the administrative authority is brought before the administrative court, and the procedural position of the authority that issued the contested act is altered.[50] First, the court *ex officio* examines admissibility of the complaint in order to determine if there are grounds for its rejection.[51] The complaint is the primary legal measure causing administrative court proceedings to be initiated. Whereas an application for the initiation of the proceedings is an exceptional measure and is submitted when the acts of law – both the PbAC and separate Acts[52] – provide for this (e.g., in cases regarding competence injunction). The complaint and the application are pleadings that should meet the formal requirements for such letters specified in Article 46 of the PbAC and include additional elements specified in Article 57(1) points 1 to 4. Provisions of the PbAC do not set too stringent formal conditions for complaints, which is in line with the legislator's tendency to deformalize administrative court proceedings and the principle of not binding the court within the limits of the complaint. Separate provisions (of Article 57a of the PbAC) apply to complaints against written interpretations of tax law issued in individual cases (tax rulings). This Article provides for additional formal conditions for complaints against such interpretations, which may be based only on an allegation of breach of procedural regulations, an error of interpretation or an incorrect evaluation as to the application of a provision of substantive law. The complaint must voice the allegation of breach of the substantive or procedural law and specify the form of such an infringement.[53]

---

49 M. Jaśkowska, M. Masternak, E. Ochendowski, *Postępowanie sądowoadministracyjne*, Warszawa 2004, p. 125.

50 T. Woś, H. Knysiak-Molczyk, M. Romańska, *Postępowanie sądowoadministracyjne*, Warszawa 2017.

51 M. Jagielska, *Skarga*, w: *Prawo o postępowaniu przed sądami administracyjnymi. Komentarz*, R. Hauser, M. Wierzbowski (eds.), Warszawa 2013.

52 Judgement of the SAC of 13 March 2007, ref. No. II GZ 31/07, CBOSA.

53 B. Dauter, A. Kabat, M. Niezgódka-Medek, *Prawo o postępowaniu przed sądami administracyjnymi. Komentarz*, Warszawa 2016, p. 318.

The provisions on complaints apply to applications as well. The consequences of lodging of a complaint or an application depend on meeting the conditions for filing them.

The PbAC contains an open catalogue of grounds for the admissibility of a complaint. The legislator has not only established conditions allowing the court to find that a complaint does not meet the requirements laid down for this procedural document but also regulated the procedure to be initiated in such a case. In principle, if the court discovers formal defects in a complaint, it is rejected. This means that the court will not decide on the merits of the case but will only rule on the impossibility of issuing a judgement. In such a case, the court will rule in a closed session about rejection of a complaint so, in practice, if a complaint does not meet the formal requirements, it precludes the possibility of effective initiation of administrative court proceedings and consideration of the case in terms of its substance. It should be noted, however, that before the court rejects a complaint, it is obliged to call the complainant to remedy its formal flaws. If the complainant fails to remove these deficiencies within the time limit set by the court, the complaint will then be rejected as inadmissible.

The conditions for admissibility of a complaint are formal requirements for correct challenging specified in the procedural law, which are concerned with the contested claim, its form, and substance. If they are met, the compliance of the contested act or action of the public administration authority may be controlled by the administrative court.

The entry into force, as of 1 January 2004, of the provisions establishing two-instance administrative courts meant that an institution of the second instance had to be set up in order to deal with appeals against rulings of Regional Administrative Courts. Invalid judgements (i.e., rulings and – in principle – judgements ending the proceedings) taken by the courts of the first instance (i.e., RACs) may be appealed to the SAC due to the fact that a cassatory model of proceedings has been adopted for the purposes of the Polish administrative court proceedings. The means of appeal available in case of contested judgements of the RACs are a cassation appeal and a complaint. A cassation appeal may be filed against any RAC's ruling issued for any type of action of public administration authorities and so cassation appeal applies to any judgement, whether it takes the complaint into consideration or rejects it.[54] Under the legal circumstances

54 A. Wiktorowska, *Środki odwoławcze*, w: *Prawo o postępowaniu przed sądami administracyjnymi. Komentarz*, R. Hauser, M. Wierzbowski (eds.), Warszawa 2013, p. 668.

applicable since 15 August 2015, the cassation appeal is relatively devolutive in character; the Regional Administrative Court may actually exercise self-control of its ruling pursuant to Article 179a of the PbAC. Previously, it was fully devolutive as the regulations did not provide for the possibility of making self-corrections.[55] The cassation appeal is also suspensive in nature as its submission suspends the validity of the contested judgement until the SAC issues its ruling. As the principal means of appeal, the cassation appeal serves primarily to protect the interests of the parties to the proceedings by enabling them to verify the judgement of the court of the first instance. Due to the fact that one of the parties to the proceedings before administrative courts is the authority, the cassation appeal also allows to protect the public interest by way of contributing to legitimate case law of such authorities.

Owing to the special powers of certain authorities responsible for upholding the rule of law (e.g., the Prosecutor or the Ombudsman), the provisions of the PbAC provide for the right to a cassation appeal. As indicated in the doctrine, that way these authorities fulfil their duties related to the protection of special constitutional values (e.g., protection of the rule of law or the rights of the citizens). There is no cassation appeal against the rulings of the SAC, which are valid from the moment of their issuance *ex officio*. A cassation appeal is not a means of directly challenging decisions or other acts of administrative authorities; the pleas contained therein must contest the ruling of the RAC. The premises for a cassation appeal may be such a flaw of a ruling that may lead to the repeal or alteration of the contested judgement. The provision of Article 174 of the PbAC provides for two grounds for lodging a cassation appeal, that is breach of the substantive law due to misinterpretation or misapplication and violation of procedural rules, if the deficiency could seriously affect the outcome of the case. The issue of incorrect application of substantive law gave rise to doctrinal disputes and has consequently led to a resolution adopted by the full composition of the SAC, which stated that "presentation of basis for cassation understood as an indication of the provisions that – according to the appellant filing a cassation appeal – have been violated by the RAC obliges the NSA, pursuant to Article 174(1) and (2) and Article 183(1) of the PbAC to address all the charges cited

55 R. Hauser, A. Skoczylas, W. Piątek, *Środki odwoławcze w postępowaniu sądowoadministracyjnym w świetle ustawy nowelizującej z dnia 9 kwietnia 2015 r. – analiza najistotniejszych zmian*, „Zeszyty Naukowe Sądownic-twa Administracyjnego" 2015, No. 4, p. 14.

as the basis for the cassation."[56] A cassation appeal must indicate a specific provision of the law and how it has been infringed as the court should not have to figure out the appellant's intention; therefore, the cassation appeal ought to be drafted in a way that leaves no room for doubts of interpretation. Deficiencies in terms of indication of the grounds for cassation are not subject to rectification. The cassation appeal is a highly formalised means of appeal, so the legislator provided for a compulsory representation by a lawyer when compiling it (with some exceptions concerning judges, prosecutors, notaries public, and Professors or Doctors of Law).[57] The amendment to the PbAC of 2015 allows the RAC to self-review the contested judgement. These courts have been awarded the power to consider cassation appeals and to re-examine cases, if the court finds that the grounds of the cassation appeal are clearly justified or if the proceedings are declared invalid.

A ruling issued in a case considered within the framework of self-review is subject to appeal under general principles. The amendment of PbAC of 2015 has, therefore, concluded the next stage of streamlining adjudication and broadening the possibility of substantive adjudication.

1.5. Computerisation

Contemporary society is a product of the digital age. It has formed as a result of the development and popularisation of modern information technologies. The Internet has played a special role in this process. It has caused an explosion of civilisational changes and, consequently, the development of a new type of society: An information society whose essence is an altered view of the world and interpersonal relations. In such a community, mechanisation, automation, and unlimited possibilities in terms of information flow create new quality in public life, and the individual is presented with an opportunity to have unlimited access to information. As far as communication of the authorities with the citizens is concerned, there is a shift from the "paper era" to the "computer technology era.Both the public authorities and the individual must rise to these challenges. Digitalisation opens up opportunities for rendering public services of an increasingly high quality and thus becomes beneficial for both the state

56 Resolution of the full composition of the SAC of 26 October 2009, ref. No. I OPS 10/09, CBOSA.

57 B. Dauter, A. Kabat, M. Niezgódka-Medek, *Prawo o postępowaniu przed sądami administracyjnymi. Komentarz*, Warszawa 2016, p. 742 et seq.

and the individual. The public authority thus faces the challenge of meeting such social expectations."[58]

The changes taking place in the society should be accompanied by appropriate amendments to the law. Therefore, contemporary wide-ranging legislative activity as well as the actions of the public administration authorities cause administrative courts to cope with new tasks and issues to be resolved. Hence the doctrine of administrative law has been inclining towards a view that the challenges of the present day influence the understanding of the concept of "public administration." The factors producing the most profound impact on public administration are globalisation, information society, and economisation of public services.[59] The development of the information society elicits important changes in social life. Information and communication technologies also affect law-making and application of the law, including administrative procedural law. Computerisation of administrative court proceedings consists in the introduction of new legal solutions within the framework of this procedure, which enable the use of information and communication technologies in the course of taking procedural actions by the administrative court and the parties.[60]

The Act of 17 February 2005 on Computerisation of the Activities of Public Entities[61] has, among others, amended the CAP to make it possible to settle public administration matters through information and communication systems. In line with the Act, electronic means of communication could be used by the authority for submitting and the service of letters. Clearly, the amendments have not ensured complete computerisation of the administrative procedure. According to the doctrine, this led to a situation where – despite the use of electronic means of communication in the proceedings – the authority printed out electronic documents onto paper for example in order to allow the party to view the case files or in order to send the files to a higher level authority or to an administrative court.[62] The Act of 10 January 2014 amending the Act on Computerisation of

58 Z. Niewiadomski, M. Zirk-Sadowski, *Prawo wobec wyzwań epoki cyfryzacji*, w: *Cyfryzacja gospodarki i społe-czeństwa – szanse i wyzwania dla sektorów infrastrukturalnych*, J. Gajewski, W. Paprocki, J. Pieregud (eds.), Gdańsk 2016.

59 Z. Niewiadomski, *Wyzwania współczesności i ich wpływ na treść pojęcia „administracja publiczna"*, in: *System prawa administracyjnego*, t. 1, *Instytucje prawa administracyjnego*, R. Hauser, Z. Niewiadomski, A. Wróbel (eds.), Warszawa 2015, p. 30.

60 P. Pietrasz, *Informatyzacja polskiego postępowania przed sądami administracyjnymi a jego zasady ogólne*, Warszawa 2020, p. 122.

61 Journal of Laws No. 64, item 565.

62 X. Konarski, G. Sibiga, *Zastosowanie środków komunikacji elektronicznej w postępowaniu administracyjnym ogólnym po nowelizacji KPA*, „Monitor Prawniczy" 2006, No. 2.

Activities of Entities Performing Public Tasks and Certain Other Acts[63] altered the PbAC (in Article 4 thereof) by way of, among others, introducing a solution based on mechanisms of electronic document management that would support the current way of handling court case files, provide the party to the proceedings with online access to case files, allow for the possibility of submitting procedural documents in an electronic form, and regulate the issue of electronic service of documents by administrative courts (with three conditions for the admissibility of electronic service, i.e.,: request/application of the party, consent of the party, submission of a letter to the court in an electronic form). As indicated in the justification to the draft amendment,[64] the drafted law was to have a positive impact on the sector of public finances. The amendments proposed in the Act were intended to simplify contact of the citizens and the entrepreneurs with the offices. Additionally, it was expected that electronic means of communication with the administration would be used more and more commonly, which would result in, among others, saved time and financial resources for the administration as well as the citizens. It was estimated that the society would save PLN 34.5 each time a matter were handled electronically instead of with the use of paper (which was an individual benefit); whereas the administration would save between PLN 5 and PLN 6.9 in the same case.[65]

Therefore, computerisation of the administrative court proceedings was meant to have a positive impact on public finances. The provisions amending the PbAC as regards computerisation of the proceedings came into force on 31 May 2019.

The relevant literature indicates that computerisation of administrative court proceedings may influence the effectiveness of protection provided by these courts by ensuring unrestrained access to the justice system, which is not unreasonably burdensome. The principle of ensuring reliability and efficiency of operation of public institutions, which arises from the Preamble to the Constitution, encourages modernisation of the right to trail by adapting it to the social and technological reality. Information and communication technologies have brought about changes, especially in terms of rules governing identification of the entities in the proceedings, the methods for submitting letters, the means

---

63 Journal of Laws, item 183, as amended.

64 Print No. 1637, http://www.sejm.gov.pl/Sejm7.nsf/druk.xsp?nr=1637 (accessed on: 5/11/2020).

65 The estimated data are available in the justification to the drat and include, among others, postal fees, employee remunerations or cost of printing documents, etc.

of ensuring access to files and a possibility of viewing them, and the service of letters. The adoption of electronic means of communication may replace traditional communication through post offices and limit personal contact of the participants in the proceedings with the court to a minimum. This aspect of the operation of administrative courts has recently acquired special significance due to the introduction of the pandemic state of emergency on the territory of the Republic of Poland.[66] The administrative courts made use of the system of Information and Communication Technology (ICT) in place, which has been servicing the court proceedings since 31 May 2019, and so direct contact could be minimised. The ICT system in place in administrative courts allows for submitting complaints and documents, handling correspondence, and having access to case files via electronic means of communication. Restrictions following from the pandemic state of emergency proved the validity and effectiveness of the measures that have been adopted so far and may also become an incentive to expand the possibilities offered by the ICT system. The administrative courts are currently working on developing a secure application that would serve to, for example, hold conference calls enabling real-time communication and allowing transmission of sound or sound and image between the participants of the conference. Establishment of a separate simplified procedure model based on an electronic complaint could also be considered. A certain category of cases might be singled out, which – on a larger scale than now – might be proceeded using the ICT system (e.g., complaints against tax interpretations, complaints against acts of supervision over the activities of self-government officers or matters regarding the cohesion policy); moreover, regulations could be developed to authorise the President of the Republic of Poland to hand over other matters for consideration in a new mode. Establishment of this mode could contribute to streamlining the proceedings, shortening their duration, making full use of the possibilities of the court's ICT system, unlocking the potential of the judges in smaller RACs, and improving the efficiency of administrative courts. The special mode devoted to this type of proceedings should be equipped with interactive forms and a system allowing for making payments or issuing instructions, etc. Understandably, such conclusions call for intensive organisational and analytical work (such as development of separate modules in the existing ICT system,

66 Regulation of the Minister of Health of 20 March 2020 Announcing the Pandemic State of Emergency on the Territory of the Republic of Poland (Journal of Laws, item 491, as amended).

creation of an e-court or e-departments) and ultimately drafting and adoption of relevant legal acts.

Furthermore, additional automation of decision-making in administrative court cases could also be considered. There are already systems employed in administrative proceedings, which allow to discover violations, e.g., of traffic regulations, and impose penalties for them (e.g., for speeding, prohibited forms of moving around or failing to pay a toll). Most commonly, simple algorithms are used for the purposes of making decisions, which serve to determine whether a violation has been committed, identify the perpetrator, and determine the legal penalty. Automatic systems are also prevalently employed for the purposes of mass issuance of decisions granting benefits; the system verifies, if the conditions are met and calculates the benefit.[67] As far as administrative court proceedings are concerned, it is also possible to indicate examples of cases that could be dealt with "automatically", e.g., lack of registration or failure to meet the deadline or perform the required action. The relevant literature[68] also advocates the need to advance computerisation further, that is, to introduce the possibility of participation in court hearings online with the use of computer facilities installed in Regional Administrative Courts and make it available to the parties and their representatives as well as the representatives of the authorities. It is noteworthy that the administrative court hearing, unlike the one before a common court, does not require evidence proceedings; it is highly formalized and quite perfectly meets the prerequisites for conducting it online. Such a regulation would be highly desirable from the point of view of public finances, for example due to reduced travelling cost as the representatives of the authorities would not need to be physically present at the hearing before the Supreme Administrative Court.[69]

---

67 Opinion of 24 April 2020 on the Amendments Proposed by the Legislative Council to the Provisions of the Civil Procedure Code, https://www.gov.pl/web/radalegislacyjna/opinia-z-24-kwietnia-2020-r--na-temat-proponowanych-przez-rade-legislacyjna-zmian-w-przepisach-kodeksu-postepowania-cywil-nego#_ftn29 (accessed on: 24/05/2020).

68 M. Kwietko-Bębnowski, *Informatyzacja sądów administracyjnych – próba oceny i poradnik praktyczny*, „Prze-gląd Podatkowy" 2020, No. 6.

69 M. Kwietko-Bębnowski, *op. cit.* points out that "the options introduced and implemented so far as regards conducting administrative court cases using IT tools deserve full acceptance and promotion, especially in the era of restrictions arising from the pandemic state of emergency. (...) All that remains is to wish courage and perseverance to those involved in the process of implementing the changes under discussion, which I believe place the Polish administrative judiciary at the forefront in terms of accessibility via IT tools."

In many matters, administrative courts were pioneers as regards good and well-thought-out solutions (among others, there has been a Central Database of Case Law since 2007, which grants the public unlimited access to the case law of administrative courts). In an address to the Minister of Justice delivered on 2 June 2020, the Ombudsman admitted[70] that computerisation of the proceedings works better in administrative courts. Attorneys-at-law also positively assess the possibility of conducting administrative court cases using IT measures. Simultaneously, they voice demands and offer directions to be considered as regards further work on the implementation of computerisation in administrative courts.

The restrictions associated with the pandemic as well as progressive computerisation of many areas of life contribute to increased interest in contacts with the court via modern information technologies exclusively. The year 2020 marked the 40th anniversary of the establishment of the Supreme Administrative Court and perhaps that is a good moment to reflect *de lege ferenda* on further digitisation of administrative court proceedings, which has already made the Polish administrative court the leader in terms of application of IT tools.

Summary

In the process of transformation of the administrative judiciary, one can witness increasing reinforcement of the position of administrative courts whose adjudicating powers are constantly expanding (e.g., Poland's accession to the European Union enabled applying for EU subsidies and appealing against the decisions in such cases). Administrative courts must quickly respond to any changes in social and economic life, which often means that they have to face phenomena they have not come into contact before (such as cryptocurrencies or drones). For the administrative judiciary to be effective, it must operate efficiently. If a party had to wait for the judgement for a long time, it would lose interest in that judgement and find the final ruling useless. If a valid judgement arrives after a long period of time, the outcome of winning the case becomes futile. As far as tax-related matters are concerned, lengthy proceedings might cause taxpayers to lose liquidity. The most important factor determining economic performance is the effectiveness of law enforcement. An effective and impartial system of law as well as the courts that can quickly enforce the conferred rights and obligations

70 No.: IV.510.21.2020. MC, https://bip.brpo.gov.pl/sites/default/files/Wystapienie%20do%20MS,%202.06.2020.pdf 2.06.2020.pdf (accessed on: 5.11.2022).

are most certainly vital. The administrative courts rapidly respond to the changing reality and adapt their activities to the emerging new conditions. This claim finds confirmation in the provisions on the introduction of the pandemic state of emergency as relevant for the operation of the administrative judiciary.[71] Readiness to promptly consider applications for suspension of the execution of an act or actions as well as cases that could put human or animal life or health in danger or result in serious harm to social interest or an irreparable economic loss in case of failure to consider the case or when necessary for the sake of the justice system – all proves that the courts skilfully react to the fluctuating environment. Thus, there are no doubts as to the fundamental importance of the administrative judiciary in the system of protection of human rights and freedoms and ensuring compliance with the standards of a democratic state ruled by law.

71 Act of 2 March 2020 on Special Solutions Related to the Prevention, Counteracting, and Combating of COVID-19, Other Infectious Diseases and Crisis Situations Caused by Them (Journal of Laws, item 374, as amended).

Dominik J. Gajewski (SGH Warsaw School of Economics)

Kamil Joński (SGH Warsaw School of Economics)

2. Administrative Judiciary between 2004 and 2022: Statistical Analysis

Abstract: The chapter compares assumptions underlying the creation of a two-instance model of administrative judiciary with actual caseload recorded over the years 2005–2022. Incoming cases were divided into sub-categories in order to explain changes in the caseload. Specifically, cases related to the structural changes of the economy and cases that can be traced-back to the specific legislative interventions had been identified. Interestingly, some categories of cases (most notably taxation-related ones) exhibited changes similar to the cyclical fluctuations in the economy (and such a hypothesis is verified in Chapter 3). The effectiveness of the first-instance administrative courts and the Supreme Administrative Court was examined, and the impact of the COVID-19 pandemic was briefly reviewed.

Keywords: Administrative Courts, Supreme Administrative Court, caseload changes, court efficiency, COVID-19

Introduction

From the perspective of the purpose of this elaboration – which is to present an interdisciplinary picture of the functioning of administrative judiciary as a component of the institutional environment of the Polish economy – the considerations presented in the previous chapter should be supplemented with statistical analyses of the "demand" for judicial control of the administration (i.e., in other words, of the number of cases brought before administrative courts).

On the one hand, it illustrates the importance of administrative judiciary for the sphere of legal and economic transactions. On the other hand, it shows the scope of tasks that the administrative judiciary must deal with in order to secure the guarantees offered by Article 45 of the Constitution. This chapter presents changes in the number of cases brought before the RAC and the SAC between 2004 and 2022 and attempts to explain reasons behind the changes.

Next, the efficiency of the RACs and SACs is discussed in detail owing to its vital role in ensuring the right to trial. The chapter ends with an analysis of the impact of restrictions introduced in connection with the COVID-19 pandemic on the operation of administrative courts.

2.1. Cases Brought before the Regional Administrative Courts

Between 2004 and 2021, the number of cases that came before the RAC fluctuated between 57 thousand in 2008 and 87 thousand in 2021. The number of cases was changing quite dynamically; for example, in 2010, the number of cases increased by 15 % in comparison to the previous year; in 2021, there was a 26 % rise; and in 2016, a decrease by 8 %.

Obviously, such considerable fluctuations in the number of cases have a clear impact on the working conditions in the RACs and their efficiency (see Chapter 2). Therefore, it is practical to explain the reasons behind them.

Depending on the subject matter, the cases brought before the RAC are recorded in one of the three registers:

(1) "SA" – complaints against acts and other actions of the administrative authorities;
(2) "SAB" – complaints about failure to act and lengthy proceedings; and
(3) "SO" – other cases examined on the basis of the PbAC (including applications for granting the right to legal aid).

The structure of cases brought before the RAC in the years 2004–2021 is presented in Figure 2.1.

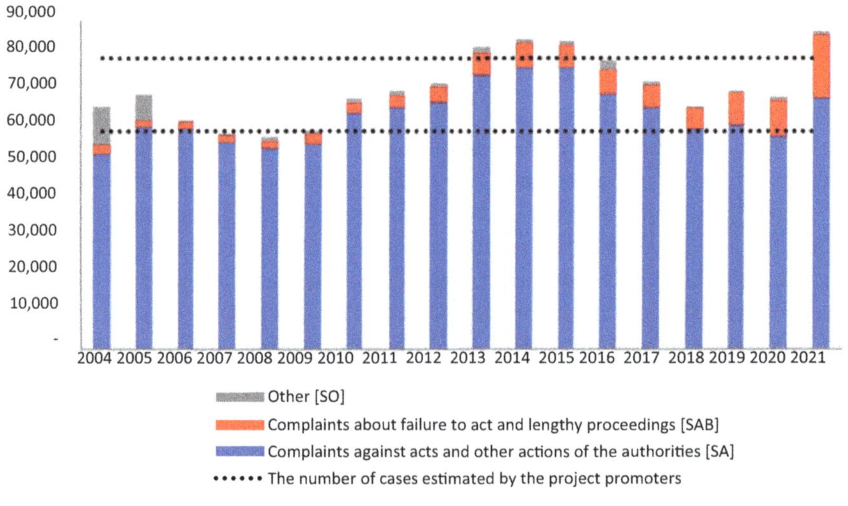

Figure 2.1. The structure of cases brought before the RAC in the years 2004–2021

Source: Movement of Cases in the RAC, http://www.nsa.gov.pl/statystyki-wsa.php (accessed on: 5/11/2022).

First, it is worth to compare the presented data with the forecasts that the authors of the concept of two-instance administrative judiciary formulated in 2001. As indicated in the justification to the draft law on the System of Administrative Courts presented by the President of the Republic of Poland[1], "analysis of the number of cases brought before the administrative court in recent years allows to estimate that the inflow of cases to the courts of first instance [i.e., the RAC] will reach the level of between 60,000 to 80,000 complaints per year." As it has turned out more than 20 years following the formulation of this forecast, it proved to be incredibly accurate as it quite precisely determined the range of fluctuations in the number of cases coming before the RACs.

Analysis of the number of complaints submitted to the RACs is of fundamental importance from the point of view of their operation. As far as cases recorded as "SO" are concerned, their number has remained very small over the last decade (and amounted to only several hundred per year), which does not validate detailed analyses of this group of cases to be carried out within the framework of this study. As a side note, it can be pointed out that a noticeable increase in the number of cases within this category in 2016 by more than a thousand occurred in the RAC in Warsaw and was caused by the activity of one person[2]. As regards complaints about failure to act and lengthy proceedings, four categories of complaints can be distinguished.[3] They are presented in Figure 2.2.

---

1 Print No. 18, the 4th term of office, documentation of the legislative process, http://orka.sejm.gov.pl/proc4.nsf/opisy/18.html (accessed on: 5/11/2022).

2 The query regarding final rulings announced in 2016 and the first half of 2017 with the complainant being P.S. and the premise – Article 55 of the PbAC retrieves 1241 judgements. In all cases, the complainant applied for a fine to be imposed on the Local College of Appeal in Warsaw. Cf., e.g., justification to the judgement of 5 June 2017, ref. No. I SO/Wa 1564/16.

3 For the purposes of statistical reporting, complaints are assigned symbols corresponding to their subject matter. The list of case symbols, their designations, and descriptions as well as the list of subject matters assigned each symbol are annexed to the Ordinance No. 14 of the President of the Supreme Administrative Court of 6 August 2015 on the Establishment of the Rules of Office at Administrative Courts.

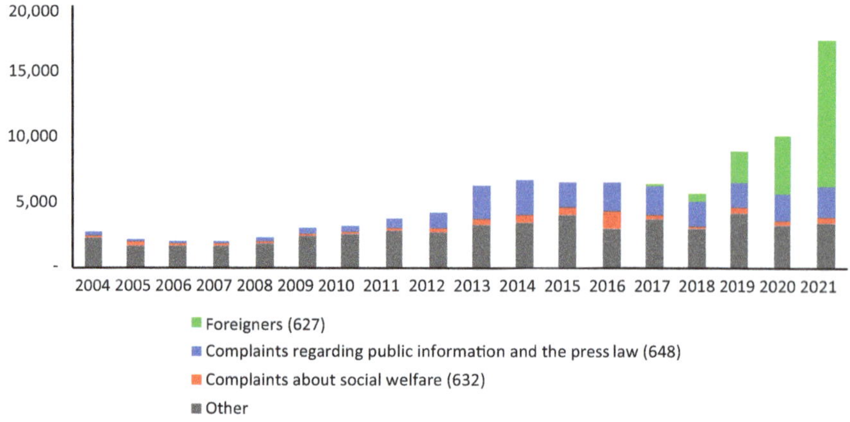

Figure 2.2. Number of complaints about failure to act and lengthy proceedings submitted to the RAC in the years 2004–2017 broken down by selected three-digit symbols

Source: Movement of Cases in the RAC, http://www.nsa.gov.pl/statystyki-wsa.php (accessed on: 5/11/2022).

The first category comprises complaints about the authorities' failure to act as regards social welfare; their number changed considerably in 2013 and then in 2016. In 2013, there was also a clear rise in the number of complaints against the authorities' actions as regards social welfare. Whereas in 2016, the number of complaints against the actions of the authorities as regards social welfare decreased noticeably (cf. part 1.1.b.). The second and the most variable category of cases are complaints about the authorities' failure to act as regards issues related to foreigners (627). There has been a sharp increase in their number observable from 2019 onward. Importantly, depending on the year, between 60 % and 80 % of all the cases in this category came before the RACs in Wrocław. This is a perfect illustration of how deficiency of particular public administration authorities can generate movement of cases noticeable at the level of aggregate statistical data presenting the movement of cases within the entire administrative judiciary.

The third category includes complaints about public information. It is difficult to assess the reasons behind the significant increase in their number, which occurred in 2013.

The third category of complaints about failure to act covers all the remaining groups of cases (assigned in total 45 different three-digit symbols). During the period under examination, their number ranged from two to four thousand cases per year.

However, as illustrated in Figure 1, the largest – and the most variable – group of cases brought before the RAC includes complaints against acts and other actions of the authorities. Therefore, they have been analysed in detail further in this chapter. Figure 2.3 shows the number of complaints submitted to the RAC in the years 2004–2021; the groups with the most variable number of cases are highlighted. As it turns out, complaints responsible for the majority of the fluctuations fall into seven categories.

Tax-related cases (symbol 611), which make up almost a third of the total number of complaints, vary the most. In the period under analysis, their number fluctuated between 13 and 26 thousand per year. The number of cases concerned with social welfare varies considerably as well. It is also worth noting the number of complaints concerning business activity, which increased in 2015 by more than 250 % compared to the previous year and remained similar in 2016 only to quickly decrease to the previous level afterwards. In turn, in 2020 and 2021, there was a sharp increase in the number of complaints registered as concerning public funds and not covered by other symbols (653). In addition, in 2021, the number of complaints concerning employment and business relations, including those related to labour inspection, tripled in comparison with the previous year.

In contrast, the number of other types of complaints remains relatively stable. In the years 2004–2021, it revolved around 30 thousand cases per year (there were between 26 and 33 thousand complaints per annum).

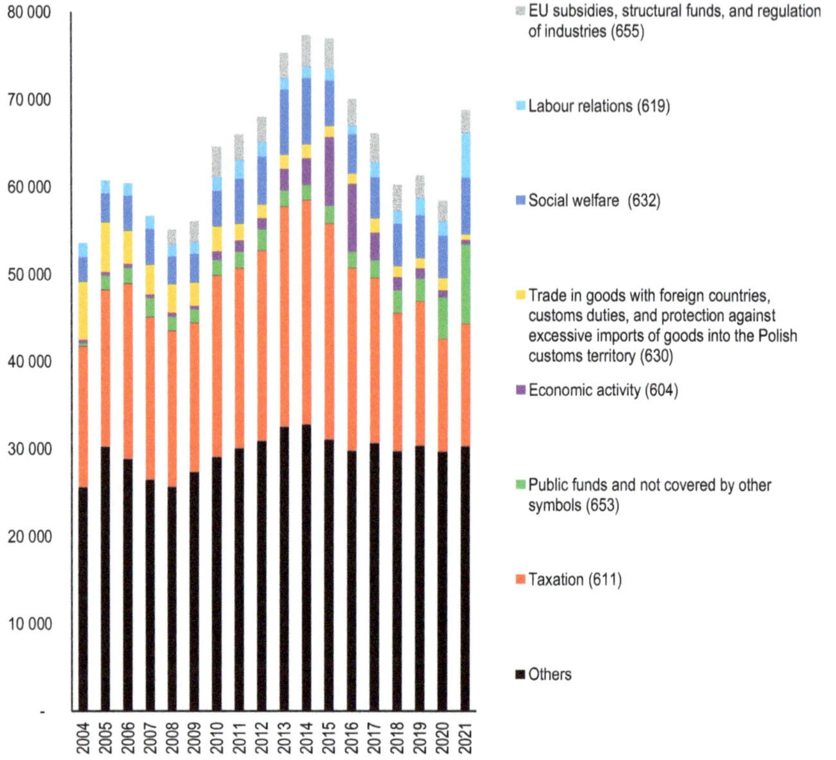

Figure 2.3. Number of complaints against acts and other actions of the authorities submitted to the RAC in the years 2004–2021, broken down by the selected three-digit symbols.

Source: Complaints against acts and actions – with symbols, http://www.nsa.gov.pl/statystyki-wsa.php (accessed on: 5/11/2022).

Based on Figure 2.3, it is possible to single out the following four main groups of complaints against acts and actions of the authorities:

(1) Complaints whose number remains relatively stable (which is the category of other in Figure 2.3);
(2) Complaints whose fluctuations can be attributed to cyclical changes (e.g., those related to taxes and social welfare);
(3) Complaints whose number is affected by structural economic changes (e.g., matters related to customs or EU structural funds);
(4) Complaints whose number is affected by systemic changes in law (e.g., those concerned with tax rulings or business activity).

These groups of complaints are analysed in detail later in this chapter. What is more, it seems that changes in the number of certain categories of complaints were brought about by the outbreak of the COVID-19 pandemic as well as the restrictions imposed by public authorities to counter it.

2.2. Complaints Whose Number Remains Relatively Stable

Analysis of data from the period between 2004 and 2021 allows to include almost 50 categories[4] of cases in this group. Its structure is also very fragmented; usually, the number of complaints with each symbol amounts to several thousand per year (however, it does not exceed two thousand in most categories).

Nevertheless, there seem to be some cyclical fluctuations in this group, if it is analysed as a whole. For example, between 2005 and 2008, when the economic situation had been improving, the number of such cases fell from 33 to 29 thousand, and then – along with the economic downturn – it increased again up to 36 thousand in 2013 and 2014.[5] Importantly, the number of cases falling into this category remained stable during the COVID-19 pandemic.

It is worth emphasising, however, that a category of complaints whose number has been stable for a long time may start to fluctuate sharply, for example, when systemic changes in the law or other unforeseen events occur. This is exemplified by complaints related to economic activity (symbol 604) – see Figure 2.7. – or the ones concerned with business relations and complaints about failure to act and lengthy proceedings regarding foreigners – see Figure 2.2.

2.3. Complaints Whose Number Is Affected by Structural Economic Transformations

Regardless of cyclical fluctuations, the number of complaints submitted to the RAC may also be influenced by long-term structural changes taking place in the Polish economy, e.g., due to the process of integration with the European Union.

Such a correlation is exemplified by complaints concerning trade in goods with foreign countries, customs duties, and protection against excessive imports of goods into the Polish customs territory (symbol 630). Until 2004, these complaints had formed the second – after complaints concerning taxes – largest category of complaints submitted to the RAC (comprising 30 % and 12 % of the

4 With tree-digit symbols.

5 See Section 1.1.b for more information on the correlation between the economic situation and the number of cases brought before court.

total number, respectively). During the first five years of Poland's membership in the European Union, their number had fallen by four thousand. Following a decade of EU membership, they comprised only about 2 % of all the complaints submitted to the RAC, and their number decreased further in 2021, which may be attributed to the impact of the COVID-19 pandemic.

This change corresponds to trade liberalisation accompanying accession to the European Union. The scale of this change manifests itself as a decrease in tax revenue from customs that has been observable over the last 15 years (while one should bear in mind that a certain amount of time passes between occurrence of certain facts and submission of a complaint to the RAC).

Fluctuations in the number of complaints on customs and the decrease in the significance of revenues from customs[6] are illustrated in Figure 2.4.

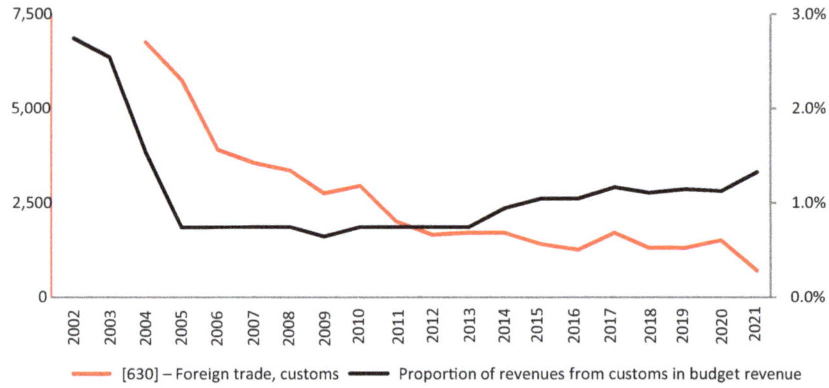

Figure 2.4. Reduction in the number of complaints about trade in goods with foreign countries and customs matters in the context of a decrease in revenues from customs.

Source: Number of cases: Complaints Against Acts and Actions – with Symbols, http://www.nsa.gov.pl/statystyki-wsa.php (accessed on: 5/11/2022); budget data: Annual Analyses of the Implementation of the State Budget, the Supreme Audit Office.

Apart from affecting the customs policy, accession to the European Union required absorption of a considerable amount of EU funds. As a result, there was an increase in the number of complaints categorised as EU subsidies, structural funds, and regulation of industries (symbol 655 introduced in 2008), as illustrated in Figure 2.5.

6 Same conclusions can be drawn from a juxtaposition of revenues from customs and the GDP.

Conclusion of the EU Financial Framework for 2007–2013 could also have affected the dynamics of complaints to some extent.

Figure 2.5. Number of complaints concerning EU subsidies, structural funds, and regulation of industries in the years 2008–2021

Source: Number of Cases: Complaints against Acts and Actions – with Symbols, http://www.nsa.gov.pl/statystyki-wsa.php (accessed on: 5/11/2022).

2.4. Complaints That Can Be Attributed to Legislative Changes

Naturally, another potential reason behind changes in the number of complaints submitted to administrative courts are amendments to the law, for example, introduction of new legal institutions and extension of the RAC's cognition to include them (and consequently the SAC's as well).

It is exemplified by the introduction – into the Polish legal order in 2007 – of the institution of tax rulings concerning future events and the possibility of challenging them before the RAC.[7] Due to the fact that this category of tax complaints can be easily attributed to a specific legislative change, it was excluded from previous analyses (cf. part 1.1.b.) so that it can be elaborated on separately.

The process of popularisation of the institution of tax rulings is illustrated in Figure 2.6.

---

7 Cf. respectively: Article 14b(2) of the Tax Ordinance and addition of point 4a to Article 3(2) of the PbAC through the Act of 16 November 2006 amending the Tax Ordinance and Some Other Acts (Dz.U.2006.217.1590).

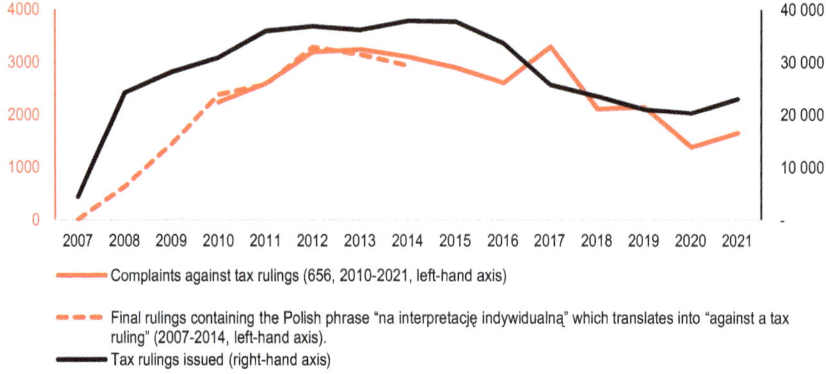

Figure 2.6. Number of tax rulings issued[8] as well as complaints against them submitted to the RAC (symbol 656)

Source: Number of Cases: Complaints against Acts and Actions – with Symbols, http://www.nsa.gov.pl/statystyki-wsa.php (accessed on: 5/11/2022); issued tax rulings: the Ministry of Finance, National Tax Information – 10 years in Poland, https://www.mazowieckie.kas.gov.pl/documents/3554560/0/20160720.10+lat+KIP.pdf (accessed on: 5/11/2022), and the annual Information on the Activities of the National Revenue Information, https://www.kis.gov.pl/dzialalnosc/raporty-z-dzialalnosci (accessed on: 5/11/2022).

Clearly, the fact that the new legal institution has become widespread caused (with slight delay) between 2.5 and 3 thousand new complaints to be submitted to the RAC. It is worth noting that popularisation of tax rulings coincided with a period of economic slowdown, which was accompanied by an increase in the number of other tax complaints (see Figure 2.7).

---

8 Cases with the symbol 656 have been registered separately since 2010; previously, they were recorded under the symbol 611 as tax cases. Therefore, in order to illustrate the number of cases regarding tax rulings, which were brought before the court between 2007 and 2009, a query was searched on the basis of on a Polish phrase "na interpretację indywidualną" (which translates into "against a tax ruling") among the final judgements. It is worth noting that the query was searched among concluded cases (with issued judgements) and not submitted complaints. These figures are thus only approximate.

Another example of a situation where a legislative change has led to a significant increase in the number of complaints submitted to the RAC is concerned with complaints about business activity, specifically organising games on slot machines[9] (see Figure 2.8).

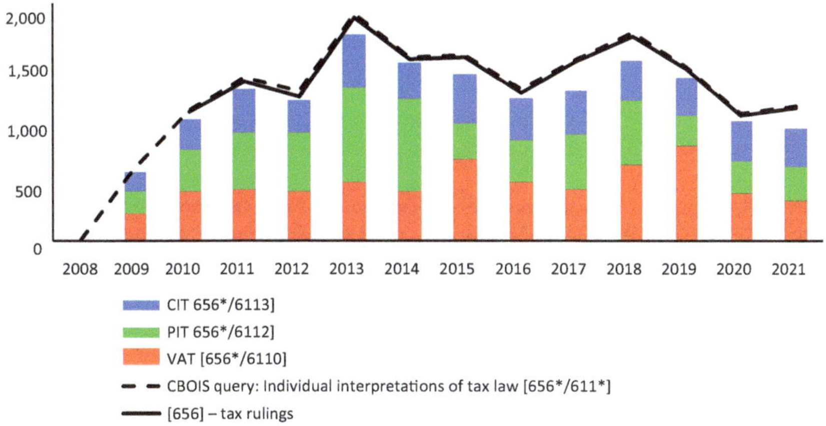

Figure 2.7. Structure of complaints about tax rulings (symbol 656) submitted to the RAC, broken down by key taxes (with four-digit symbols)

Source: Number of Cases: Complaints against Acts and Actions – with Symbols, http://www.nsa.gov.pl/statystyki-wsa.php (accessed on: 5/11/2022); data on the number of cases broken down by four-digit symbols after CBOIS.

9 This example is described in K . Jonski, (2020) *Legislacja a funkcjonowanie sądownictwa* [in:] M. Mazuryk, M. Kaczocha (eds.), *Legislacja w Polsce w latach 1918–2018. Sto lat doświadczeń tworzenia prawa*, Wydawnic-two Sejmowe, Warszawa 2020.

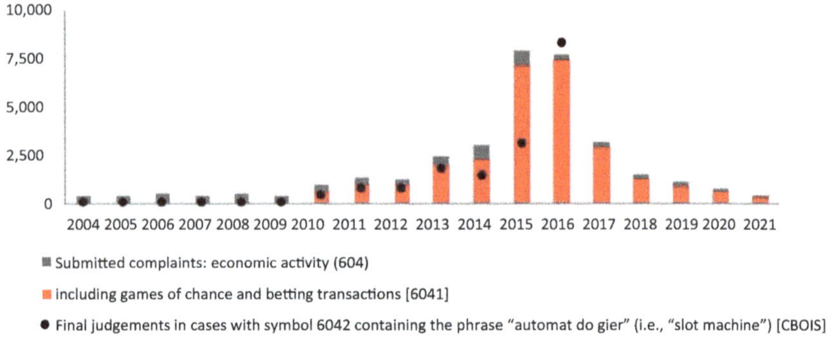

Figure 2.8. Number of complaints* about economic activity (symbol 604) submitted to the RAC in the years 2004–2021; complaints on games of chance and betting transactions are highlighted

* Statistical reporting does not allow to single out complaints about slot machines – therefore, a query was made to search judgements issued between 2008 and 2016 in cases with the symbol 6042, which contain the Polish phrase "automat do gier" (i.e., "slot machine"). Noteworthy, the query was made to search concluded cases (with issued judgements) and not submitted complaints.. Respectively, the bars represent cases brought before the court and the dots – the concluded ones. This explains the value obtained for 2016 when the number of recognised complaints exceeded the number of submitted complaints (as the RAC considered unresolved complaints from the previous year).

Source: Complaints against Acts and Actions – with Symbols, http://www.nsa.gov.pl/statystyki-wsa.php (accessed on: 5/11/2022).

The Act of 19 November 2009 on Gambling[10] introduces, among others, a legal definition of playing on a slot machine[11] and financial penalties for organising it outside casinos[12] (Article 89(1)(2) of the Act on Gambling).[13] Nevertheless, in accordance with the transitional provisions (Article 129 of the Act on Gambling),

10 Journal of Laws of 2009 No. 201, item 1540.

11 In line with Article 2(3) of the Act, it is a game "on mechanical, electromechanical, or electronic devices, including computer devices, for monetary winnings or winnings in kind, which is randomized to some extent."

12 According to Article 4(1)(a) of the Act on Gambling, a casino is considered to be a "separate place offering roulette games, card games, dice games or slot games, which operates based on an approved rulebook, with the minimum total number of roulette games and card games being 4 and the number of installed slots – between 5 and 70."

13 As indicated in the RIA of the government submission, "In pursuit of the fundamental and systemic objectives, especially the goal of enhancing protection of the society and the rule of law from the effects of gambling, there can be no randomized slot machine games offered outside casinos." Cf. print of the Sejm of the 6th term of office, No. 2481.

business activity concerned with the so-called low-prize gaming machines and the so-called gaming arcades, if carried out on the basis of permits issued for a period of six years[14], could continue until their expiry.

2.5. Complaints Whose Number Appears to Be Related to Cyclical Changes – Matters Concerning Taxes (611) and Social Welfare (632)

For millennia, it has been typical for the functioning of the economies to show cyclical fluctuations of activity, that is, the so-called business cycles.[15] Contrary to the hopes commonly expressed at the beginning of the 21st century[16] at the time of Great Moderation, it does not seem that they might be eliminated in the foreseeable future.

Although from the time of systemic transformation until the Covid-19 pandemic, Poland had not fallen into a recession[17], cyclical fluctuations were noticeable in our economy as well. One of the indicators that allow to illustrate them is the so-called output gap. This measure is intended to reflect the difference between the actual (observable) and potential level of the gross domestic product; in other words, it informs whether the economy is developing above or below its potential.

There is an estimation of the output gap compiled by the European Commission[18] presented in Figure 2.9 in the context of complaints on taxes (symbol 611) and social welfare (symbol 632) submitted to the RAC. Tax rulings and advance opinions (symbol 656) were excluded from the pool of complaints about taxes because they are discussed in more detail in section 1.1.c.

---

14 Article 36(1) of the Act of 29 July 1992 on Games and Betting Transactions (Dz.U.2004.4.27, consolidated text).

15 An example of that can be a story described in the Book of Genesis (Genesis 41).

16 For example, in the famous and often quoted speech of the Nobel Laureate R. Lucas delivered at the 115th meeting of the American Economic Association, which took place in 2003, he stated that "macroeconomics in this original sense has succeeded: Its central problem of depression prevention has been solved, for all practical purposes, and has in fact been solved for many decades."

17 More on the so-called transformational recession, e.g., in: R. Zukowski (1993), *Stabilization and Recession in a Transitional Economy: The Case of Poland*, "World Development" 1993, Vol. 21, No. 7, s. 1163–1178; G. Kolodko, *Globalization and Catching-up: From Recession to Growth in Transition Economies*, "Communist and Post-Communist Studies" 2001, No. 34, pp. 279–322.

18 Cf. The AMECO database, https://economy-finance.ec.europa.eu/economic-research-and-databases/economic-databases/ameco-database_en

The presented value of the output gap indicates that before 2007 the Polish economy was developing below its potential and the number of complaints under examination was increasing at that time.[19] After 2006, at the apex of the economic upturn (and with growth exceeding the potential), the number of complaints decreased slightly only to increase again in 2010 and 2013 – which can be linked to the subsequent phases of the economic downturn:

the financial crisis[20] and the European debt crisis[21] (2010). The drop in the number of complaints that happened after 2014 also seems to be linked to the improvement in the economic situation reflected by the closing of the output gap.[22] The growth noticeable between 2017 and 2019, which clearly exceeded the potential of the Polish economy, was accompanied by a record low number of complaints on taxes. However, it turned out that the number of cases of this type was further decreasing during the COVID-19 pandemic (but in contrast to complaints on taxes, the number of complaints about social welfare increased).

---

19 However, one should bear in mind that these were the first years of the operation of two-instance administrative judiciary – which could have affected the number of submitted complaints (and so considerable caution is advised when interpreting data for this period).

20 Which was symbolically initiated by the fall of Lehman Brothers (15/09/2008).

21 Which had been unfolding since the turn of 2010 and 2011 and was symbolically brought to an end by M. Draghi's speech of 26 July 2012.

22 Interestingly, although there is a survey (see the BOSE indicator shown in Appendix 1, which reflects the current economic situation based on comparison of companies in a good condition with those in a poor condition – in simplified terms) indicating that the most severe economic downturn occurred in the recessionary year of 2009, the values of the output gap suggest that the deepest slowdown occurred in 2013.

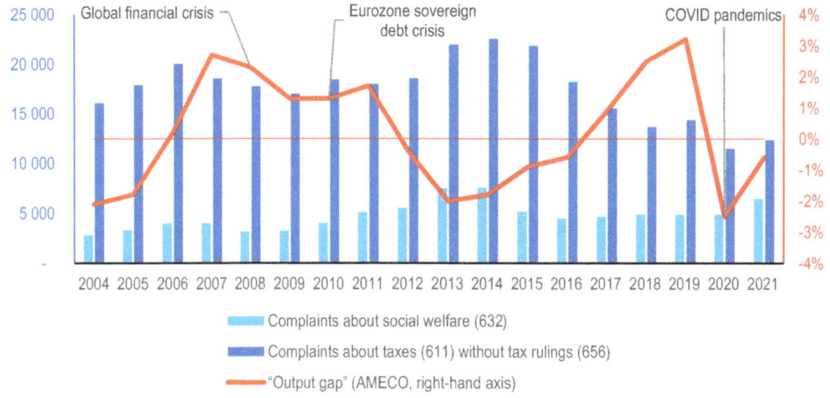

Figure 2.9. Changes in the number of submitted complaints about taxes* and social welfare in the context of economic changes (and the output gap)

* Cases with symbol 611, excluding complaints about tax rulings and advance opinions (symbol 656).

Source: Number of Complaints: Reports, http://www.nsa.gov.pl/statystyki-wsa.php; output gap (between actual GDP and potential GDP, percentage of the potential GDP): the European Commission, the AMECO database, https://economy-finance.ec.europa.eu/ economic-research-and-databases/economic-databases/ameco-database_en (accessed on: 5/11/2022).

All the above point to the existence of a correlation between the changes in the economic situation and the number of complaints about taxes and social welfare submitted to the RAC.

However, an in-depth analysis of complaints about taxes (symbol 611) reveals quite an unexpected correlation: The cyclical fluctuations observed in Figure 2.9 are essentially the consequence of changes in the number of complaints on excise duty as well as changes in the number of complaints about personal income tax, although to a much smaller degree. Additionally, contrary to complaints about excise duty, complaints regarding the second key indirect tax – VAT – do not follow the course of the business cycle. Moreover, their number was slightly declining during the period of widening and then narrowing of the so-called "VAT gap" (see Chapter 3). These dynamics are presented in Figure 2.9.

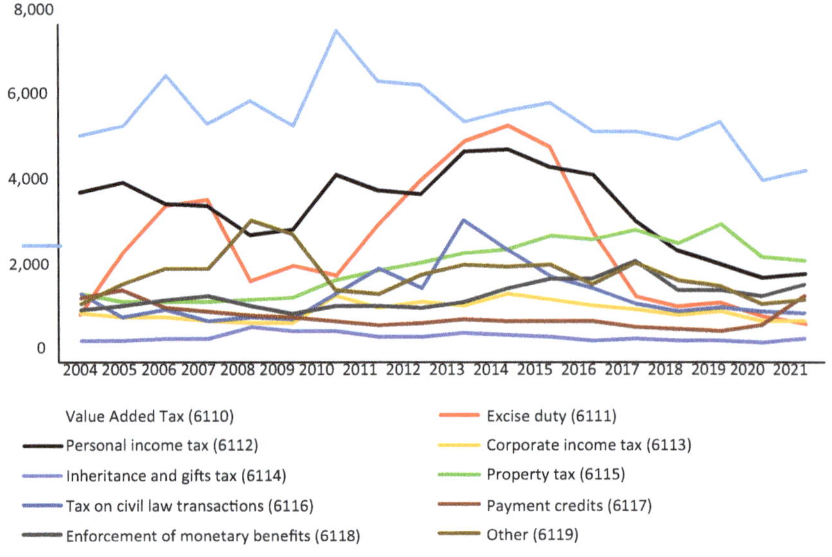

Figure 2.10. Changes in the number of submitted complaints against acts and activities regarding taxes broken down by four-digit symbols

Source: Number of Complaints: Reports, http://www.nsa.gov.pl/statystyki-wsa.php (accessed on: 5/11/2022).

2.6. Summary of Changes in the Number of Complaints Submitted to the RAC

To sum up the considerations so far, let us attempt to illustrate to what extent each group of complaints contributed to the fluctuations in the total number of complaints submitted to the RAC.

Figure 2.10 shows percentage changes in the total number of submitted complaints each year[23] and their decomposition taking into account the key groups analysed above.

The presented analysis once again demonstrates considerable variability in the number of complaints lodged with the RAC. It turns out, however, that a group of about 30 thousand complaints categorised in this chapter into the "stable" group only fluctuated up to 5 %.[24] The only exception was the year 2005

23 Which is the total of complaints on activities of the authorities (SA) and complaints about failure to act and lengthy proceedings (SAB).

24 After 2010, this category of cases accounted for fluctuations ranging +/– 2 %.

compared to 2004. However, one should not forget that these were the first years of operation of two-instance administrative judiciary and so caution is advised when interpreting data for this period.

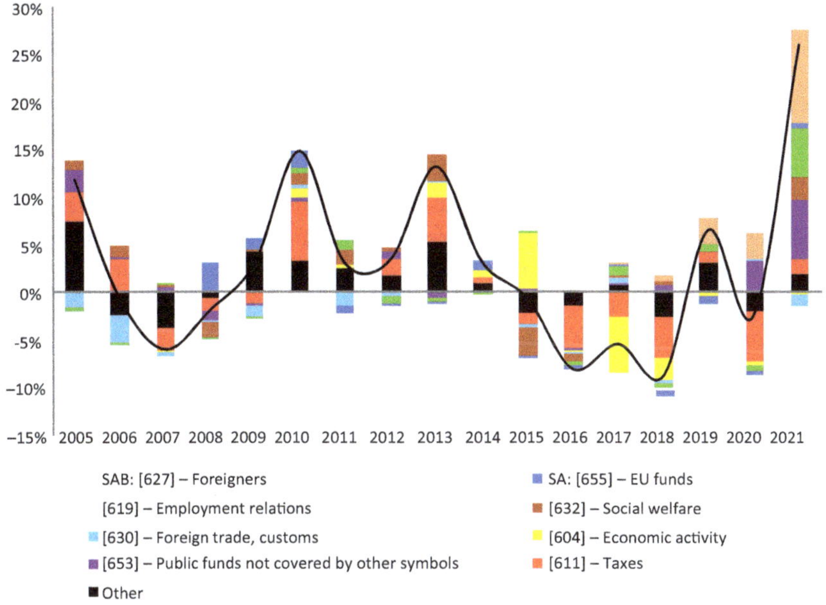

Figure 2.11. Decomposition of changes in the number of complaints submitted to the RAC in the years 2005–2021: percentage change compared to the previous year

Source: Complaints on acts and actions with symbols and complaints on failure to act and lengthy proceedings: http://www.nsa.gov.pl/statystyki-wsa.php (accessed on: 5/11/2022).

In principle, before 2019, complaints about the authorities' failure to act and lengthy proceedings had little impact on the changes in the total number of complaints lodged with the RAC in the period under examination. This situation changed unexpectedly in 2019 as there was a sharp increase in the number of cases concerning foreigners, in particular those submitted to the RAC in Wrocław (see Figure 2.2). Evidently, the unusual consequence of the deficiency of public administration authorities may be a burden placed on the administrative judiciary. Furthermore, changes that can be attributed to structural transformations of the Polish economy related to the accession to the EU have also contributed to the increase in the number of complaints only to a small extent.

The data presented in Figure 2.11 imply that before the year 2021 (which could prove unusual due to the COVID-19 pandemic), fluctuations in tax cases (including the ones arising from the introduction of the institution of challengeable tax rulings) as well as other systemic changes in the law (such as gambling regulations and other changes affecting the number of complaints about business activity) were considered key factors accounting for the fluctuations in the total number of complaints submitted to the RAC each year.

From the point of view of the management of the administrative judiciary, the presented analyses pose a question as to the possibility of forecasting changes in the number of cases brought before the RAC. Unfortunately, the experience of the 18 years of operation of the two-instance administrative judiciary teaches us to have scepticism in this regard. First and foremost, the role of unpredictable events becomes vital in this respect, for example, as in the case of complaints about failure to act and lengthy proceedings in cases involving foreigners. In the period preceding the COVID-19 pandemic, the variability in some large groups of cases – in particular those regarding taxes – seems difficult to predict. Even though analysis of statistical data (cf. Fig. 2.9.) may point to their correlation with cyclical fluctuations of the economy, effective forecasting requires the existence of cause-and-effect relationships. More detailed analyses of individual cases presented in Chapter 3 call for utmost caution in this respect.

Whereas as regards complaints whose number is related to systemic legal changes, the prerequisite for forecasting their numbers is the capability of reliably assessing the effects of the regulations (RIA).[25]

It should be noted that the RIAs of none of the draft laws that had the greatest impact on the number of complaints lodged with the RAC in the period under analysis (cf. section 1.1.d)[26] indicated that the consequence of the entry into force of the drafted law would be an increase in the number of cases brought before the RAC.

Indeed, contemporary experiences suggest that compiling an RIA is an overly complex process (both for scientific reasons and from the perspective of

25 In line with Article 28(1) of the Bylaws of the Council of Ministers (M.P.2016.1006, consolidated text), the RIA is a separate section of a justification to a draft act, which presents evaluation of the anticipated socio-economic consequences of the drafted law. This document was introduced into the state legislative process in 2001 (M.P.2001.33.547).

26 These are: amendment to the Tax Ordinance introducing challengeable tax rulings concerning future events (see Print of the Sejm of the 5th term of office, No. 731) and the Act on Gambling prohibiting the organisation of games on slot machines outside casinos (see Print of the Sejm of the 6th term of office, No. 2481).

the administrative practice[27]), and the estimates provided therein often prove considerably arbitrary and find no confirmation in verifiable facts.

For example, in the course of legislative work on the draft act amending some acts in order to prevent the use of the financial sector for tax fraud (UD232)[28], in the RIA drawn up 20 days apart, the project promoters estimated that there may be 4,650[29] and 700[30] blockades of business accounts (which could be appealed to the RAC in Warsaw). Another example is the ex-post RIA of the Act of 19 July 2019 Amending Certain Acts to Reduce Payment Backlogs[31], which assessed the expected and actual number of administrative proceedings and decisions made by the President of the Office of Competition and Consumer Protection.[32]

2.7. Cases Brought before the Supreme Administrative Court

At the outset, it is worth mentioning that in contrast to the practically perfect forecast of the number of cases brought before the RAC (cf. Section 1.1.),

the prediction accepted in the justification to the draft of the System of Administrative Courts[33] foreseeing that "about 10 % of the judgements issued by administrative courts of first instance may be appealed to the second instance" has not come true.

---

27 Cf., e.g., D.J. Gajewski, A. Werner, P. Karwat, A. Olczyk, J. Wierzbicki, *Tendencje w polityce podatkowej w kra-jach Europy Środkowo-Wschodniej: obowiązki podatkowe przedsiębiorców*, w: *Raport SGH i Forum Ekonomicznego 2020*, Oficyna Wydawnicza SGH, Warszawa 2020, s. 481–524; D.J. Gajewski, P. Karwat, A. Olczyk, A. Werner, J. Wierzbicki, *Reakcja polskiej polityki podatkowej na kryzys związany z pandemią na tle państw Grupy Wyszehradzkiej, Raport SGH i Forum Ekonomicznego 2021*, Oficyna Wydawnicza SGH, Warszawa 2021, s. 189–223, Interesujące analiz w tym zakresie, na przykładzie procesu wprowadzania restrykcji związanych z pandemią COVID-19, prezentują K. Joński, W. Rogowski, *Evidence-Based Policymaking during the COVID-19 Crisis: Regulatory Impact Assessments and the Polish COVID-19 Restrictions*, "European Journal of Risk Regulation" 2022, s. 1–13. doi:10.1017/err.2022.18.

28 Documentation of the legislative process, https://legislacja.rcl.gov.pl/projekt/12296503 (accessed on: 5/11/2022).

29 Version of 31 August 2017, p. 122, https://legislacja.rcl.gov.pl/docs//2/12296503/12421639/12421640/dokument308702.pdf (accessed on: 5/11/2022).

30 Version of 20 September 2017, p. 8, https://legislacja.rcl.gov.pl/docs//2/12296503/12421645/12421646/dokument309870.pdf (accessed on: 5/11/2022).

31 Journal of Laws 2019, item 1649.

32 https://legislacja.rcl.gov.pl/projekt/12355253/katalog/12846683#12846683 (accessed: 5/11/2022).

33 Print No. 18, 4th term of office, documentation of the legislative process, http://orka.sejm.gov.pl/proc4.nsf/opisy/18. html (accessed on: 5/11/2022).

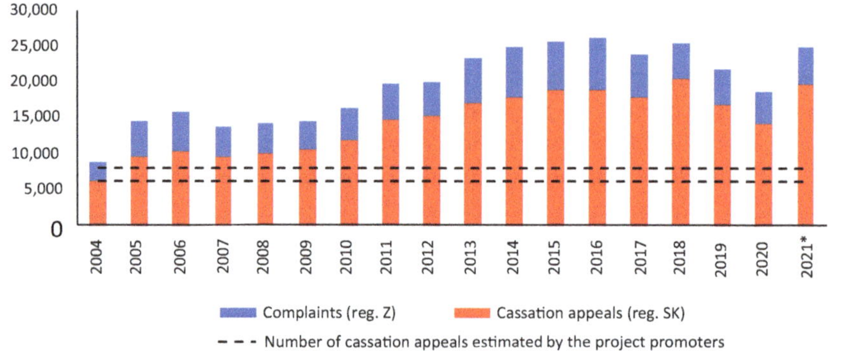

Figure 2.12. Number of cases brought before the SAC in the years 2004–2021

* As far as 2021 is concerned, more than seven thousand cases were disregarded as they were re-registered in connection with the establishment of the new departments: the General Administration Chamber and the Financial Chamber.

Source: Data on the movement of cases in the SAC, http://www.nsa.gov.pl/statystyki-nsa.php (accessed on: 5/11/2022).

In contrast to the RAC, which seemed to be dealing with a number of complaints fluctuating like a sine wave in the period under analysis, the number of complaints filed with the SAC increased significantly (see Figure 2.12), which directly affected its efficiency (see section 2.2.c). Thus, the issue of explaining the determinants of changes in the number of cassation appeals assumes high practical significance. Due to their large share (of about 70 %) in the total number of cases, their importance for the legal system as well as the working time of judges necessary to consider cases of this category (compared to complaints), subsequent part of the analysis is concerned with fluctuations in the number of cassation appeals (reg. SK). The obvious starting point is to link the number of cassation appeals lodged with the SAC with the number of complaints recognised by the RAC (reg. SA and SAB).[34]

The parameter linking these two variables is the challengeability, which can be interpreted as the probability that a given RAC's ruling will be challenged at the SAC. It may be approximated by the number of cassation appeals filed with the SAC in a

34 In order to take into account the organisational structure of the SAC for the purposes of this analysis, the division of complaints based on the jurisdiction of the Chambers of the SAC has been adopted instead of symbols used in the preceding sections. For more information on the substantive jurisdiction of the Chambers of the SAC, see: http://www.nsa.gov.pl/struktura-organizacyjna.php (accessed on: 5/11/2022).

given year divided by the number of complaints recognised by the RAC within the same period of time (in percentages). This data is shown in Figure 2.13.

Evidently, the correlation between the number of complaints recognised by the RAC and the number of cassation appeals lodged with the SAC varies in different case groups and changes over time on top of that (in particular, as regards cases considered by the Financial Chamber and the General Administrative Chamber: Before 2011, challengeability was noticeably rising).

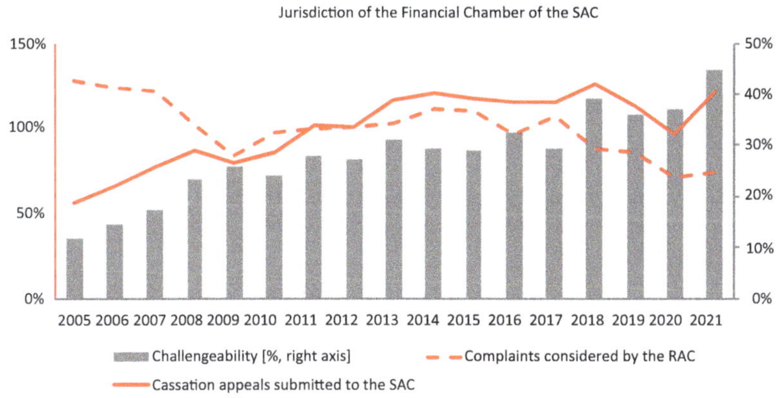

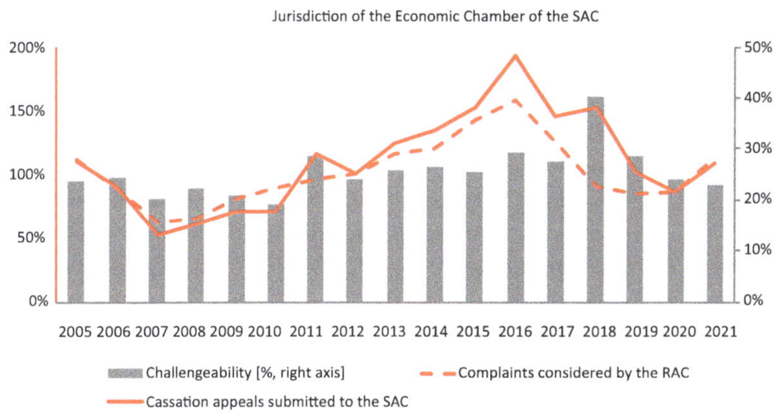

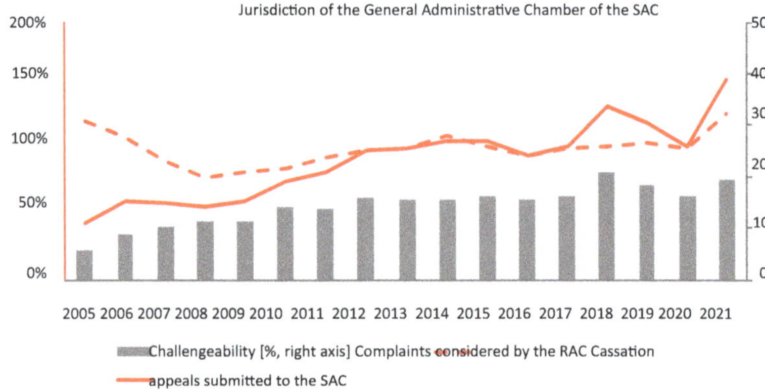

Figure 2.13. Number of cassation appeals submitted to the SAC* against the number of complaints considered by the RAC** in the years 2005–2021 (year 2012=100 %)

* Excluding re-registered cases.

** Cases registered in SA and SAB; since 2018, "settled" and "closed" cases are provided in order to ensure comparability with data from the previous years when cases categorised as "closed" were not recorded separately.

Source: Data on the movement of cases in the SAC, http://www.nsa.gov.pl/statystyki-nsa.php (accessed on: 5.11.2022); data on the movement of cases in the RAC, http://www.nsa.gov.pl/statyst yki-wsa.php (accessed on: 5/11/2022).

As regards the Financial Chamber, the dependency does not seem to be particularly strong: Throughout the whole period under analysis, there was an upward trend in challengeability, regardless of the fluctuations in the number of complaints recognised by the RAC.

As far as the Economic Chamber is concerned, the correlation between the number of cassation appeals submitted to the SAC and the number of complaints examined by the RAC appears to be more stable, except for, e.g., the years 2011 or 2018.

It is worth analysing why the number of cassation appeals filed with the Economic Chamber doubled in the years 2012–2016. As Figure 2.14 shows, this was mainly caused by an increase in the number of complaints about business activity (specifically as regards games of changes and betting transactions – with symbol 6042 – which are elaborated on more broadly in section 1.1.d and Figure 2.8). Whereas cases concerned with excise duty (symbol 6111)[35] contributed to fluctuations in the number of cassation appeals submitted to the Economic Chamber to a much smaller extent. Therefore, it seems reasonable to assume that this was a one-off event.

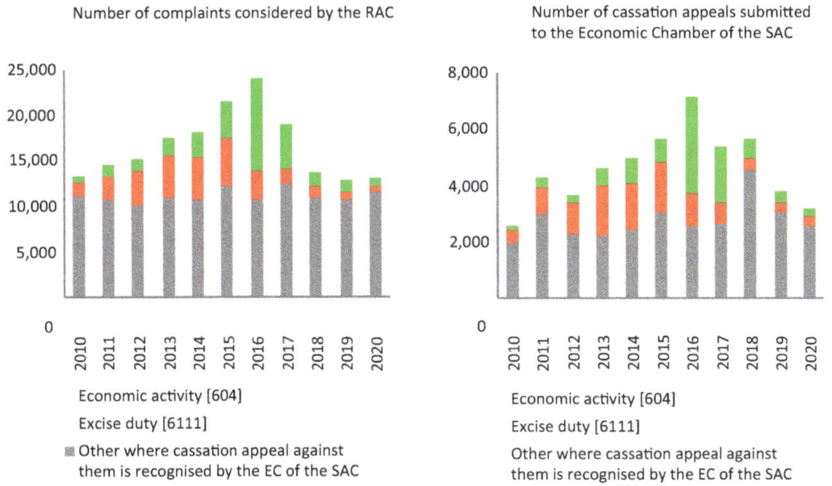

Figure 2.14. Explanation of the reasons behind the increase in the number of cassation appeals submitted to the Economic Chamber of the SAC

Source: Data on the movement of cases in the SAC, http://www.nsa.gov.pl/statystyki-nsa.php (accessed on: 5/11/2022); data on the movement of cases in the RAC, http://www.nsa.gov.pl/statyst yki-wsa.php (accessed on: 5/11/2022).

35 Recognition of cases about excise duty (with symbol 6111) was handed over to the Economic Chamber of the SAC, cf. Ordinance No. 17 of the President of the SAC of 4 December 2007 on the Establishment of Adjudicating Divisions at the Chambers of the Supreme Administrative Court and the Scope of their Operation (unpublished act) as formulated in Article 1 of the Ordinance No. 15 of the President of the SAC of 30 September 2009 amending the Ordinance on the Establishment of Adjudicating Divisions at the Chambers of the Supreme Administrative Court and the Scope of their Operation (unpublished act). Compliance of the change of jurisdiction *ratione materiae* introduced in such a way with Article 45(1) in conjunction with Article 176(2) and Article 2 of the Constitution was contested in case SK 41/15 which was dismissed by the Constitutional Tribunal by way of its judgement of 5 April 2016 (since submission of a constitutional complaint must be linked to the adoption of specific rules for using this instrument protecting the constitutional rights and freedoms. Failure to comply with these rules prevents the effective initiation of the proceedings before the Tribunal, irrespective of the factual and legal circumstances surrounding the case that the appeal is connected with; cf. Judgement of the Constitutional Tribunal of 5/04/2016, SK 41/15, OTK-A 2016, No. 5).

The level of challengeability in each category of cases is also interesting to examine. In particular, it turns out that challengeability of cases concerning excise duty is the highest, which corresponds to a particularly high level of challengeability of cases that have cassation appeals against them recognised by the Financial Chamber of the SAC. In the case of the General Administration Chamber, the correlation between the number of complaints recognised by the RAC and the number of cassation appeals submitted after 2010 seems relatively stable, however, greater fluctuations have been observable in the recent years. To sum up, the number of cassation appeals submitted to the SAC in the period under examination fluctuated in a somewhat similar fashion as the number of complaints recognised by the RAC. By definition, the parameter linking these two variables is the challengeability which also varied in the period under analysis and reached the highest value in cases concerned with taxes. It also appears important that the RAC's judgements regarding tax rulings (656) are challenged particularly frequently.

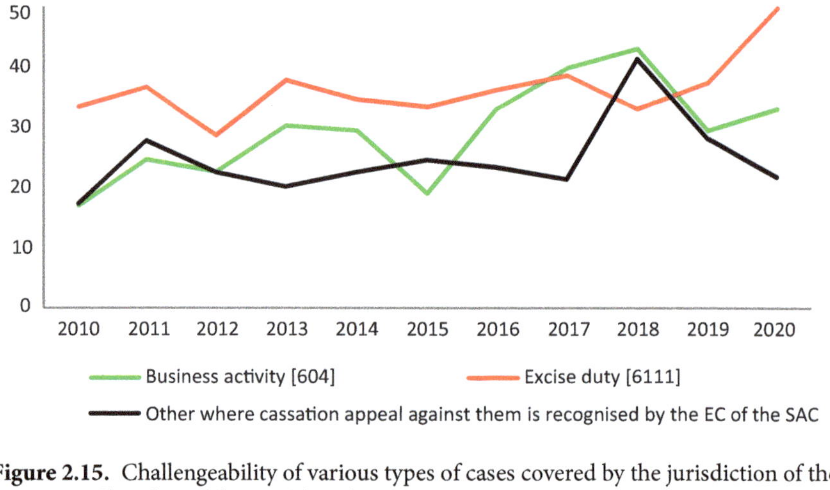

Figure 2.15. Challengeability of various types of cases covered by the jurisdiction of the Economic Chamber of the SAC (in %)

* Before 2013, the number of cases in this category was exceedingly small (that is, 124–312 cassation appeals; in 2013, there were 400–600), which affects the reliability of the challengeability calculated based on it – see Figure 2.12.

Source: Data on the movement of cases in the SAC, http://www.nsa.gov.pl/statystyki-nsa.php (accessed on: 5/11/2022); data on the movement of cases in the RAC, http://www.nsa.gov.pl/statystyki-wsa.php (accessed on: 5/11/2022).

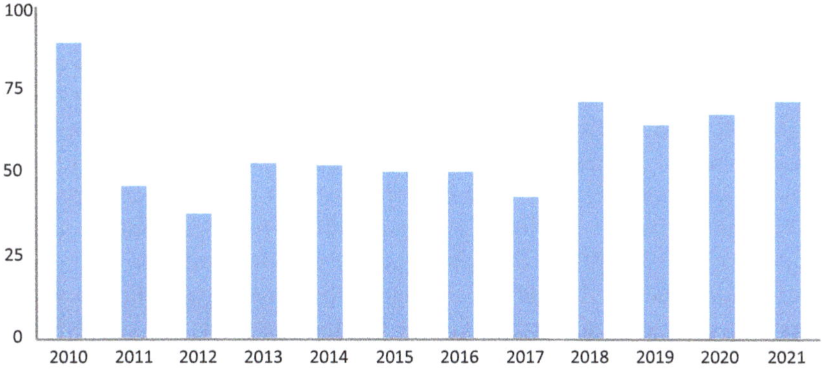

Figure 2.16. Challengeability in cases concerning tax rulings (656, in %)

Source: Data on the movement of cases in the SAC, available at http://www.nsa.gov.pl/statystyki-nsa.php (accessed on: 5/11/2022); data on the movement of cases in the RAC, available at http://www.nsa.gov.pl/statystyki-wsa.php (accessed on: 5/11/2022).

In the context of fluctuations in the challengeability of RAC's rulings, it is also worth mentioning the resolution of the full composition of the SAC of 26 October 2009 (I OPS 10/09) which shaped the current and uniform case law practice in terms of the obligation of the SAC to refer to all the allegations cited as the bases for a cassation appeal.[36] In the justification to the resolution, the substance of the right to trial arising from Article 45(1) and Article 77(2) of the Constitution was evoked and then elaborated upon further in the case law of

36 Resolution of the SAC of 26/10/2009, I OPS 10/09, ONSAiWSA 2010, No. 1, item 1., see also H. Knysiak-Molczyk's critical commentary: Gloss to the Resolution of the SAC of 26 October 2009, I OPS 10/09, Przegląd Sejmowy 2010/4/218-226 and the approving gloss by G. Borkowski: Basis for a Cassation Appeal – Interpretation of Article 174 of the Act on Law on Proceedings before Administrative Courts. Gloss to the resolution of the SAC of 26 October 2009, I OPS 10/09, Gloss 2009/4/137-148. By the way, it is worth pointing out that at the time when the said resolution was passed, the issue of the basis for a cassation appeal was also the subject of constitutional complaints (cf., e.g., Judgement of the Constitutional Tribunal of 19/10/2010, SK 8/09, OTK-A 2010, No. 8, item 94 and the approving gloss by W. Piątek and A. Skoczylas: Basis for a Cassation Appeal in Administrative Court Proceedings. Gloss to the Resolution of the CT of 19 October 2010, SK 8/09, PiP 2011/5/119-124).

the Constitutional Tribunal. According to the SAC, the purpose of a cassation appeal is to allow a party dissatisfied with the judgement of the first-instance court, which assessed infringement of the administrative procedure, to have the SAC verify the correctness of this assessment within the limits set out in the basis for the cassation appeal as defined in Article 174(2) of the PbAC. Consideration of the case by the SAC means that the Court examines it within the limits of all the allegations listed in the basis for the cassation appeal. The SAC claims that failure to address all the allegations reported must be qualified as an unjustified derogation from the principle of being bound by the limits of the cassation appeal and should be assessed in the same way as going beyond the limits of the appeal. It was stressed in the justification to the resolution that the cassation basis understood in this way makes the cassation appeal an effective appeal measure in the sense that its submission enables substantive resolution of a case in the proceedings before the SAC (see p. 38 of the justification).[37] It is also worth comparing the probability of the repeal of the RAC's judgement in each Chamber of the SAC (see Figure 2.17).

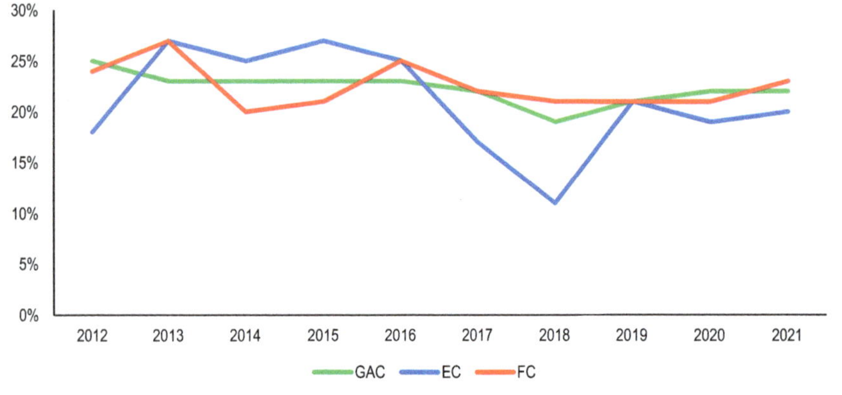

Figure 2.17. Proportion of cassation appeals upheld in the years 2012–2021
Source: Data on the movement of cases in the SAC, available at http://www.nsa.gov.pl/statystyki-nsa.php (accessed on: 5/11/2022).

37 Cf. Gloss to the Resolution of the CT of 19/10/2010, SK 8/09, OTK-A 2010, No. 8, item 94.

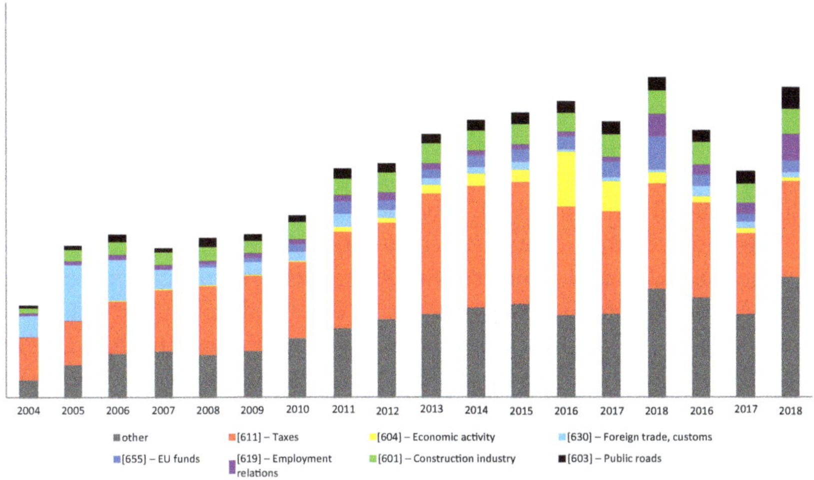

Figure 2.18. Number of cassation appeals (excluding the re-registered ones) submitted to the SAC in the years 2004–2018, broken down by the selected three-digit symbols (as in Figure 2.3)

Source: Data on the movement of cases in the SAC, http://www.nsa.gov.pl/statystyki-nsa.php (accessed on: 5/11/2022).

Figure 2.18 supplements the previous analysis – where cassation appeals were divided based on the jurisdiction *ratione materiae* of each Chamber of the SAC – by presenting the number of cassation appeals filed with the court broken down by selected three-digit symbols previously used for the analysis of the RAC.

2.8. Effectiveness of the Regional Administrative Courts

From an economic point of view, administrative control exercised by administrative courts may be seen as independent arbitration in disputes between the private and the public sectors. The conditions for exercising it properly are set out in Article 45 of the Constitution, which grants everyone "the right to a fair and open examination of a case by a competent, independent, and impartial court without undue delay." Traditionally, this standard is considered with reference to two aspects; one is related to the systemic position of the courts (i.e., their impartiality and independence) and the other with their organisation (their effectiveness). Considering the high variability in the number of complaints submitted to the courts, this chapter analyses the capacity of administrative courts to live up to the constitutional standard for the recognition of complaints without undue delay. In order to pursue this goal, two concepts need to be defined: effectiveness and efficiency of the court. Effectiveness of the court will be understood as its ability to quickly recognise cases that are brought before it.[38]

Whereas efficiency will refer to the relation between expenditure (e.g., of work) and achievement of results (i.e., recognition of cases). In other words, one might picture in their imagination that a very effective court could be very inefficient (if a disproportionately large number of judges effectively recognise very few cases) or that a very efficient court could be highly ineffective (if a disproportionately small number of judges cannot avoid lengthy proceedings despite hearing an above-average number of cases). Obviously, from the point of view of enforcement of the constitutional right to trial, effectiveness is of key significance, however, efficiency of the system determines the way the society evaluates how successfully this right is enforced.

The following two basic measures can be used to assess the effectiveness of the Regional Administrative Courts:

(1) Timeliness of complaint resolution at the RAC: That is, the typical lapse of time between submission of a complaint and its resolution; and
(2) The clearance rate, that is, the ratio of the number of recognised complaints to the number of submitted complaints,[39] which is a measure of the court's capability of recognising cases on an ongoing basis.

Of course, there is a logical relationship between these two measures (and it should be expected that the inability to recognise complaints on an ongoing basis will be accompanied by an increase in the duration of the proceedings), and so changes in one allow to better understand the dynamics of the other.

In the relevant literature, two approaches are employed to measure the timeliness of case recognition.

---

38 One should note that the analyses presented below make use of statistical categories which are average figures and refer to a large number of cases. Thus, they describe the effectiveness of the court (or the judicial system) as a whole – as a public institution. They are intended to diagnose systemic barriers that exist at this level. The case is different with the assessment of a particular case of lengthy proceedings when considering the institution of filing a complaint on the violation of a party's right to have their case recognised in court proceedings without undue delay. In such a case, a systemic cause (e.g., case overload) is only one possible reason behind the lengthiness of the proceedings.

39 Clearance Rate (CR)" por. np. CEPEJ, *European judicial systems Efficiency and quality of justice*, Edition 2016 (2014 data), "CEPEJ STUDIES" 2016, No. 23, p. 48.

The first one uses data on the time elapsed since the case was brought before the court until its resolution.[40] Therefore, the average values calculated on this basis only take into account a sample of cases settled within a given period. The advantage of this way of calculation of the typical time of complaint resolution is the direct reference to the perspective of the party awaiting the judgement and possible intuitive interpretation. The disadvantage, however, is its susceptibility to outliers; on the one had, there are cases dealt with in a very short period of time (which are usually formalistic) and, on the other hand, there are cases settled in a given year, which took many years to be recognised. Moreover, the indicator only takes into consideration the proceedings that have been completed (as it does not take into account outstanding cases until they are settled). Thus, its value may be highest not at the moment of deterioration of the effectiveness but afterwards, when the crisis has already been tackled and the delay remedied.

The second approach uses the queueing theory[41] in order to approximate the theoretical time of case recognition based on their number.[42] The advantage of this method is reduction of the reporting scope, elimination of the impact of outliers, and the fact that it does not ignore the outstanding cases. The problem is interpretation. Although the indicator is expressed in months, it is not an approximation of the actual time of case recognition but only a theoretical measure of system capacity.

Therefore, depending on the nature of the case, it may or may not correspond to the actual typical time of case recognition.[43] Figure 2.19 presents the timeliness

40 In practice, these data are usually juxtaposed in tables in specific ranges. As regards the RAC, there are seven ranges of different length: 0–2, 2–3, 3–4, 4–6, 6–12, 12–24 and more than 24 months. Thus, in order to calculate the average, certain values need to be adopted for each range (and these are the middle values within a range), which reduces the accuracy of the obtained results.

41 Cf., e.g., rozdział 4 „Paganini kolejek" w Z. Jędrzejczyk, K. Kukuła, J. Skrzypek, *Badania operacyjne w przy-kładach i zadaniach*, Wydawnictwo Naukowe PWN, Warszawa 2015.

42 The Disposition Time (DT) indicator is defined as the number of cases waiting to be settled on the last day of a given period divided by the number of cases settled within that period and then multiplied by the length of the period (e.g. 12 months). Por. CEPEJ, *op. cit.* Thus, the use of this indicator does not require that recording case recognition time.

43 It is worth pointing out that this approach is adopted to construe the measure "Effectiveness of proceedings in Regional Administrative Courts – recognition time of cases registered as SA, SAB, and SO", which is calculated for the purposes of

of complaint resolution[44] by the RAC illustrated with both of the above-mentioned approaches for the sake of verifying whether they lead to consistent conclusions. Additionally, Figure 2.19 also shows the third measure of typical complaint resolution time: The time interval representing a median (i.e., half of the complaints are resolved quicker than this value indicates and half of them are resolved within a longer period of time than indicated by this value).

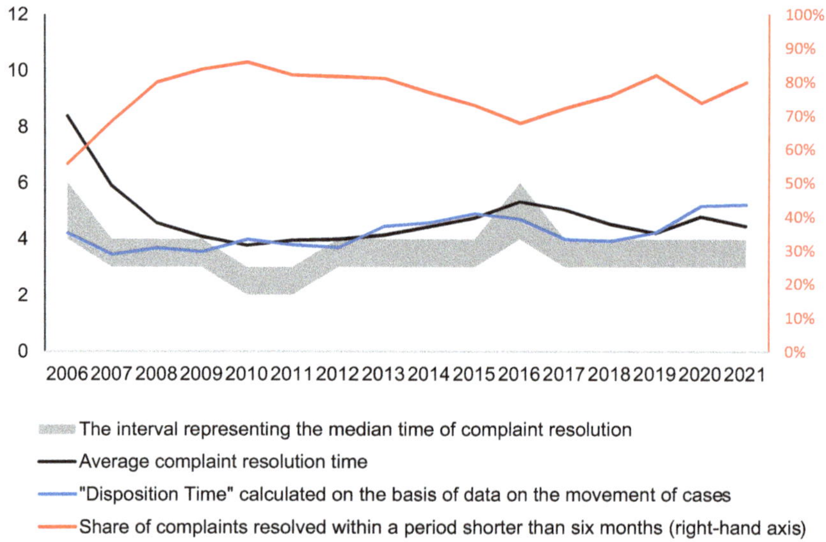

Figure 2.19. Timeliness of case recognition at the RAC in the years 2006–2021 expressed in months – alternative measures of the central tendency

Source: Annual reports: Legal Aid, Timeliness, and Other, http://www.nsa.gov.pl/statystyki-wsa.php (accessed on: 5/11/2022).

One should also note that in the official communication, the SAC (unlike the Ministry of Justice as regards common courts) does not use measures of the central tendency (such as the average or median) to talk about the duration

the Multi-Annual State Financial Plan and the juxtaposition of planned budgetary expenditures as per task basis (where target value is less than six months).

44 The total of all complaints on acts and actions (in reg. SA) and complaints on failure to act (in reg. SAB) is taken into account.

of the proceedings. The presented data illustrate the distribution of complaint resolution time; that is, information on what percentage of complaints was recognised within a period of time not exceeding three, four or six months.[45] This allows to present a clear, easy-to-interpret measure of effectiveness, which is not burdened with errors of estimation (e.g., due to the influence of extreme values) and describes a broader group of cases instead of just the "typical values". Therefore, Figure 2.19 also shows the percentage of complaints that have been recognised within a period of less than six months.

The analysis of four alternative measures of timeliness of the RAC's examination of cases leads to consistent conclusions.[46]

First of all, one must acknowledge that despite significant fluctuations in the number of complaints (which are analysed in Chapter 1) lodged with the RAC, the Court managed to maintain a relatively satisfactory level of effectiveness of the proceedings in the period under analysis. Importantly, the situation did not deteriorate considerably in the aftermath of the COVID-19 pandemic.

2.9. The Effectiveness of the Supreme Administrative Court

Similarly as the case with the Regional Administrative Courts, the following two basic measures were used to assess the effectiveness of the Supreme Administrative Court:

(1) Timeliness of appeal resolution at the SAC: That is, the typical lapse of time between submission of an appeal to its consideration; and

---

45 Cf. "Information on Administrative Courts' Activities" submitted annually to the Sejm by the President of the SAC.

46 As expected due to the character of administrative judiciary – in particular, the fact that cases are very often settled during a single court sitting – analysis of both measures of the average time of appeal consideration (i.e., the average time calculated on the basis of data on the time of case consideration and the Disposition Time indicator based on data about case movement) leads to almost identical results. The exception is the period of the first years of operation of the two-instance administrative judiciary when the RAC struggled with a significant backlog from the previous years (cf. Figure 2.4). This led to the underestimation of the Disposition Time that indicated high system capacity (however, the actual time of complaint recognition was higher because there were outstanding cases from the previous years).

(2) The clearance rate, that is, the ratio of the number of recognised appeals to the number of submitted appeals,[47] which is a measure of the court's capability of recognising cases on an ongoing basis.

Moreover, the analysis is limited to cassation appeals (reg. SK) that make up the largest and, at the same time, the most laborious and time-consuming category of cases dealt with by the SAC (cf. Section 1.2).

However, one should note that in the period under analysis – as a result of changes in the internal organisation of the Financial Chamber[48] and the General Administrative Chamber of the SAC – the reported statistical data have been severely distorted owing to re-registration of cases.[49] Though statistics on the movement of cases have been adjusted in this respect by way of adding a category of "closed" cases in contrast to the "settled" cases, data on the "timeliness of settling cases"[50] have not been adjusted in this respect. This causes unreliability of the indicators based on these data; as regards the FC in 2020 and the GAC in 2021, respectively.

Table 2.1. Data on the number of cases in reg. SK "closed" or "settled" in each Chamber of the SAC in the years 2018–2021

		2018	**2019**	**2020**	**2021**
General Administrative Chamber	Settled	6,516	6,515	5,783	5,416
	Closed	7	12	5	4,092
Financial Chamber	Settled	5,905	5,672	4,237	4,540
	Closed	4	12	3,124	48
General Administrative Chamber	Settled	6,547	4,238	2,625	3,004
	Closed	51	8	12	11

Source: Annual Reports; Movement of Cases at the SAC, http://www.nsa.gov.pl/statystyki-nsa.php (accessed on: 5/11/2022).

47 Por. np. CEPEJ, op. cit., p. 48.

48 Cf. interview with the Vice-President of the SAC, the President of the Financial Chamber J. Rudowski, https://www.rp.pl/sady-i--trybunaly/art321371-nowy-wydzial-nsa-zwiekszy-specjalizacje-rozmowa-z-prezesem-izby-finansowej-ja-nem-rudowskim; accessed on: 5/11/2022.

49 I.e., closure of a case with the current reference number and its re-registration with a new reference number in the new department. In this chapter, the cassation appeals submitted to the SAC are, therefore, analysed based on the category of cases brought before the court, excluding the ones that have been re-registered.

50 A period of time lapsed between submission of a case in a given or previous reporting period until the date of its settlement.

Figure 2.20 illustrates the timeliness of cassation appeal recognition (reg. SK) by the SAC. Similarly as the case with the RAC, two methods of calculating the typical time of appeal resolution were employed: the average time and the Disposition Time based on case movement. Additionally, Figure 2.20 also shows the third measure of typical appeal resolution time: The time interval representing a median (i.e., half of the cassation appeals are resolved quicker than this value indicates and half of them are resolved within a longer period of time than indicated by this value).

It should be stressed again that in the official communication, the SAC (unlike the Ministry of Justice as regards common courts) does not use measures of the central tendency (such as the average or median) to discuss duration of the proceedings. The presented data illustrate the distribution of appeal resolution time; that is, information on what percentage of the appeals was recognised in the period not exceeding a year.[51] This allows to present a clear, easy-to-interpret measure of effectiveness, which is not burdened with errors of estimation. Therefore, Figure 2.20 also includes the percentage of appeals recognised within a period not exceeding one year.

51 Cf. Information on Administrative Courts' Activities submitted annually to the Sejm by the President of the SAC.

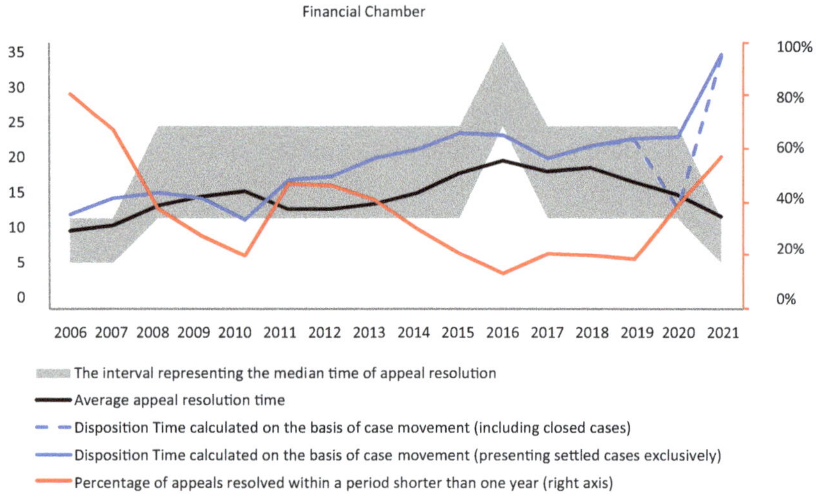
Financial Chamber
35
30
25
20
15
10
5
0
100%
80%
60%
40%
20%
0%
2006 2007 2008 2009 2010 2011 2012 2013 2014 2015 2016 2017 2018 2019 2020 2021
The interval representing the median time of appeal resolution
Average appeal resolution time
Disposition Time calculated on the basis of case movement (including closed cases)
Disposition Time calculated on the basis of case movement (presenting settled cases exclusively)
Percentage of appeals resolved within a period shorter than one year (right axis)

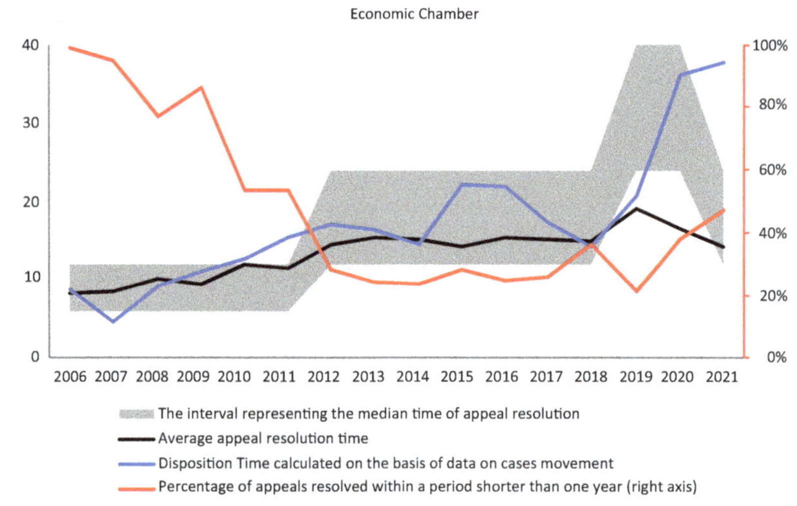
Economic Chamber
40
30
20
10
0
100%
80%
60%
40%
20%
0%
2006 2007 2008 2009 2010 2011 2012 2013 2014 2015 2016 2017 2018 2019 2020 2021
The interval representing the median time of appeal resolution
Average appeal resolution time
Disposition Time calculated on the basis of data on cases movement
Percentage of appeals resolved within a period shorter than one year (right axis)

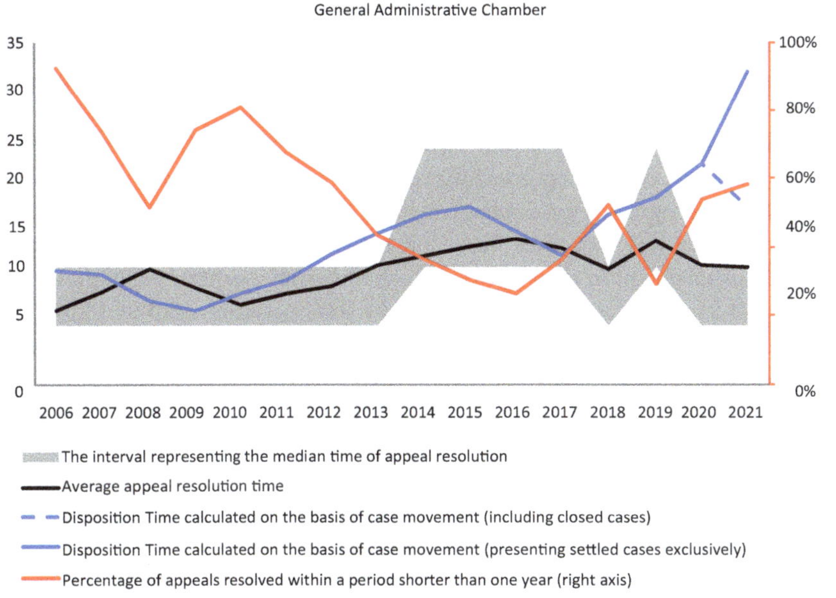

Figure 2.20. Timeliness of appeal resolution (reg. SK) at the SAC in the years 2006–2021 expressed in months – alternative measures of the central tendency

Source: Annual reports: Complaints, Requests, Special Complaints, and Other, http://www.nsa.gov.pl/statystyki-nsa.php (accessed on: 5/11/2022).

Analysis of four alternative measures of timeliness of case recognition by the SAC leads to consistent conclusions. During the period under examination, a clear deterioration in the effectiveness of cassation appeal recognition could basically be observed in all three Chambers of the SAC, which was reflected in an increase in the typical duration of the proceedings[52] and a significant reduction in the percentage of appeals recognised within a year.

---

52 Differences between the average cassation appeal resolution time and the Disposition Time calculated on the basis of case movement are relatively large, however, there are no doubts as to what direction the changes are heading in. One should pay attention to the fact that the indicator of average appeal recognition time at the Financial Chamber has been understated in the recent years. This is due to the fact that the duration of the proceedings is recorded in ranges and the last range is "over 24 months". In 2016, there were 54 % of the completed proceedings included in this range, and so the median time of cassation appeal recognition time at the Financial Chamber exceeded two years. By

The main reason for that is most likely the significant increase in the number of cassation appeals lodged with each Chamber of the SAC (cf. Section 1.2.). Without disregarding the issues arising due to the introduction of the category of closed cases, the situation during the COVID-19 pandemic appears to be particularly noteworthy as at that time alternative measures of effectiveness of the SAC suggest conflicting conclusions. Although the measures of the court's capability of recognising cases on an ongoing basis indicate a clear deterioration in effectiveness, the measures based on recognition time of concluded cases suggest improvement in this regard. This results from a general reduction in the number of cassation appeals handled by the SAC between 2020 and 2021 (see Table 2.1). More detailed information on this is provided in the next section.

2.10. Restrictions Related to the COVID-19 Pandemic versus Operation of Administrative Courts

From the point of view of social life in Poland and more broadly – in the world, one of the most remarkable events that took place in the period under analysis was the pandemic of the coronavirus causing the COVID-19 disease.

It led to the introduction of restrictions that were unprecedented in terms of their inconvenience for the citizens, the degree of interference in the constitutional rights and freedoms as well as their consequences for the functioning of the economy.

The impact of the pandemic-related restrictions on the administrative judiciary should be analysed on two levels. The first is concerned with changes in the "demand" for judicial control of the administration that was carrying out tasks bordering on health care and protection of public order on an unprecedented scale, which contributed to the increase in the number of cases coming before the administrative courts. The second is concerned with the impact of the restrictions on the operation of administrative courts themselves – in particular, suspension of holding court hearings in the traditional form.

In the initial period of the pandemic (i.e., the so-called first lockdown), the RAC's operation had collapsed, however, the consequences for the SAC turned out to be less severe (see Figure 2.22). Undoubtedly, it was largely due to the fact that the system of administrative courts had entered the pandemic already equipped with extensive IT facilities (see Section 1.5).

It is worth pointing out that the initial reaction (which took place under the pre-pandemic legal conditions) to the introduction of restrictions preventing holding hearings was an attempt to follow a simplified procedure under Article 119(2) of the PbAC. It stipulates that a case may be heard in a simplified mode upon a request from a party, if none of the other parties requests a hearing at the court within 14 days of having been notified that such a request has been made. In practice, however, this regulation has not proven to be an adequate tool for effective recognition of cases during a lockdown.

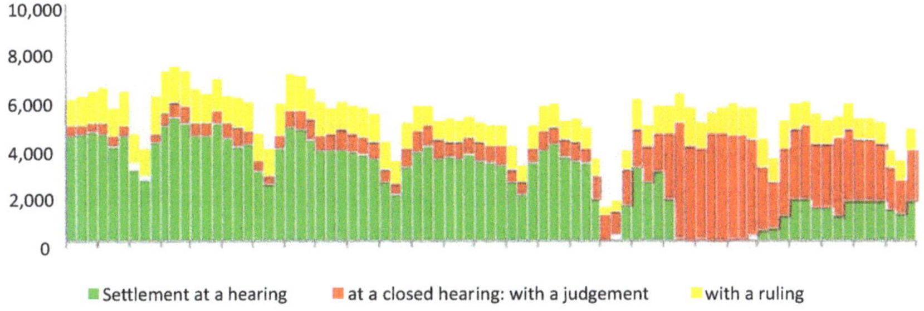

Figure 2.21. Number and structure of concluded cases regarding complaints about acts and actions of the authorities (reg. SA) submitted to the RAC in the years 2016–2022 – monthly

Source: Own study based on statistical data, http://www.nsa.gov.pl/statystyki-wsa-1.php (accessed on: 5/11/2022).

The legislative intervention that turned out to be crucial for the effective operation of administrative courts during the pandemic was the so-called "Covid Act,"[53] which was a kind of a functional equivalent of the introduction of a state of emergency that the political leadership had not decided to introduce. The amendment of 14 May 2020[54] introduced Article 15 zzs[4] to this Act (and not to the PbAC), which regulated the issue of recognition of a cassation appeal by

---

the way, it is worth adding that this justifies changing the form of statistical records in a way that enables ongoing monitoring of the effectiveness of the Financial Chamber (by way of adding further ranges).

53 Act of 2 March 2020 on Special Solutions Related to the Prevention, Counteracting, and Combating of COVID-19, Other Infectious Diseases, and Crisis Situations Caused by Them, Journal of Laws of 2021, item 2095, as amended.

54 Act of 14 May 2020 Amending Certain Acts as Regards Shielding Activities in Connection with the Spread of SARS-CoV-2 Virus; Journal of Laws, item 875, as amended.

the SAC at a closed sitting and holding "remote hearings" (i.e., a trial with no location) at the SAC and the RAC.

In accordance with section 1 of that Article, during the "state of epidemic threat" or the "state of epidemic" announced due to the COVID-19 pandemic and within one year following cancellation of the last of them, in cases where a party lodging a cassation appeal has not renounced the hearing or where another party has requested that a hearing be held, the SAC may consider the cassation appeal at a closed sitting (with three judges present), if all parties agree to it within 14 days from the date of notification of the intention to recognise the case at a closed sitting.

In turn, Section 2 of the above Article allowed (in the same period) for hearings to be held at the RAC and the SAC with the use of technological devices that allow holding them remotely with simultaneous direct transmission of the image and sound and the participants to such a hearing do not need to be inside a court building, unless conducting a hearing without the use of such devices posed no excessive risk to the health of the participants. At the same time, Section 3 of the above Article stipulated that the Chairperson may decide on holding a closed sitting, if they consider it necessary to recognise a case and holding a hearing required by law would pose an excessive threat to the health of the participants and it could not be held remotely. In consequence of application of the regulations in question, there was a clear shift back to recognising cases "at a hearing" remotely both at the SAC and the RAC – which is visible in Figures 2.21 and 2.22.

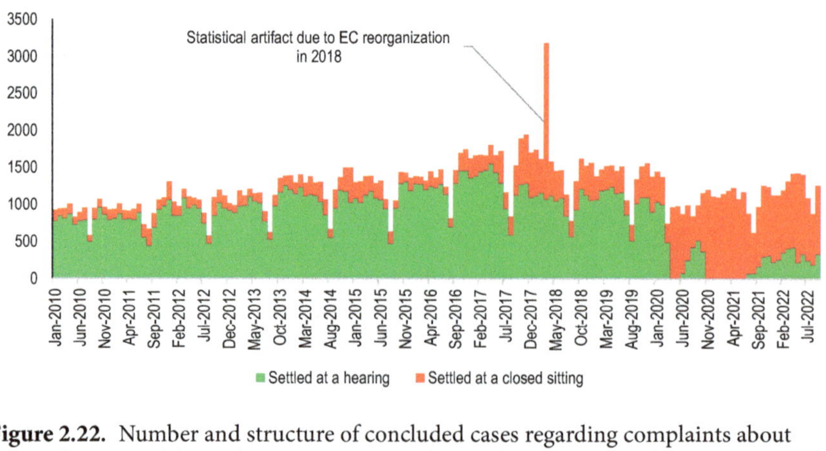

Figure 2.22. Number and structure of concluded cases regarding complaints about acts and actions of the authorities (reg. SK) submitted to the SAC in the years 2016–2022 – monthly

Source: Own study based on statistical data, http://www.nsa.gov.pl/statystyki-nsa-1.php (accessed on: 5/11/2022).

The Article 15 zzs[4] of the "Covid Act", which is under analysis, was amended by the Act of 28 May 2021.[55] In particular, section 1 thereof – concerning recognition of cases at closed sittings with a composition of three judges – was amended to facilitate using this solution. The new wording states that during the "state of epidemic emergency" or the "state of the epidemic" announced due to COVID-19 and within one year of cancellation of the last of them, the SAC "is not bound by the party's request to hold a hearing." At the same time, the condition of lack of excessive threat to the health of the participants to a "classic" hearing (which was intended to reduce their number in favour of remote hearings) was removed from Section 2 of the provision under analysis; the mention of "excessive health risk" for the participants of a hearing as a condition for holding a closed sitting with three judges based on the President's decision was also removed from Section 3 of the provision.

Summary

The analyses presented herein indicate that in the years 2004–2021, the number of cases brought before the RAC oscillated in the range between fewer than 60 and more than 80 thousand, which falls within the limits forecast by the authors of the concept of two-instance administrative courts. However, the significant scale of observable changes is noteworthy. Their main causes are fluctuations in the number of complaints regarding excise duty or social welfare, the consequences of systemic changes in the law (such as introduction of the institution of challengeable tax rulings and changes in organisation of games on slot machines) as well as the impact of weaknesses of certain public administration bodies (e.g., complaints about lengthy proceedings and failure to act in cases regarding foreigners, which were predominantly submitted to the RAC in Wrocław). Although it is currently (in November 2022) difficult to comprehensively assess the impact of the COVID-19 pandemic on the number and structure of cases brought before administrative courts, it seems that the pandemic has contributed to an increase in the number of specific categories of cases (regarding e.g., employment and business relationships). It is also

55 Act of 28 May 2021 Amending the Act on the Civil Procedure Code and Some Other Acts (Journal of Laws, item 1090).

interesting to note that fluctuations in the number of cases, which can be linked to legislative changes, were, in principle, unexpected for the authors of the draft acts that have led to these changes.

As far as the SAC is concerned, the number of cassation appeals lodged with this court was systematically increasing at a rate exceeding the pace of trends in the number of RAC's judgements between 2004 and 2011. Thus, the challengeability of first-instance judgements had been increasing. After 2012, this parameter has stabilised, thus making the number of RAC's judgements the basic factor determining the number of cassation appeals.

A noteworthy fact is that despite significant fluctuations in the number of complaints submitted to the courts, the administrative judiciary – seen as a system – is characterized by a satisfactory level of effectiveness.

Even during the COVID-19 pandemic, following the initial collapse, the SAC and the RAC have regained their previous effectiveness (largely owing to the legislative solutions adopted *ad hoc* at that time). However, the manner of hearing cases before these courts has changed fundamentally. Separate in-depth research would be necessary to determine whether this change produced an impact on enforcement of the right to trail before the SAC and the RAC (as well as the social view of their functioning).

Dominik J. Gajewski (SGH Warsaw School of Economics)

Kamil Joński (SGH Warsaw School of Economics)

3. Tax Complaints (611) – Analysis of Microdata[1]

Abstract: Chapter 3 attempts to verify the hypothesis on a possible link between the inflow of tax cases and the business cycles of the Polish economy, which is suggested in Chapter 2. Emphasis is placed on VAT cases (which is the biggest category) and the cases regarding excise duty (due to volatility of caseload). The unique Case Law and Case Information Central Database (CBOIS) was queried in order to link dates of the underlying economic activities, dates of the relevant tax administration decisions and the administrative court cases regarding VAT and excise duty. The obtained results reveal substantial lags between the underlying economic activities and the court proceedings. Therefore, it is unlikely that the caseload dynamics might result form the business cycle.

Keywords: VAT cases, cases regarding excise duty, case-level data, caseload changes, business cycle

Introduction

As indicated in the previous chapter, analysis of aggregated data allows to hypothesize that the number of complaints in two categories – concerning taxes (611) and social assistance (632) – may be correlated to cyclical fluctuations in the economy (cf. Figure 2.9). Verification of such a hypothesis requires more detailed research that goes beyond analysis of aggregated statistical data.

This is the purpose of this chapter; given the number of tax-related complaints (which burdens the system of administrative courts as a whole) and their importance from the point of view of the institutional environment of the economy, this chapter focuses exclusively on these cases.

Examination of the structure of tax complaints submitted to the RAC (with symbol 611) – presented in Figure 2.9 – demonstrates that fluctuations in their number, which give the impression of reflecting the cyclical fluctuations in the Polish economy, are shaped almost entirely by a single category of cases and that

---

1 The results presented in the second part of this chapter were previously published in D.J. Gajewski, K. Joński, *Liczba skarg wnoszonych do wojewódzkich sądów administracyjnych a cykliczne wahania gospodarki*, „ZNSA" 2020, No. 5, pp. 89–98.

category is comprised of complaints about excise duty (6111). This correlation, however, is almost undetectable in the case of other taxes, including indirect taxes such as VAT (6110).

On the other hand, data illustrating the activity of the administrative authorities – in particular, tax audit authorities – may suggest special importance of enforcement of VAT within the framework of their activities (and significant intensification of such endeavours after 2013). This validates detailed analysis of these two categories of cases.

The study covers two aspects: First is the time elapsed since an economic event until issuance of a challenged decision on excise duty and VAT and then until submission of a complaint to the RAC[2], and second is the structure of complaints about excise duty as regards the aspect *ratione materiae*. Such analysis, which is carried out on a micro level (of individual judgements), is possible due to the use of the Case Law and Case Information Central Database (CBOIS). Such research will make it possible to better understand the relationship between the events taking place within the framework of business transactions and the functioning of a component of the institutional environment of the economy, which is the system of administrative judiciary.

However, the point of departure fir such research should be analysis of statistical data illustrating the activity of administrative authorities as regards tax matters.

3.1. Activity of Administrative Authorities as Regards Tax Matters

Analysis of statistical data illustrating the activity of the administrative authorities as regards tax matters requires brief presentation of the scope of tasks and institutional structure of these authorities.

At the outset, a distinction should be made between situations where the taxpayer's interaction with the authority is concerned with (1) actual economic events (or facts) and situations where (2) hypothetical facts are described by the

---

2 It is suggested in the public debate that there might be delays of several years, which is linked to the prescription period for tax liability, cf., e.g., Waśko, *Wszczynanie postępowań karnych skarbowych w trakcie postępowań kontrolnych – analiza praktyki wybranych urzędów kontroli skarbowej*, "Przegląd Podatkowy" 2017, No. 2, pp. 44–49; A. Ladziński et al., Instrumentalne wszczynanie postępowań karnych skarbowych w trakcie postępowań kontrolnych i podatkowych – analiza praktyki stosowania art. 70 § 6 pkt 1 Ordynacji Podatkowej, Toruń 2019.

taxpayer in an application for a tax ruling.[3] The administrative courts exercise control over the activities of the authorities in both cases. As far as interaction between the taxpayer and the authority based on actual economic events is concerned, it principally manifests itself with a tax decision (within the meaning of the TO) made by a tax authority or a decision issued by a tax audit authority. According to the provisions of the TO and Act on Tax Audit, the taxpayer is entitled to an appeal against decisions issued at the first instance.

Until 2017, in accordance with Article 13 of the TO, the tax authorities of the first instance were: The Head of the Tax Office, the Head of the Customs Office, the Wójt (i.e., the Head of a Gmina – which is a municipality), the Burmistrz (i.e., the Mayor of a City), the Starosta (i.e., the Head of a Poviat – which is a county) or the Marshal of a Województwo (i.e., Voivodship).

Whereas the Head of the Tax Chamber and the Head of the Customs Chamber could act as:

(a) A review body for decisions of the Head of the Tax Office or the Head of the Customs Office, respectively;
(b) The first-instance body, on the basis of separate provisions;
(c) The review body for decisions made by that body at the first instance.

In turn, pursuant to Article 8 of the Act on Tax Audit (ATA),[4] tax audit authorities include:

(a) The Minister competent for Public Finance (who is the supreme tax audit body);
(b) The Inspector General for Tax Audit as a higher tier authority over the Heads of Tax Audit Offices;
(c) The Head of the Tax Audit Office (TAO).

In accordance with Article 24(1)(1), a tax audit authority concluded audit proceedings with a decision (within the meaning of the TO), among others, when the audit findings were concerned with taxes determined by the Heads of Tax Offices or excise duty and tax on extraction of certain minerals. The taxpayer could appeal against the decision of the Head of the TAO – in accordance with Article 26(1) of the ATA – to the Head of the Tax Chamber or the Head of the Customs Chamber (depending on the tax that the decision was concerned with).

---

3 This is an institution introduced into the Tax Ordinance in 2007 (Dz.U.2006.217.1590).
4 Dz.U.2004.8.65, consolidated text.

To sum up, in the years 2005–2017, there were the following separate departments under the Minister of Public Finances:

(1) Tax administration, regulated by Act of 29 August 1997 on the Tax Ordinance, comprising 16 Tax Chambers and 400 Tax Offices;
(2) Tax audit, regulated by the Act of 28 September 1991 on Tax Audit,[5] comprising 16 Tax Audit Offices (TAO) along with 8 Remote Offices;
(3) Customs service, regulated by the Act of 27 August 2009 on Customs Service,[6] comprising 16 Customs Chambers and 45 Customs Offices along with 143 Customs Divisions.

Based on the existing structures, the National Tax Administration (NTA) was established as of 1 March 2017, which was regulated by the Act of 16 November 2016 on National Tax Administration.[7] It comprises 16 Tax Administration Chambers (which are equivalents of Tax Chambers), 400 Tax Offices, 16 Tax and Customs Offices (created by the merger of Tax Audit Offices and Customs Chambers), 45 Delegations of the Tax and Customs Office (created on the basis of Customs Offices and Remote Offices of the TAO), and 143 Customs Divisions.

There is the Head of the NTA in charge of the NTA, who has the rank of the Secretary of State, and their Deputies, who have the rank of the Under Secretary of State. There is also a uniformed formation within the NTA: the Tax and Customs Service. In addition, the National Tax Information (NTI) was established, which took over the tasks of the National Tax and Customs Information (fig. 3.2. and 3.3.).

5 Dz.U.1991.100.442.

6 Journal of Laws of 2009 No. 168, item 1323, earlier Act of 24 July 1999 on Customs Service, Journal of Laws of 1999 No. 72, item 802.

7 Journal of Laws of 2016, item 1947.

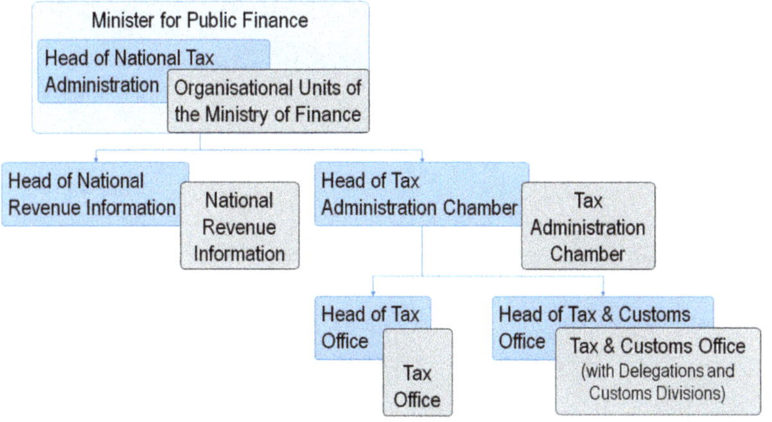

Figure 3.1. The bodies and units of the NTA

Source: Ministry of Finance, National Tax Administration, https://www.kis.gov.pl/documents/6609173/6751991/bro-szura+KAS.pdf (accessed on: 5/11/2022); https://www.gov.pl/web/kas/struktura-kas (accessed on: 5/11/2022).

It is worth emphasising that tax authorities may conduct tax audit aimed at verifying whether a party subjected to audit meets the obligations arising from the provisions of tax law (see section VI of the TO).

The purpose of tax audit conducted by the tax authorities was "to protect the interests and property rights of the State Treasury and to ensure effectiveness of fulfilment of tax obligations and collecting other receivables that comprise the revenues of the state budget or the state special purpose funds" (Article 1(1) of the ATA); in other words, it is to combat the most serious cases of tax avoidance. Following the reform of the NTA, these tasks have been taken over by the tax and customs audit authority (see section V of the ANTA). After a review, the Supreme Audit Office (SAO) positively assessed "the usefulness of the reform of the tax and customs administration in Poland." According to the SAO, "consolidation of the tax and customs services has created conditions allowing for improvement of the effectiveness of the entire system of collection of public levies," while "the biggest concern of the SAO is the sphere of human resources in a broad sense."[8]

8 The SAO (2019); Information on the results of audit: CONDITION OF THE NATIONAL ORGANISATION OF TAX ADMINISTRATION, No. 159/2019/P/18/009/KBF, https://www.nik.gov.pl/plik/id,21676, vp,24326.pdf (accessed on: 5/11/2022).

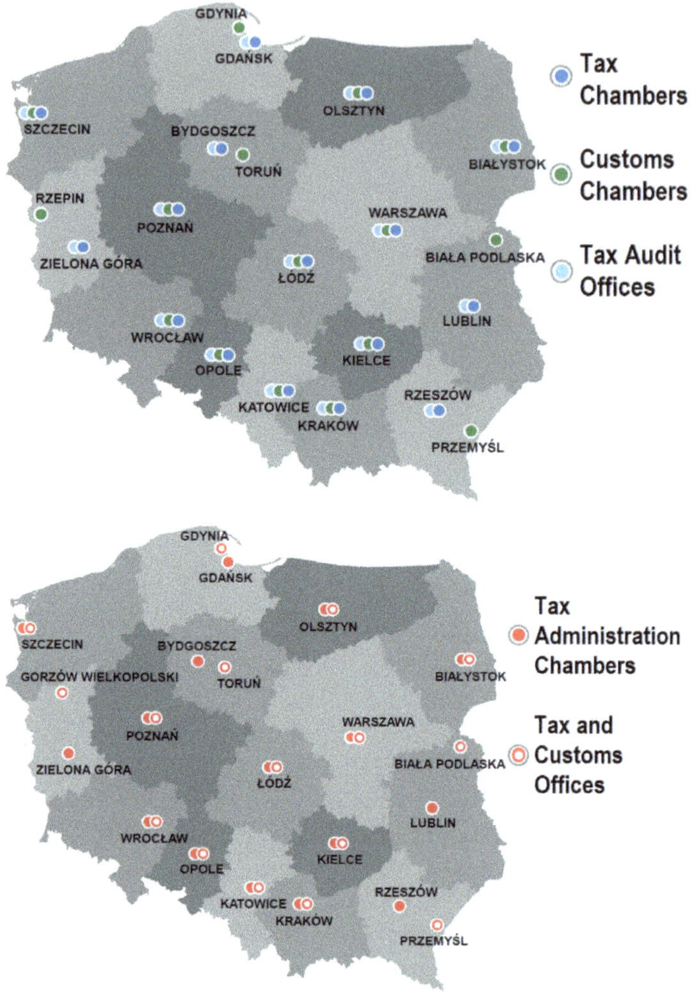

Figure 3.2. Location-based organisation before and after the reform of the NTA

Source: Ministry of Finance, presentation: National Tax Administration, https://www.gov.pl/attachment/4d35e6d-4-7fbc-4c3a-82bc-a9e158868381 (accessed on: 5/11/2022).

As regards fiscal audit activities, detailed information for the years 2006–2016 is provided in the annual reports of the Inspector General for Tax Audit. They cover in particular: The number of audit proceedings concluded with a decision and proceedings where corrections of tax returns were made as well as the total amount determined in effect of audit proceedings broken down by (1) findings related to decisions issued by tax audit authorities and (2) findings related to voluntary corrections of tax returns.[9] In addition, the reports contain data on other TAO activities: (1) the total amount of prevented VAT refunds and (2) loss reduction arrangements. More detailed information on the activities of the TAOs and the Tax and Customs Offices (TCOs) was presented by the Under Secretary of State at the Ministry of Finance P. Dziedzic in response to Interpellation No. 32784, the 8th term.[10] It supplements the data covered by the reports on the number of audit proceedings concluded with a decision and proceedings where corrections of tax returns were made as well as the amount derived from the findings of audit proceedings broken down by (1) findings related to decisions issued by tax audit authorities and (2) findings related to voluntary corrections of tax returns – taking into account the years 2017 and 2018.

What is particularly important is that the response presents data on the number of findings and the amount derived from the findings, which are covered by appeals against tax assessments (in the case of tax and customs audits)[11].

In order to obtain more extensive relevant information, the author of the present elaboration applied to the Ministry of Finance, Investment, and Development within the framework of access to public information with a request for information about data regarding second-instance decisions as well as complaints to the RAC (i.e., on the number of and amount derived from findings covered by appeals – see Appendix).

In addition, there are data on tax and customs audits presented, which led to withholding undue VAT refunds; the data for the years 2012–2016 correspond to the data on "prevented VAT refunds" in the reports.

Furthermore, data on decisions of the Heads of Tax Offices as regards withholding VAT refunds are provided; these are data on the number of such decisions and the amount of withheld refunds within a year as well as the number and amount of refunds withheld at the end of the year for the period 2012–2018.

As far as the amount of established losses of revenue related to VAT is concerned, information is provided in the response of the Under Secretary of

---

9 On the basis of Article 14 of the Act on Tax Audit, which was introduced in 2006 and provided for such a possibility (Dz.U.2006.191.1413).

10 https://orka2.sejm.gov.pl/INT8.nsf/klucz/ATTBFMHQE/%24FILE/i32784-o1.pdf (accessed on: 5/11/2022).

11 D.J. Gajewski (ed.), *VAT Gap in Poland: Policy Problem and Policy Response*, Peter Lang 2024.

State at the Ministry of Finance P. Cybulski to the Interpellation No. 31643, the 8th term of office.[12]

3.2. Tax Audits (Tax and Customs Audits)

The structure of findings from the tax (and customs) audits in PLN million, which were carried out between 2006 and 2018, is presented in Figure 3.3. The analysis takes into consideration breakdown both by tax types and by the findings related to decisions issued by tax audit authorities versus the findings related to voluntary corrections of tax returns.

It is noteworthy that in terms of amounts derived from the relevant findings, the predominant group comprises decisions on tax assessments issued by the tax (and customs) audit authority.

Interestingly, the category of the findings that has been largest since 2007 (and unquestionably dominant since 2010) is the one concerning VAT. From 2013 onwards, the scale of and growth rate in this category have been plainly spectacular. The increase occurred at a time when the so-called VAT gap was reaching its largest size.

It is advisable to compare the data on the amount derived from tax audit findings with data on appeals against tax assessments, submitted by the taxpayers, which were considered in the second instance by the Tax Chambers (fig. 3.4.); the same can be done with data on the amount derived from findings upheld in the appeal proceedings (fig. 3.1.).

12 https://orka2.sejm.gov.pl/INT8.nsf/klucz/ATTBDNHWQ/%24FILE/i31643-o1.pdf (accessed on: 5/11/2022).

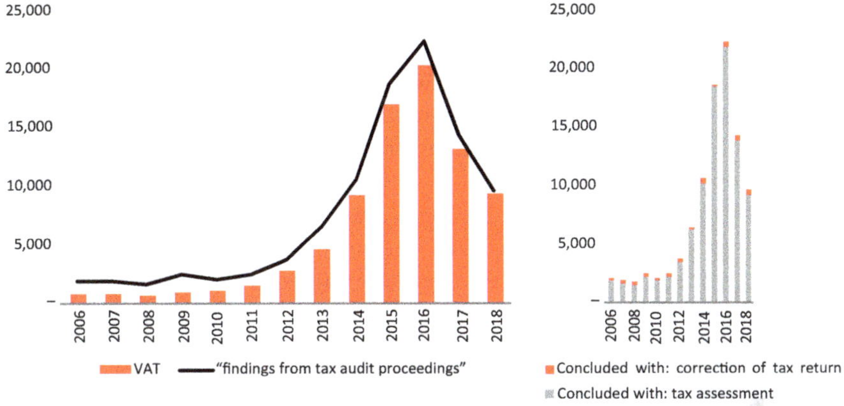

Figure 3.3. Findings from tax and customs audits (in PLN million) broken down into audits that have led to submitting corrections of the tax return or to a decision on tax assessment; VAT is highlighted (in the left panel)

Source: Annual Reports of the Inspector General for Tax Audit for the years 2006–2016 and data presented by the Under Secretary of State at the Ministry of Finance P. Dziedzic in response to Interpellation No. 32784, the 8th term of office.

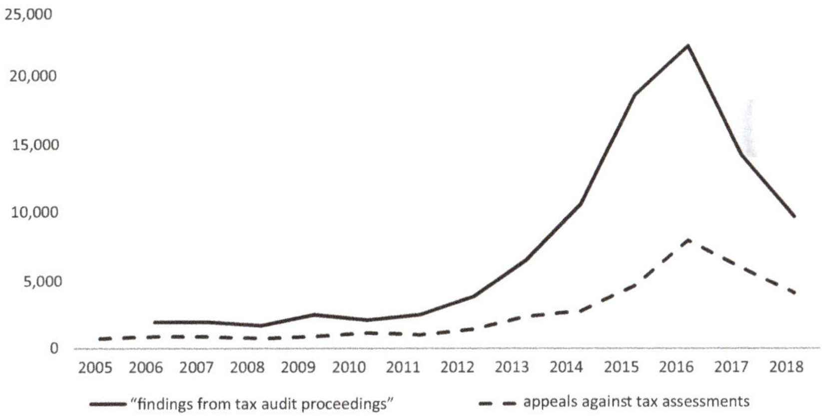

Figure 3.4. Findings from tax and customs audits (in PLN million); decisions challenged by the taxpayers are highlighted (i.e., amount derived from findings contested in appeals against decisions)

Source: Annual Reports of the Inspector General for Tax Audit for the years 2006–2016 and data presented by the Under Secretary of State at the Ministry of Finance P. Dziedzic in response to Interpellation No. 32784, the 8th term of office.

It is valuable to note that the majority of the findings related to decisions on VAT assessments (in terms of value – i.e., the amount – that the decisions were concerned with) were not challenged in the second instance. In combination with the rapid decline in the value of findings from VAT-related audits, which was observable in 2017 and 2018, it is justified to inquire about the nature of this phenomenon[13].

In accordance with the response to the request for access to public information submitted by the author of this text (see the request and the reply in the Appendix), data on the amounts covered by tax assessments that were appealed against to the RAC are only available for the year 2013 and onwards. They are presented in Figure 3.1.

Table 3.1. The amount covered by tax assessments appealed against to the RAC (in PLN million)

	2013	2014	2015	2016	2017	2018
Complaints lodged with the RAC against tax assessments	3,230.749	3,082.503	6,061.905	6,067.914	6,016.094	6,651.314
Judgements upholding the authorities' view	1,223.159	1,693.24	3,285.178	499.195	3,578.634	4,780.802

Source: A. Niekłań-Wudarska, Response of the Deputy Head of the Minister's Office at the Ministry of Finance to the request of 9 October 2019 for sharing public information (cf. the Appendix).

Apart from analysis of data on findings from tax (and customs) audits, it is necessary to examine data on the amounts of losses of revenue determined as a result of the audits carried out by the Tax Offices. Table 3.2 presents data on VAT in this respect; the data provided in the Response to Interpellation No. 31643, the 8th term, indicate that about 60 % of this type of audits were concerned with VAT. Moreover, the activities of the tax authorities in respect of VAT refunds ought to be examined.

As already indicated above, there are data available on VAT refunds both prevented by the tax (and customs) authorities and withheld by the tax authorities.

13 D.J. Gajewski (ed.), *VAT Gap in Poland: Policy Problem and Policy Response*, Peter Lang 2024.

Table 3.2. The amounts of losses of revenue (from VAT) determined as a result of audits carried out by the Tax Offices

	2014	2015	2016	2017	2018
Number of VAT audits carried out by the Tax Offices	49,434	29,975	23,233	16,981	12,861
Losses of revenue (in PLN million)	3,421.35	5,108.77	7,529.08	5,198.50	4,153.50

Source: Data provided by the Under Secretary of State at the Ministry of Finance P. Cybulski in response to Interpellation No. 31643, the 8th term of office.

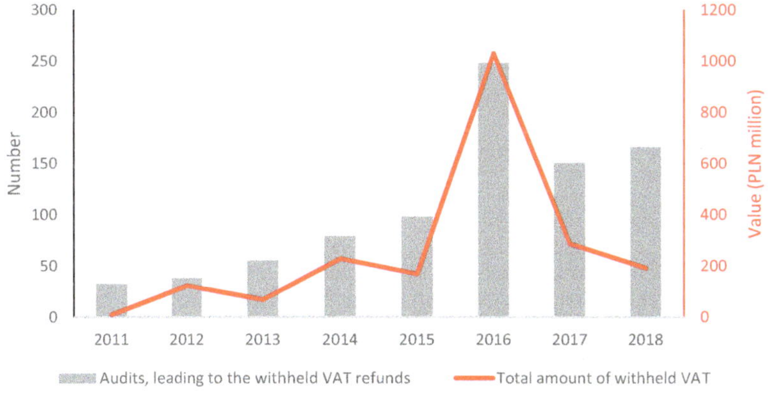

Figure 3.5. The number of withheld VAT refunds and the total amount of withheld VAT refunds (in consequence of tax and customs audits)

Source: Data provided by the Under Secretary of State at the Ministry of Finance P. Dziedzic in response to Interpellation No. 32784, the 8th term of office.

As far as tax and customs audits are concerned, it is noteworthy that the number of audits that prevented undue VAT returns increased significantly in 2016 leading to a considerably greater amount of withheld returns (fig. 3.5).

The average value of a withheld return was then PLN 4.15 million; in contrast, this value ranged between PLN 1.21 and 3.2 million in the previous years, while in 2017 and 2018, it amounted to PLN 1.91 and 1.15 million, respectively[14].

The year 2016 also turned out to be a record year as regards VAT refunds that had a payment deadline extended by way of decision made by the Heads of Tax

14 D.J. Gajewski (ed.), *VAT Gap in Poland: Policy Problem and Policy Response*, Peter Lang 2024.

Offices (fig. 3.6). The amount of VAT refunds exceeding PLN 1 billion remains withheld every year since 2015 (and in 2017, it was PLN 0.9 billion).

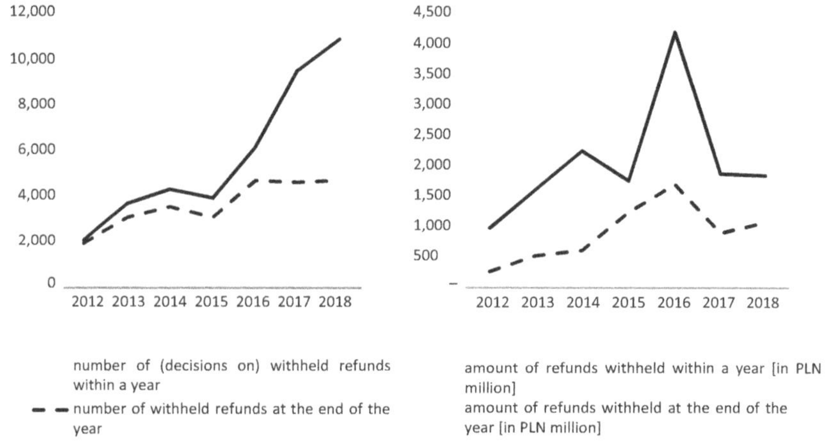

Figure. 3.6. The number and amount of withheld VAT refunds that had a payment deadline extended by way of a decision of the Heads of Tax Offices

Source: Data provided by the Under Secretary of State at the Ministry of Finance P. Dziedzic in response to Interpellation No. 32784, the 8th term of office.

3.3. Research Methodology for Measuring the Time Elapsed between the Occurrence of an Economic Event, Issuance of an Administrative Decision, and Submission of a Complaint to the RAC[15]

The Case Law and Case Information Central Database (CBOIS) was used for the purposes of this study. The following query was used: RAC's judgements with symbols 6110 and 6111 made between 1 January 2005 and 31 December 2018;

15 Part of the presented results were published in D.J. Gajewski, K. Joński (2020) Liczba skarg wnoszonych do wojewódzkich sądów administracyjnych a cykliczne wahania gospodarki, Zeszyty Naukowe Sądownictwa Administracyjnego – No. 5/2020(92) and D.J. Gajewski, K. Joński (2020) Country Note: Procedures of the Polish Tax Authorities and the VAT Gap: Evidence from Administrative Court Files, 48, Intertax, Issue 11, pp. 1012–1019, https://kluwerlawonline.com/journalarticle/Intertax/48.11/TAXI2020102

narrowed down to final judgements that are available on the Internet. As regards VAT, there were 68.2 thousand judgements retrieved.

At the next stage of selection, cases regarding tax rulings were rejected (symbol 656);[16] afterwards, the sample was further narrowed down to judgements where the operative part indicated that it was concerned with complaints "against a decision" (and not, for example, against a tax ruling). In the majority of such cases, the operative part of the judgement provided information on the date of issuing the decision that the complaint was lodged against. Whereas, in 64 % of the cases (i.e., in 32 thousand of them), it was also possible to establish the year of occurrence of the economic event that the decision referred to.[17] Due to the way VAT is settled and the way the operative part of judgements is worded, the year that the tax applied to is provided only.

Although such an outcome can be considered satisfactory and validates further analysis, it must be concerning that in some years (e.g., in 2007) the number of judgements with a successfully determined date of the economic event was smaller than half of all the judgements for which the date of issuance of the challenged decision was established (cf. Figure 3.7).

This is largely due to regional differences in the practice of formulating the operative parts of judgements. For example, the year of the economic event was determined in the case of over 92 % of the judgements of the RAC in Wrocław, 77 % of the judgements of the RAC in Kraków, 69 % of the judgements of the RAC in Warsaw, and 0 % of the judgements of the RAC in Gliwice[18] (and the latter comprise 8.7 thousand judgements and that is almost half of all the judgements for which it was impossible to establish the date of the economic event).

As far as excise duty is concerned, 33.8 thousand judgements were retrieved. Just as the case with VAT cases, the ones concerning tax rulings (symbol 656) were

---

16 This symbol has been registered since 2010 and so, at this stage, complaints concerning tax rulings from before 2010 are still included in the research sample. They will be singled out at the next stage when the sample will be narrowed down to complaints about decisions.

17 The following is an example of the wording of an operative part of a judgement: "The Regional Administrative Court in (...) in the following composition: (...) after considering – at a closed session on 22 March 2018 – a complaint (...) against the decision of the Head of the Tax Administration Chamber in (...) of 12 October 2017, No. (...) concerning Value Added Tax for the months between January to June 2015 rules: (...)."

18 The operative part of the judgements of that Court merely states that the challenged decision was concerned with Value Added Tax.

rejected, and the sample was then further narrowed down to judgements whose operative part indicated that they were concerned with complaints "against a decision." In almost all those cases, it was also possible to establish the issue date of the decision that the complaint was lodged against. In contrast to judgements on VAT, however, it was possible to establish the date of the economic event in only every fifth case (which is fewer than 7 thousand cases). This is due to the fact that the operative parts of judgements in cases regarding excise duty do not usually specify the period that the decision was concerned with but are limited, for example, to a statement such as the following: "concerning determination of tax liability for excise duty arising from intra-Community acquisition of a passenger car."[19]

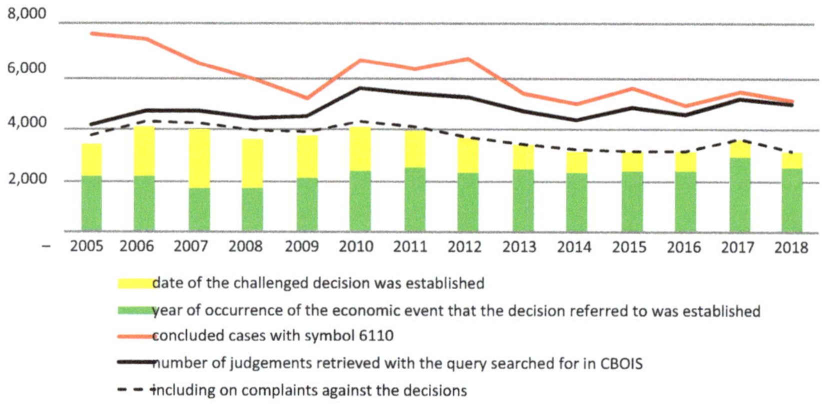

Figure 3.7. Research sample: Judgements concerning VAT
Source: Own study based on data from CBOIS.

What is important from the methodological point of view is that it does not seem that the group of judgements whose operative parts state the settlement period of excise duty could be a random sample. The cases where this happened were rather unusual and, therefore, the judges decided to include such information in the operative part of the judgement.

As indicated above, in VAT cases, lack of data was due to, for example, regional differences (as the case with the RAC in Gliwice). Therefore, it is impossible to

19 Cf. judgement of the RAC in Gdańsk of 25 April 2012, I SA/Gd 10/12.

draw conclusions from the available data. Unfortunately, the available sample of judgements regarding excise duty, where the year of the economic event that the decision referred to was established, is relatively small and likely unrepresentative (fig. 3.8). It can be speculated that since the decisions on VAT were concerned with tax returns for a particular month, it was thus indicated in the operative part of the judgement, but the decisions regarding excise duty were usually concerned with a single transaction (e.g., purchase of a car) and, therefore, the date of the transaction did not appear in the operative part of the judgement. Therefore, conclusions drawn from analysis of the available data cannot be used to generalise about all the cases regarding excise duty.

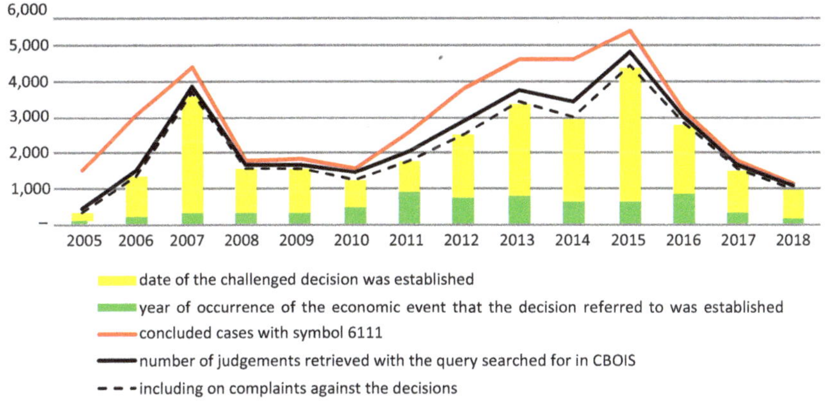

Figure 3.8. Research sample: Judgements concerning excise duty
Source: Own study based on data from CBOIS.

3.4. Results: Cases Concerning Excise Duty and VAT

Since the study covered a large sample of available judgements and the issue dates of the administrative decisions as well as dates of occurrence of the relevant economic events were extracted automatically rather than manually, a possible number of errors should be taken into account. It might also be the case that there were mistakes made at the time the operative parts of the judgements themselves were drawn up.[20] Therefore, a decision was made not to

20 For example, judgement of the RAC in Poznań of 8 September 2005, I SA/Po 2597/03. The date when the case was brought before the Court is 24 October 2003, but the date of issue of the challenged decision indicated in the operative part of the judgement

use the arithmetic average, which is sensitive to extreme observations or errors, and employ measures of position instead, such as the median and the first and third quartile.[21] The cases concerned with VAT and excise duty were analysed separately. In both cases, the following was highlighted: (1) The time elapsed from the date of issue of the challenged decision to the date when a case was brought before the RAC (as registered in the CBOIS); (2) The time elapsed from the year of occurrence of an economic event that a decision referred to until the date of issue of the decision.

It has already been pointed out that due to the way VAT is settled and the way the operative part of judgements is worded, the year that the tax applied to was provided only. Therefore, the date of 30 June was used for the calculations (in order for the inaccuracy at the level of a single case not to exceed six months). In about 12 % of the cases under examination, the decisions were concerned with tax for a period longer than one year. In such cases, 30 June of the last year that the decision was concerned with served as the date for the purposes of calculations.[22]

The results for VAT complaints are presented in Tables 3.3 and 3.4, and for excise duty in Tables 3.5 and 3.6.

---

is 23 September 2005. It is evident from the contents of the statement of reasons that there was an obvious clerical error with the date 23 September 2003. In this case, the period between issuing the decision and submission of the case to the RAC would be minus 700 days.

21 Quartiles divide the sample into four groups with the same number of observations. The first quartile (Q1) represents 25 % of the observations with the lowest value of an attribute (e.g., the shortest time); there are 50 % of the typical observations found between the first and the third quartile (Q3) (which are split in half by the median – Q2); and in the fourth quartile (Q4), there are 25 % of the observations with the attribute value (e.g., the longest time) higher than the ones in the third quartile. Despite exercising caution in terms of selection of the measure to be used in research, employment of the average values leads to the same conclusions.

22 For example, judgement of the RAC in Wrocław of 24 January 2005, I SA/Wr 69/04, on the case regarding a complaint against the decision "concerning settlement of Value Added Tax for the following months: June, September, and December 1998, January, March, April, May, July, August, September, October, November, and December 1999, March, May, June, July, September, October, November, and December 2000, each month from January to December 2001 and from January to June 2002." In this case, 30 June 2002, which is the last year that the decision was concerned with, served as the date for the purposes of calculations.

Table 3.3. Typical time elapsed from issuance of the challenged VAT decision to submission of a complaint to the RAC (in days)

		Median (Q2)	First quartile (Q1)	Third quartile (Q3)	Number of analysed cases
Year of submission of the case to the RAC	2004	65	60	70	1,483
	2005	65	59	74	3,269
	2006	66	59	78	3,636
	2007	66	61	75	3,405
	2008	67	60	74	3,629
	2009	67	60	78	3,900
	2010	65	59	72	4,334
	2011	66	61	72	3,892
	2012	65	61	73	3,327
	2013	66	61	77	3,454
	2014	67	61	76	3,418
	2015	66	60	74	3,277
	2016	66	61	73	3,327
	2017	68	62	76	3,155
	2018	67	62	73	1,778

Source: Own study based on data from CBOIS.

Evidently, the typical time elapsed between the issue of a challenged decision regarding VAT and submission of a case to the RAC was stable in the period under examination and it was about two months, which is clearly linked to procedural regulations.

As regards the time elapsed between the occurrence of an economic event that a decision referred to until issuance of the decision, it was not that stable (see Table 3.4). As for the challenged decisions issued between 2003 and 2006, the median time elapsed between the occurrence of an economic event until issuance of the decision was around 3.5 years; and in half of the typical cases, it was between 2 and 5 years. In the years 2012–2014, the median reached five years, and the range of the 50 % typical values stretched from 3.5 to 6 years. Since 2014, the typical time between the occurrence of an economic event and issuance of the challenged decision has shortened and stabilised at the level of 4.5 years.

Data on decisions issued in 2018 must be deemed unreliable because the sample of the RAC's judgements ended with this year. Thus, it is probable that many cases concerning decisions issued at that time have not yet concluded with a judgement and so they were not included in the research sample; the small number of cases compared to the previous years confirms this supposition (see Table 3.4).

Table 3.4. Typical time elapsed between the economic event (or fact) that the challenged VAT decision was concerned with and issue date of that decision (in years*)

		Number of analysed cases	Median (Q2)	First quartile (Q1)	Third quartile (Q3)	Arithmetic average**
Year of issuance of the decision appealed to the RAC	2003	1,034	2.9	1.9	3.9	3.0
	2004	1,336	3.4	1.9	4.7	3.4
	2005	1,537	3.3	2.0	4.8	3.5
	2006	1,523	3.5	2.0	4.9	3.6
	2007	1,776	3.9	2.5	5.4	4.0
	2008	1,801	3.9	2.7	5.3	4.0
	2009	2,084	4.3	2.9	5.5	4.3
	2010	2,533	4.7	3.3	5.6	4.6
	2011	2,712	4.7	3.4	5.8	4.7
	2012	2,257	4.9	3.5	5.9	4.9
	2013	2,432	5.3	3.7	6.2	5.1
	2014	2,432	4.9	3.2	6.0	4.8
	2015	2,474	4.5	3.0	5.9	4.6
	2016	2,773	4.4	3.0	5.7	4.6
	2017	2,271	4.4	3.0	5.6	4.5
	2018	749	4.7	3.5	6.0	4.8

* Calculations were based on the date of 30 June of the year that tax in the relevant decisions applied to (and so the inaccuracy does not exceed six months).
** The arithmetic average is presented for illustrative purposes, and, in practice, it turns out to be extremely close to the median.
Source: Own study based on data from CBOIS.

Table 3.5. Typical time elapsed from issuance of the challenged decision regarding excise duty to submission of a complaint to the RAC (in days)

		Median (Q2)	First quartile (Q1)	Third quartile (Q3)	Number of analysed cases
Year of submission of the case to the RAC	2005	122	64	210	969
	2006	62	52	82	1,896
	2007	**76**	**62**	**416**	**3,441**
	2008	62	54	69	1,427
	2009	62	49	68	1,738
	2010	65	56	73	1,529
	2011	66	57	77	2,174
	2012	61	54	68	3,294
	2013	64	56	71	4,027
	2014	63	56	70	3,814
	2015	**68**	**58**	**413**	**4,424**
	2016	**71**	**61**	**724**	**2,549**
	2017	66	57	74	1,104
	2018	63	56	70	674

Source: Own study based on data from CBOIS.

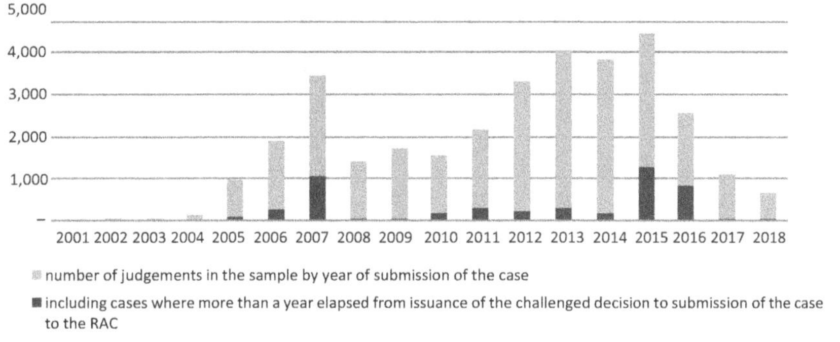

Figure 3.9. Judgements on excise duty by year of submission of the case to the RAC
Source: Own study based on data from CBOIS.

As far as cases on excise duty are concerned, the typical time elapsed between issuance of the challenged decision and submission of the case to the RAC was, as a rule, close to about two months (similarly as with VAT cases). However, two spectacular exceptions compel careful attention; in the years 2007 and

2015–2016, there was a large number of complaints that were filed more than one year after the challenged decision was issued (see Table 3.5 and Figure 3.9).

Table 3.6 presents data about the time elapsed between the occurrence of the economic events a decision was concerned with and the issue date of the decision. However, it should be reiterated that – given the small number of judgements whose operative parts contained information about the settlement period that the challenged decision applied to (cf. Figure 3.8) and their likely lack of representativeness – the results must be approached with particular caution.

Table 3.6. Typical time elapsed between the economic event (or fact) that the challenged decision regarding excise duty was concerned with and the issue date of that decision (in years*)

		Number of analysed cases	Median (Q2)	First quartile (Q1)	Third quartile (Q3)
Year of issuance of the decision appealed to the RAC	2005	117	2.3	1.6	4.1
	2006	276	2.6	1.8	3.6
	2007	281	2.5	1.5	3.9
	2008	320	3.5	2.2	4.6
	2009	436	4.0	2.8	5.3
	2010	467	4.4	3.1	5.4
	2011	910	4.3	2.4	5.4
	2012	800	4.4	2.8	5.5
	2013	817	4.7	2.8	5.7
	2014	818	3.5	2.2	5.2
	2015	414	4.0	2.6	5.5
	2016	814	3.8	2.6	5.0
	2017	258	5.3	3.7	7.0
	2018	81	5.5	4.0	7.6

* Calculations were based on the date of 30 June of the year that tax in the relevant decisions applied to (and so the inaccuracy does not exceed six months).
Source: Own study based on data from CBOIS.

3.5. Structure of Cases Regarding Excise Duty

In order to analyse the structure of the complaints lodged with the RAC and appeals to the SAC as regards excise duty, a series of queries was searched for in the CBOIS database. The queries were used to search for judgements on cases with symbol 6111, which concluded the proceedings and were issued between 1 January 2005 and 31 December 2021; next, cases brought before the court between 1 January 2005 and 31 December 2019 were then singled out from among them.

The basic goods subject to taxation with excise duty were used as keywords, such as alcohol, tobacco products (and so the actual words were: tytoń [tobacco], papieros [cigarette], nikotyna [nicotine]), electricity, and diesel fuel. In addition, the query included passenger cars. The results of the analysis – broken down into complaints lodged with the RAC and cassation appeals lodged with the SAC – are presented in Figures 3.10 and 3.11.

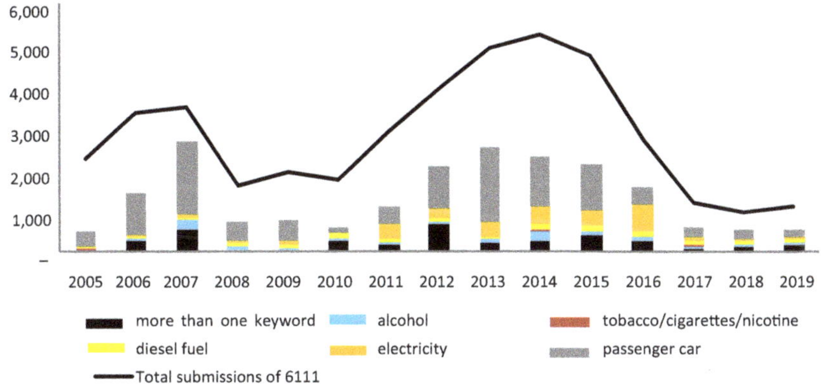

Figure 3.10. The structure of cases regarding excise duty brought before the RAC in the years 2005–2019

Source: Own study based on statistical data, http://www.nsa.gov.pl/statystyki-wsa-1.php (accessed on: 5.11.2022) and analyses of data obtained from the CBOIS.

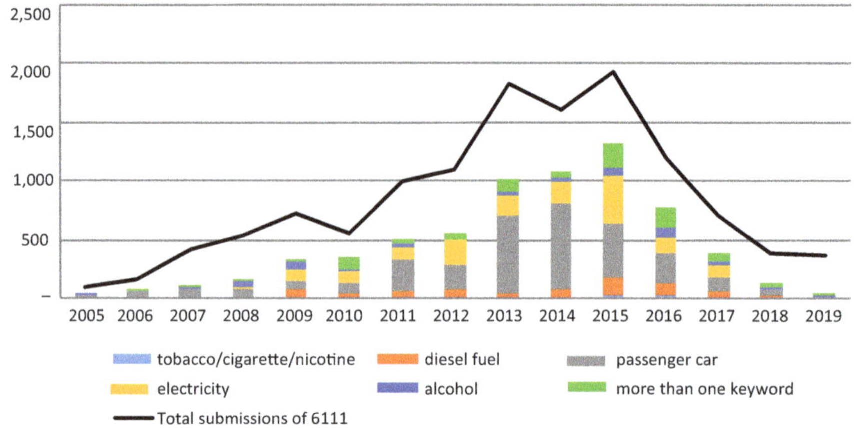

Figure 3.11. The structure of cases regarding excise duty brought before the SAC in the years 2005–2019

Source: Own study based on statistical data, http://www.nsa.gov.pl/statystyki-wsa-1.php (accessed on: 5.11.2022) and analyses of data obtained from the CBOIS.

The key words that were used allowed to classify about half of all the complaints about excise duty, which were filed during the period under review. At the same time, they showed the way cases concluded with judgements containing the phrase "passenger car" influenced fluctuations in the number of cases with the symbol 6111.

This result encourages scepticism when considering the hypothesis linking changes in the number of cases regarding excise duty to the cyclical fluctuations in the economy. It seems that such a correlation, which was observable on aggregated statistical data, was merely a statistical artefact.

Summary

The objective of the study was to explain the potential correlations between the number of tax complaints lodged with the RAC (with symbol 611) and cyclical fluctuations in the economy. Statistical data on the number of cases filed between 2004 and 2021 allow to validate putting forward a hypothesis that such a correlation exists for cases regarding excise duty. Verification of this hypothesis is possible through analysis of the time elapsed from the occurrence of an economic event that the challenged decision was concerned with (and which may be related to the economic situation, including fluctuations in the economy) until the time of submission of the relevant complaint to the RAC; hence, analysis of the structure of cases was carried out. To this end, judgements on VAT and excise duty were singled out from the CBOIS database and their operative parts were used.

As regards VAT, the obtained results indicate that the typical time elapsed between the occurrence of an economic event affecting tax assessment and issuance of a decision that was challenged at the RAC is about five years (with half of the typical observations being between three and six years). This result corresponds to claims made within the framework of the public debate that tax audits are usually initiated not immediately after the occurrence of the contested events but shortly before expiry of the five-year prescription period for tax liabilities.[23]

Therefore, it is a rule that economic conditions may affect the burden placed on administrative judiciary with a delay of up to several years. An additional – probably no less important – factor is also the pragmatics of the way the tax authorities work.

As far as excise duty is concerned, it is interesting to take a look at the periods when there was a large number of complaints filed with the RAC against decisions that were issued more than one year before. In the period under examination, the typical time elapsed from the occurrence of economic events affecting the assessment of excise duty until the moment of issuing the decision that would be challenged at the RAC was getting longer, starting from about two years and reaching about five years. However, one should bear in mind that only every fifth judgement had the reference period of the challenged decision specified in its operative part. It is, therefore, reasonable not to treat these results as valid for all cases concerned with excise duty.

An additional study of the structure of the cases concerned with excise duty (6111) made it possible to classify around half of the complaints using five groups of keywords. The study illustrated the role that cases concluded with judgements containing the phrase "passenger car" played in the fluctuations in the number of cases with symbol 6111.

---

23 Information emerges in the public debate indicating that these might be delays of several years, which is linked to the prescription period for tax liability, cf., e.g., J. Waśko, *Wszczynanie postępowań karnych skarbowych w trakcie postępowań kontrolnych – analiza praktyki wybranych urzędów kontroli skarbowej*, „Przegląd Podatkowy" 2017, No. 2, pp. 44–49; A. Ladziński et al., *Instrumentalne wszczynanie postępowań karnych skarbowych w trakcie postępowań kontrolnych i podatkowych – analiza praktyki stosowania art. 70 § 6 pkt 1 Ordynacji Podatkowej*, Toruń 2019.

This result encourages scepticism toward the hypothesis that the number of cases concerned with excise duties (and consequently tax complaints, 611, cf. Figure 2.10) is correlated with the cyclical fluctuations in the economy. It seems that such a correlation, which is observable based on the aggregated statistical data (cf. Figure 2.9), is as merely a statistical artefact.

Dominik J. Gajewski (SGH Warsaw School of Economics)

Kamil Joński (SGH Warsaw School of Economics)

4. "Demand" for Resolution of Disputes by the Administrative Court: From the Number of Cases to the Disputed Value

Abstract: The chapter attempts to shift the analysis of the administrative court caseload (i.e., the demand for adjudication) from the considerations of "volume" (i.e., the number of incoming cases) to "value" (i.e., the value of a claim). To this end, court files were analysed using a randomly selected 10 % sample od VAT cases lodged with the Supreme Administrative Court in 2019. Cases with high disputed values are discussed in greater detail, and the structure of court fees is illustrated.

Keywords: VAT cases, value of claim, analysis of court files, Supreme Administrative Court, court fees

Introduction

So far analyses of the "demand" for judicial settlement of disputes with public administration have focused on the number of disputes (i.e., submitted complaints) but did not take into account their subject-matter. Meanwhile, based on the economic analysis of the law, it can be argued that the significance of complaints – from the point of view of their consequences for economic turnover – differs depending on the amount of monetary claim covered by the contested acts of administrative authorities.

Unfortunately, statistical reports drawn up in administrative courts offer no possibility of determining the amount of monetary claim covered by the administrative authorities' acts challenged at the RAC.

The revenue from court fees charged in the course administrative proceedings, which is recorded in state budget implementation reports, seems to point to certain conclusions as to the value of these claims and its changes over time.[1] However, this measure is highly imprecise and can only be treated as being illustrative in character. This mainly arises from two facts: (1) collection of a proportional or fixed court fee depending on case type (Article 230(1) of the

1 In section 069 Proceeds from Various Fees, Part 05 – Supreme Administrative Court.

PbAC) and (2) nonlinearity of proportional fees (section 1 of the Regulation of the Council of Ministers of 16 December 2003 on the Amount of and Detailed Rules for Collecting Court Fees in Proceedings before Administrative Courts.[2]) Therefore, although an increase (or decrease) in budgetary revenue from court fees indicates a rise (or drop) in the value of monetary claims covered by the acts challenged at administrative courts, it will not reflect its scale.[3]

The amount of budgetary revenue from court fees collected in the course of administrative court proceedings is presented in Figure 4.1.

A sharp increase in revenue from court fees collected in the course of proceedings before administrative courts after 2009 as well as its considerable volatility in the subsequent years certainly capture attention.

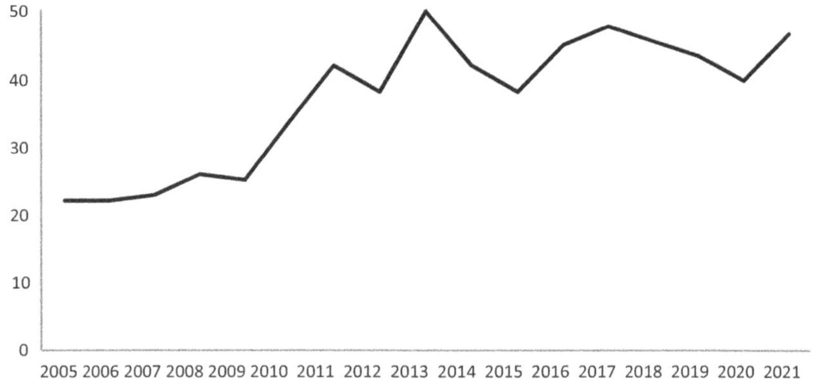

Figure 4.1. State budget revenue from court fees collected at administrative courts (in PLN million)

Source: Section 069 Proceeds from Various Fees; since 2017 – section 063 Proceeds from Court Fees and Costs, Part No. 5 – Supreme Administrative Court, the Supreme Audit Office, annual Information on the Results of State Budget Implementation Audit, https://www.nik.gov.pl/kontrole/analiza-budzetu-panstwa/ (accessed on: 5/11/2022).

2 Journal of Laws of 2003 No. 221, item 2193.

3 The case is different with common courts where the amount of the proportional fee is principally 5 % of the value of the disputed claim but no more than 100 thousand PLN (however, cases where the value of the disputed claim exceeds PLN 2 million are rare) – see Article 13(1) of the Act of 28 July 2005 on Court Costs in Civil Cases (Journal of Laws of 2005 No. 167, item 1398).

4.1. Court Fee in Administrative Proceedings

As pointed out in the relevant literature[4], the purpose of court fees is both financing the operation of judicial authorities (though indirectly because the fees are a source of state budgetary revenue as a whole and not income of the system of administrative courts) and influencing procedural decisions so that excessive use of the judiciary is prevented. This purpose is reflected, for example, in the method of determining the sequence of proportional fees delineated in section 1 of the Regulation of the Council of Ministers of 16 December 2003 on the Amounts of and Detailed Rules for Collecting Court Fees in Proceedings before Administrative Courts.[5] They are degressive in character – the percentage value of the court fee decreases along with the increase in the amount of the disputed claim (for example, if the value of the claim in the first instance is PLN 100, the court fee will be 100 %; if the disputed claim is PLN 100 million – 0.1 %), which is intended to "lower the attractiveness" of court proceedings in the case of low values of the disputed claim (fig. 4.2.). It is worth mentioning that the amounts of court fees have not been updated for 17 years, which may affect the practical effectiveness of these regulations.

Similar as the case with proportional fees, the structure of fixed court fees may also influence parties' decisions regarding proceedings. In principle, it is more complex (the regulations cited above provide for 49 separate categories of cases where fixed fees are collected in 11 different amounts).[6] At the same time, the fees themselves are much lower than the proportional fees, which raises a justified question as to their proportionality, given the nature and level of complexity of the issues that the court decides on in both categories of cases.

4 Cf. M. Wild (ed.), M. Dziurda, P. Rylski, J. Sadomski, *Ustawa o kosztach sądowych w sprawach cywilnych. Analiza funkcjonowania – wnioski* de lege ferenda, Instytut Wymiaru Sprawiedliwości, 2015.

5 Dz.U.2003.221.2193, as amended.

6 PLN 100, 200, 300, 500, 800, 1,000, 1,500, 3,000, 5,000, 8,000 and 10,000.

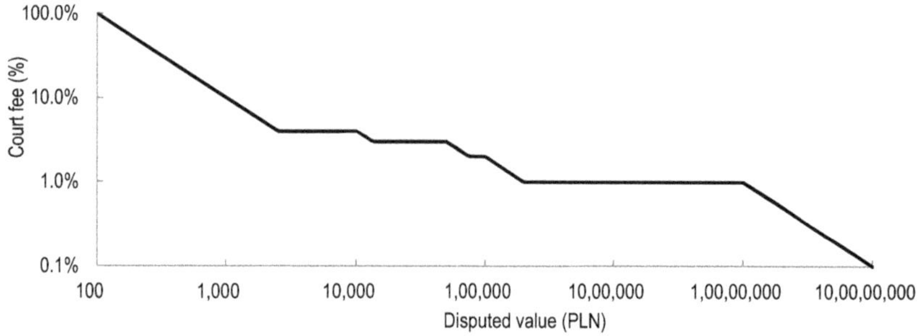

Figure 4.2. Percentage value of the fee in proceedings before the RAC compared to the disputed value

Source: Section 1 of the Regulation of the Council of Ministers of 16 December 2003 on the Amounts of and Detailed Rules for Collecting Court Fees in Proceedings before Administrative Courts.

As far as the economic consequences of the case law of administrative courts are concerned, it should be noted that the total amount of the disputed claims considered in the courts is often seen as a benchmark of the importance of the disputes for the functioning of the economy.[7] Such an approach seems to be inherently conservative since it is justified to believe that the case law of courts (especially supreme courts) shapes application of the law to a broader extent than the actually recognised cases. However, due to methodological issues undermining the attempts to quantify such an indirect (and therefore impossible to directly observe) impact, analysis of recognised cases serves as an important starting point, which also validates such research.

Moreover, the analysis of cassation appeals regarding VAT lodged with the SAC in 2019 (which is the last year before the COVID pandemic) may spark an interesting discussion on the activities of tax authorities as regards improvement of VAT collection (in other words, reduction of the VAT gap).[8]

4.2. Research Methodology and Sample Selection

Unfortunately, the RAC's and SAC's statistical reports do not record the disputed value. There is no possibility to establish it directly through the Case Law and

7 C. Costello et al., *Economic value of the judiciary: A pilot study for five countries on volume, value and duration of large commercial cases*, 2020, https://www.encj.eu/node/563 (accessed on: 5.11.2022).

8 CASE, *Study and Reports on the VAT Gap in the EU-28 Member States*, 2020, https://op.europa.eu/s/wNXJ (accessed on: 5.11.2022).

Case Information Central Database (CBOIS) either. Therefore, it is necessary to carry out a study of case files on a representative sample of cases.

4.2.1. Sample Selection Method

Appeals regarding VAT form the largest category of tax cases brought before the SAC (see Table 4.1). Such appeals were randomly selected for the sample according to the order of registration of cases in the SAC, which is reflected in their subsequent reference numbers. In 2019, there were I FSK cases registered at Division 1 of the Financial Chamber of the SAC with reference numbers from 1 to 2387. In order to carry out the study, a decision was made to analyse a random sample of 10 % of the cases brought before the court: Thus, every 10th case was included in the sample based on subsequent reference numbers (ending with 5).

If case files of the selected case were unavailable (e.g., because they were in the hands of the adjudicating panel or the chairpersons of the divisions), the case with the highest reference number preceding it was selected instead.[9]

Table 4.1. Structure of tax cases registered at the SAC in 2019

Symbol	Case substance per symbol	Number of submitted cases	Percentage of tax cases lodged in 2019
6110	Value Added Tax	2,373	39 %
6115	Property tax	966	16 %
6112	Personal income tax	795	13 %
6119	Other with the core symbol 611	461	8 %
6113	Corporate income tax	443	7 %
6111	Excise duty	373	6 %
6118	Enforcement of monetary benefits	335	6 %
6116	Tax on civil law transactions, stamp duty, and other taxes and fees	176	3 %
6117	Payment credits (discharge, deferral, arrangement of instalments, etc.)	59	1 %
6114	Inheritance and gifts tax	42	1 %

Source: SAC Statistics, http://www.nsa.gov.pl/statystyki-nsa.php (accessed on: 5/11/2022).

9 E.g., case I FSK 113/19 was analysed instead of case I FSK 115/19 owing to the unavailability of the selected case files as well as files No. I FSK 114/19 at the time of examination.

For each case included in the sample, the reference number at the SAC and the reference number at the RAC were recorded as well as the dates of the RAC's judgement and of submission of the case to the SAC. These metrics make it possible to verify correctness of the collected data through comparing them with the information (on cases) provided in CBOIS.

The variable that is key from the point of view of this study – which is the disputed value (DV) – was recorded on the basis of information contained in the complaint lodged with the RAC (or in a supplement to it). If the tax authority quoted a different DV in response to the complaint and the Court decided to set it as per the authority's indication, this value was recorded for the purposes of the study. It was also verified whether this amount was consistent with the DV indicated in the cassation appeal.

Moreover, the amounts of court fees that had been paid at the first- and second-instance courts were recorded and it was also noted whether in each case the taxpayer had been granted legal aid in the form of full or partial exemption from the court fee. Comparison of the recorded DVs and the amounts of court fees paid in was the next stage of verification of the accuracy of the collected data.

4.2.2. Verification of the Representativeness of the Research Sample

In line with the adopted methodology, the study covered 239 cassation appeals with symbol 6110, which is 10 % of the total of this category of cases brought before the SAC in 2019. In 37 cases (i.e., 15 %), the case files with the selected reference number were not available, so in accordance with the adopted selection method, they were replaced with the available cases with a lower reference number.

The study of a sample of 10 % of the total number of cases makes it possible to expect that its results will be representative and will lead to conclusions allowing for making generalisations. The first stage of the study was verification of this assumption (and thus of the credibility of the obtained results).

To this end, the characteristics of cases under analysis were collected on the basis of information that are available in CBOIS for all 2,387 cases registered in Division 1 of the Financial Chamber of the SAC in 2019. Such characteristics, which are relevant from the point of view of this study, include the geographical distribution of the cases (by the RAC whose judgement was appealed) and its subject-matter (e.g., a tax ruling or other matters). Juxtaposition of all cases (as per CBOIS) and the research sample is provided in Table 4.2.

It can be concluded that the random selection of cases correctly reflects the structure of all cassation appeals concerning VAT in terms of the geographical aspect (although the cassation appeals against judgements of the smallest RACs remain underestimated).

In the sample under examination, one third (33 %: 80 out of 239) of the cases were appeals against tax rulings, which precisely reflects their proportion in the total number of cassation appeals with symbol 6110 brought before the SAC in 2019. However, Table 4.1 shows that the higher the level of detail of analysis (of the proportion of cases concerning tax rulings divided by the RACs that passed the first-instance judgement), the looser the fit (in this respect, the RAC in Gdańsk appears to be particularly interesting as the research sample contained no cassation appeals against the judgements on a VAT ruling passed by this RAC). This naturally arises from the fact that, for example, the number of cassation appeals against judgements on VAT rulings amounted to 36 in the RAC in Gdańsk, 48 in the RAC in Bydgoszcz, and 24 in the RAC in Białystok. With a random sample size of 10 %, there should respectively be three, five, and two cases, if the fit was perfect, and so a difference of as few as several cases becomes noticeable; in the sample of 239 cases, including 80 cases regarding tax rulings, there were three such cases from Bydgoszcz and two from Białystok. One must bear in mind this specific characteristic of research on case files when drawing conclusions from the compiled sample. Therefore, a study of disputed values, for example, is only valid when the sample is considered as a whole (as it presents the bigger picture of the whole country, which can be deemed accurate based on the above analysis), without taking into account an otherwise interesting geographical aspect.

Table 4.2. Geographical structure of the selected sample and of all the cases (in %)

RAC	Cassation appeals 6110 (in total)		Including tax rulings		Other	
	All cases in 2019	Research sample	All cases in 2019	Research sample	All cases in 2019	Research sample
Białystok	3	2	3	3	3	2
Bydgoszcz	5	4	6	4	5	4
Gdańsk	6	7	5	0	6	11
Gliwice	8	11	9	11	8	11
Gorzów Wielkopolski	2	3	4	4	2	2
Kielce	2	2	3	1	2	3

(continued on next page)

Table 4.2. Continued

RAC	Cassation appeals 6110 (in total)		Including tax rulings		Other	
	All cases in 2019	Research sample	All cases in 2019	Research sample	All cases in 2019	Research sample
Kraków	5	6	7	9	5	4
Lublin	6	5	6	5	6	6
Łódź	7	8	8	5	7	9
Olsztyn	2	2	2	3	2	1
Opole	3	1	4	3	2	1
Poznań	5	6	6	4	5	7
Rzeszów	3	3	5	6	3	1
Szczecin	4	4	3	5	4	3
Warsaw	31	31	24	28	35	33
Wrocław	5	7	7	11	5	4

Source: Own work.

4.3. Disputed Value and Legal Aid

In view of the fact that one third of the cassation appeals (with symbol 6110) submitted to the SAC in 2019 are concerned with tax rulings, it is obvious that the disputed value was not determined in these cases.

However, collected data show that, among the other two thirds of the cases, there is a large group of cases where the disputed value was not determined either (and their subject-matter is usually referred to in CBOIS as "Value Added Tax"). This applies to another set of 50 cases under examination (21 %). In nearly half of them, the subject-matter evaluated by the court was the validity of postponing a VAT refund. In these cases, the appeals were mainly concerned with withheld returns amounting to several hundred thousand PLN.[10] This

---

10 The small number of cases under analysis allows for no reliable estimations of the measures of the central tendency (such as the average or the median) or dispersion (e.g., the range of 50 % typical observations).

value corresponds to the average amount of withheld VAT refunds in the years 2012–2018.[11]

In effect, the disputed value was determined in only 46 % of the VAT cases under analysis, which were brought before the SAC in 2019 (i.e., in 110 cases).

Finally, the DV was established in 46 % of the cases subject to examination. Their structure is shown in Table 4.3. It is delineated with six intuitive value ranges owing to the fact that this type of data is characterized by specific distributions dominated by singular very high observations (with the highest DV recorded in the sample amounting to PLN 42.3 million; the total of the five highest DVs was PLN 151 million, and the total in the remaining 104 cases – only PLN 123 million).

Table 4.3. Structure of cases regarding VAT per disputed value

Interval	Number of cases	Percentage of cases with a specified DV
below 10,000	11	10
10–100 thousand	22	20
100–500 thousand	38	35
0.5–1 million	11	10
1–10 million	18	16
over 10 million	9	8

Source: own work.

It turns out that the largest group comprising one-third of the VAT cases with a determined DV (and over 15 % of all the VAT cases under examination) are cases with a disputed value ranging between PLN 100 and 500 thousand. There was a DV lower than PLN 10,000 only in every 10th case where the disputed value was determined.

Importantly, in every 4th case regarding VAT where the disputed value was determined, it exceeded PLN 1 million, and in 8 % of the cases – PLN 10 million.

From the point of view of an attempt being made to assess the role of administrative judiciary in the economy in terms of disputes between the taxpayer and the administrative authorities directly resolved by the courts, it should be assumed that the above-mentioned set of 8 % of the cases is of crucial

11 Calculated on the basis of data provided in the reply to Question No. 32784 of 29 August 2019 (the 8th term).

importance. The total disputed value in the cases under analysis, where the DV was above PLN 10 million, amounted to PLN 202 million, which is 74 % of the total DV in all the 110 cases under examination.

In comparison, the total disputed value in 83 cases under analysis, where the DV was below PLN 1 million, amounted to as little as PLN 20 million, which is 7 % of the total DV in all the 110 cases under examination.

4.3.1. Legal Aid in Cases under Examination

In the sample of VAT cases under analysis, legal aid in the form of full or partial exemption from payment of the court fee was granted in 23 cases. It is remarkable that 14 of the exemptions were granted in cases with a DV of over PLN 1 million. In other words, legal aid was granted in more than half of the cases with a DV higher than PLN 1 million (i.e., 14 out of 27).

The problem that this signals is also relevant for cases with a DV exceeding PLN 10 million; out of nine such cases in the sample, in five of them the administrative courts granted the appellants the right to legal aid in at least one of the instances (in two cases the appellants paid no fee and in the third case – PLN 500). To sum up, the right to legal aid in the form of full or partial exemption from the court fee was granted in more than half of the cases regarding VAT with the highest disputed value. In comparison, in cases with a DV lower than PLN 1 million, such aid was granted in only 11 % of the cases.

Given the rather conservative approach of the administrative judges to the issue of granting legal aid to legal persons, this raises the question of practical enforceability of the disputed tax claims of particularly high value.

4.4. Characteristics of Cases Regarding VAT with the Highest Disputed Value

As indicated above, the total value of the claims covered by the disputes settled by courts in a given period is sometimes considered by the relevant literature to be the measure of their impact on the functioning of the economy.[12] Such an approach seems to be inherently conservative since it is justified to believe that the case law of courts (especially supreme courts) shapes the process of application of the law to a broader extent than the actually recognised cases.

---

12 C. Costello et al., Economic value of the judiciary: A pilot study for five countries on volume, value and duration of large commercial cases, 2020, https://www.encj.eu/node/563 (accessed on: 5/11/2022).

However, the methodological difficulties underlying attempts to perform such an analysis validate focus on studies based on recognised cases (as such a broad influence of case law on the economy would need to be evaluated in indirect terms since it would be impossible to observe it directly).

In view of earlier analyses devoted to the economic aspect of complaints about collection of VAT[13], it is justified to carry out an in-depth qualitative analysis of 27 cases from the sample with a DV higher than PLN 1 million. Since the majority of the proceedings before the Supreme Administrative Court have not yet ended with a judgement, the statements of reasons for judgements passed at the first instance underwent analysis.

The cases were organised in a descending order by the disputed value.

In the cassation appeal registered in the SAC on 25 September 2019 (with a ref. No. I FSK 1835/19), which was filed against judgement of 7 January 2019 (ref. No. III SA/WA 711/18), the disputed value was PLN 42.3 million. The case was concerned with a chain of transactions which was deemed to be the so-called VAT carousel. The administrative decision was issued at the first instance by the Head of the Masovian Tax and Customs Office in Warsaw on 8 June 2017 and was concerned with settlement of VAT for the period between November 2012 and August 2013. According to the Articles of Incorporation of the taxpayer's company, its main activity was wholesale sales of electronic and telecommunications equipment as well as relevant spare parts. On the basis of the collected evidence, the first-instance authority questioned the correctness of VAT settlements and stated that VAT invoices issued by the company did not document actual economic events because the activities they covered had not been performed. In line with findings made during the audit, the company was a link in a chain of unreliable transactions aimed at disguising fraud and generating fake documentation which was used to make fictitious VAT settlements in the course of subsequent transactions covering the goods indicated in the documentation. The court fee was paid in the course of proceedings before the administrative courts of both instances.

In the cassation appeal registered in the SAC on 13 February 2019 (with a ref. No. I FSK 245/19), which was filed against judgement of 28 September 2018 (ref. No. I SA/LU 261/18), the disputed value was PLN 38.7 million. The case was concerned with a chain of transactions, which was deemed to be the so-called

13 D.J. Gajewski, K. Joński, *Country Note: Procedures of the Polish Tax Authorities and the VAT Gap: Evidence from Administrative Court Files*, "Intertax" 2020, Vol. 48, No. 11, pp. 1012–1019.

VAT carousel. The administrative decision was issued in the first instance by the Head of the Tax Audit Office in Lublin on 21 December 2016 and was concerned with settlement of VAT for the period between November 2012 and June 2014. The Head of the Tax Audit Office audited the taxpayer's business activity of wholesale sales of electronic and telecommunications equipment and relevant spare parts. On the basis of the collected evidence, the first-instance authority concluded that since the taxpayer had no employees and no warehouses on their own to store various types of electronic devices to be traded, such as televisions, game consoles or mobile phones of different brands and models, they were in fact an intermediary link in 227 identified supply chains of electronic equipment, where they acted mostly as the second, third or fourth entity (the so-called buffer) after the first entity in the country that had not paid the Value Added Tax on the reported transactions (i.e., "the missing trader"). The chains of trade in the same commodity, which had been identified, had an international character, and the last participant in these supply chains on the territory of Poland was an entity that accounted for a given supply without charging Value Added Tax on it (making it intra-Community supply or export with a rate of 0 %) and declared a tax refund or reduced the amount of payable tax (the so-called broker). The taxpayer was granted the right to legal aid in the form of exemption from the court fee in the proceedings before the administrative court (however, they paid in a fee of PLN 500 in the first instance).

In the cassation appeal registered in the SAC on 12 April 2019 (with a ref. No. I FSK 715/19), which was filed against judgement of 26 November 2018 (ref. No. III SA/GL 618/18), the disputed value was PLN 25.4 million. The case was concerned with a chain of transactions, which was deemed to be the so-called VAT carousel. The administrative decision was issued in the first instance by the Head of the Tax Audit Office [HTAO] in Katowice on 14 September 2016 and was concerned with settlement of VAT for November 2016. During the audit, there were more than a dozen instances discovered where groups of devices had been traded among entities multiple times either before or after making a transaction and there were entities involved in the chain that had been offering a price below market value or entities that had been the so-called missing traders. The taxpayer was granted the right of legal aid in the form of full exemption from the court fee in the proceedings before administrative courts in both instances. In the cassation appeal registered in the SAC on 22 March 2019 (with a ref. No. I FSK 555/19), which was filed against judgement of 24 April 2018 (ref. No. III SA/WA 1575/17), the disputed value was PLN 23 million. The HTAO found an overstatement of input tax – to be deducted – amounting in total to PLN 23 million resulting from recording VAT invoices in purchase registers, which documented the taxpayer's purchase transaction covering the right of perpetual usufruct of land along with the ownership rights to two commercial and service buildings, three non-residential buildings, and equipment situated on the premises of this property.

The tax control authority declared the transaction to be an apparent act within the meaning of Article 83(1) of the Civil Code,[14] justifying this declaration by claiming, among others, that the entities participating in many of the transactions described in the decision were related to each other and did not have the means allowing to perform them. The administrative decision was issued in the first instance by the Head of the Tax Audit Office in Lublin on 28 July 2016 and was concerned with settlement of VAT for the years 2014–2015. The taxpayer was granted the right to legal aid in the form of partial exemption from the court fee in the proceedings before the SAC (however, they paid the whole court fee in the first-instance proceedings).

In the cassation appeal registered in the SAC on 3 October 2019 (with a ref. No. I FSK 1885/19), which was filed against judgement of 12 March 2019 (ref. No. III SA/WA 1891/18), the disputed value was PLN 21.9 million. The case was concerned with a chain of transactions, which was deemed to be the so-called VAT carousel. The administrative decision was issued in the first instance by the Head of the Masovian Tax and Customs Office in Warsaw on 11 August 2017 and was concerned with settlement of VAT for July 2013. The findings made in the course of audit of the company demonstrated that during the period under examination it was engaged in activity consisting in selling IT equipment, that is, electronics (and mainly smartphones), to entities operating on the domestic market and in EU countries within the framework of intra-Community purchase of goods from the Czech Republic and Cyprus. According to the auditors, the appellant was involved in a carousel fraud. The court fee was paid in the course of proceedings before the administrative courts of both instances.

In the cassation appeal registered in the SAC on 15 March 2019 (with a ref. No. I FSK 494/19), which was filed against judgement of 19 September 2018 (ref. No. III SA/WA 3732/17), the disputed value was PLN 14.6 million. The case was concerned with determination of the correct VAT rate for the traded goods and services. The taxpayer submitted a corrected tax return and as reasons for their submission they indicated that adjustment arose from the fact that the company had received a positive tax ruling from the Minister of Finance regarding recognition of sales systems such as drive in, walk through, and food court as

14 Act of 23 April 1964 – Civil Code (Journal of Laws of 2016, item 380).

supply of goods and so a 5 % VAT rate was applied to such sales (originally, the sale was treated by the company as a catering services and was taxed with an 8 % VAT rate). The Director of the Tax Audit Office did not agree with the taxpayer and also stated that the tax rulings they had received did not apply to this case because the applications for these rulings had presented facts different from the ones discovered during the proceedings (as the rulings did not determine the correctness of assignment of the products and services offered by the company to the PKWiU statistical classification categories; PKWiU stands for the Polish Classification of Products and Services). The administrative decision was issued on 5 January 2017 and was concerned with settlement of VAT for the years 2013–2014.The court fee was paid in both instances of proceedings before the administrative court.

In the cassation appeal registered in the SAC on 30 May 2019 (with a ref. No. I FSK 1035/19), which was filed against judgement of 15 February 2018 (ref. No. III SA/WA 560/17), the disputed value was PLN 12.2 million. The case was concerned with a chain of transactions, which was deemed to be the so-called VAT carousel. The administrative decision was issued in the first instance by the Head of the Tax Audit Office in Białystok on 26 August 2016 and was concerned with settlement of VAT for 2012. The authority challenged the taxpayer's right to deduct input tax arising from invoices for purchase of fuel, claiming that they did not document acquisition of goods originating from their issuers; although the actual fuel deliveries were not contested by the authority. The court fee was paid in the course of proceedings before the administrative courts of both instances.

In the cassation appeal registered in the SAC on 30 August 2019 (with a ref. No. I FSK 1665/19), which was filed against judgement of 24 January 2019 (ref. No. III SA/WA 950/18), the disputed value was PLN 12.1 million. The findings of the tax audit as regards Value Added Tax demonstrated that the taxpayer had made transactions within the framework of the so-called tax carousel and the purchase invoices for the mobile phones as well as the invoices for their resale did not document actual transactions. The administrative decision was issued in the first instance by the Head of the Tax Office in Legionowo on 26 July 2017 and was concerned with settlement of VAT for 2013. The taxpayer was granted the right of legal aid in the form of full exemption from the court fee in the proceedings before administrative courts in both instances.

In the cassation appeal registered in the SAC on 12 December 2019 (with a ref. No. I FSK 2295/19), which was filed against judgement of 19 February 2019 (ref. No. III SA/WA 1218/18), the disputed value was PLN 11.6 million. The case involved the use of invoices that do not reflect actual economic transactions (the so-called blank invoices). The administrative decision was issued in the first instance by the West Pomeranian Tax and Customs Office in Szczecin on 27 July 2017 and was concerned with settlement of VAT for the period between January and February 2016. The auditors challenged purchases and sales of fuel, claiming that the relevant VAT invoices declared transactions between entities described in them, which had not been carried out. Consequently, transport services related to these transactions, which the taxpayer had purchased and provided themselves, were contested as well. In turn, the taxpayer argued that they had made actual transactions of purchase and sale of fuel and that the tax authority had misinterpreted the evidence because the entity conducted the so-called clean trade in fuels (which means the company was an intermediary in sales of fuel); the company indicated that according to the concession issued by the President of the Energy Regulatory Office, it could only carry out the "clean trade in fuels". The taxpayer was granted the right of legal aid in the form of partial exemption from the court fee in the proceedings before administrative courts in both instances.

In the cassation appeal registered in the SAC on 29 August 2019 (with a ref. No. I FSK 1655/19), which was filed against judgement of 16 January 2019 (ref. No. III SA/WA 827/18), the disputed value was PLN 9.8 million. The case was concerned with a chain of transactions, which was deemed to be the so-called VAT carousel. The administrative decision was issued in the first instance by the Head of the Tax Office (HTO) in Otwock on 27 April 2017 and was concerned with settlement of VAT for 2013. The authority challenged the taxpayer's right to a deduction on invoices for fuel supply because – according to the HTO – the invoices originating from certain entities did not document actual economic events, which a taxpayer "exercising due diligence should at least have known about". The court fee was paid in the course of proceedings before the administrative courts of both instances.

In the cassation appeal registered in the SAC on 28 July 2019 (with a ref. No. I FSK 1455/19), which was filed against judgement of 5 December 2018 (ref. No. III SA/WA 4029/17), the disputed value was PLN 7.4 million. The case involved the use of invoices that do not reflect actual economic transactions (the so-called blank invoices) in trade in gases. The administrative decision was issued in the first instance by the Head of the Tax Audit Office in Bydgoszcz on 30 December 2016 and was concerned with settlement of VAT for the period from January to June 2012. The taxpayer was granted the right of legal aid in the form of partial exemption from the court fee in the proceedings before administrative courts in the first instance.

In the cassation appeal registered in the SAC on 1 April 2019 (with a ref. No. I FSK 615/19), which was filed against judgement of 19 December 2018 (ref. No.

I SA/GD 543/18), the disputed value was PLN 5.1 million. The administrative decision was issued in the first instance by the Head of the Pomeranian Tax and Customs Office in Gdynia on 11 May 2017 and was concerned with settlement of VAT for 2013. The authority claimed that the output tax on the sale of imported footwear had been understated due to the underselling prices, which led to the determination of the tax base by means of an external comparative assessment. In consequence, the amount of output tax estimated by the authority is the amount of tax reported by the taxpayer increased by the output tax on estimated sales of footwear and decreased by the tax arising from invoices for sales of footwear. The taxpayer was granted the right of legal aid in the form of full exemption from the court fee in the proceedings before administrative courts in both instances.

In the cassation appeal registered in the SAC on 12 August 2019 (with a ref. No. I FSK 1565/19), which was filed against judgement of 16 April 2019 (ref. No. I SA/KR 1250/18), the disputed value was PLN 4 million. The case was concerned with a chain of transactions, which was deemed to be the so-called VAT carousel. The administrative decision was issued at the first instance by the Head of the Tax Audit Office in Kraków on 28 October 2015 and was concerned with settlement of VAT for the period between April 2013 and March 2014. According to the authority, operation of the company during the period covered by the decision consisted solely in accepting fictitious invoices that did not reflect actual economic events and placing those invoices on the market. These were invoices for purchase and sales of zinc and lead, purchase and sales of construction materials, renovation and construction works, and marketing services. Owing to the lack of technical, organisational, and logistic means as well as lack of means of transport, registered office (as the headquarters were located in a virtual office), employees or warehouses, it was declared that the company was not a taxpayer within the meaning of Article 15 of the VAT Act and so it was not entitled to deduct input tax arising from invoices for purchases of goods and services. At the same time – considering Article 108(1) of the VAT Act – it was determined that the company had issued invoices that did not document actual economic events and had introduced those invoices into the business trading. The company was obliged to pay the tax indicated in these invoices. The taxpayer was granted the right of legal aid in the form of full exemption from the court fee in the proceedings before administrative courts in both instances.

In the cassation appeal registered in the SAC on 17 July 2019 (with a ref. No. I FSK 1371/19), which was filed against judgement of 16 November 2018 (ref. No. III SA/WA 2552/17), the disputed value was PLN 4 million. The taxpayer submitted a VAT-7 return with an indication of an amount to be returned. According to the tax audit authority, the transaction recorded on a VAT invoice (issued for the supply of real property) was intended to circumvent the law within the meaning of Article 58(1) of the Civil Code[15] and was concluded solely for the purpose of declaring an excess of input tax over output tax on the taxpayer's VAT return for October 2015, which was to be returned to their bank account. The Head of the Tax Administration Chamber in Warsaw found that there was no economic justification for the purchase of the above-mentioned property when mortgages were raised against it in the absence of financial means to finance it. The administrative decision was issued in the first instance by the Head of the Tax Audit Office in Rzeszów on 10 February 2017 and was concerned with settlement of VAT for October 2015. The taxpayer was granted the right of legal aid in the form of partial exemption from the court fee in the proceedings before administrative courts in the second instance (whereas the fee was fully paid in the first instance).

In the cassation appeal registered in the SAC on 2 October 2019 (with a ref. No. I FSK 1875/19), which was filed against judgement of 3 July 2019 (ref. No. I SA/ŁD 296/19), the disputed value was PLN 2.6 million. From the point of view of the effectiveness of proceedings before the administrative court and – as suggested by the frequency of repeal of rulings and judgements – from the point of view of interpretation of the law (as regards the principle of objective truth in tax proceedings), it was the most problematic case with a DV equal to or exceeding PLN 1 million among the cases under analysis. The case involved the use of invoices that do not reflect actual economic transactions (the so-called blank invoices). The authority accused the taxpayer of (1) issuing VAT invoices that did not document actual economic events in the form of promotional services; (2) overstating input tax to be deduced on invoices issued by (…) as these invoices did not reflect actual economic events, that is, purchase of prepaid cards; and (3) of the unrecorded sale of goods.

It is worth noting the course of the proceedings before the administrative authority in the case under examination. Initially, the first-instance authority issued a decision on 24 July 2013, but it was repealed by the second-instance authority on 6 December 2013. After reconsidering the case, a decision was issued by the Head of the Tax Audit Office in Łódź on 18 August 2015 and upheld by the second-instance authority on 26 February 2016.

A complaint was lodged in the Regional Administrative Court in Łódź (with a ref. No. I SA/ŁD 392/16) whose judgement of 9 August 2016 was repealed by

15 Act of 23 April 1964 – Civil Code (that is, Journal of Laws of 2017, item 459).

the SAC on 25 January 2019 (see case with a ref. No. I FSK 133/17) and handed over for reconsideration.

The Supreme Administrative Court supported the allegations concerning infringement of Article 108(1) of the VAT Act by way of applying it in connection with the discovery that the invoices issued by the complainant (in the case under analysis) to one of the companies did not reflect any transaction because it clearly surfaced from the testimonies of (...) that the complainant had not sold any services but provided this contractor with promotional vouchers. According to the Supreme Administrative Court, the sole fact of altering the classification of taxable transactions recorded on an invoice does not entitle the tax authority to apply Article 108(1) of the VAT Act, which imposes an obligation on the issuer of the invoice to pay the tax indicated on it solely due to the fact that invoice has been issued. The Supreme Administrative Court declared that – based on above mentioned provision – if an invoice documents an act that has actually been performed between entities indicated in the invoice as parties to the act, which has, however, been improperly classified as a service instead of as a sale, it does not give rise to an obligation to pay the tax indicated therein pursuant to this provision as it is not the kind of invoice that this provision applies to.

Another allegation supported by the SAC was infringement of Article 141(4) of the PbAC as regards the RAC's evaluation of the findings of the authorities with respect to the nature of the invoices for the acquisition of prepaid cards, which were issued to the appellant by one of the companies. When presenting arguments for the acceptance of this finding, the RAC followed the steps of the tax authority and invoked other judgements of the RAC in Warsaw[16] where it was accepted that the invoices issued by this entity to the complainant in the case under examination qualified the tax indicated in them to be covered by Article 108(1) of the VAT Act. However, these judgements were repealed[17] and the basis for the repeal was recognition of the validity of the procedural allegations (pursuant to Article 122, Article 187(1), Article 188, and Article 191 of the TO) that incomplete evidence was gathered for adopted assumptions about blank invoices. According to the SAC, this problem of assessing the substance of a transaction may be similar to the above-mentioned issue of selling promotional

---

16 Judgements of 11 September 2014, ref. No. III SA/Wa 2204/13, and of 22 September 2014, ref. No. III SA/Wa 2445/13.

17 Judgements of the Supreme Administrative Court of 7 December 2016 in a case with a ref. No. I FSK 692/15 and of 15 March 2017, ref. No. I FSK 832/15.

vouchers instead of providing services. In the opinion of the SAC, sufficient factual discoveries had not yet been made in this respect.

On 3 July 2019, the RAC in Łódź passed another first-instance judgement (with a ref. No. I SA/ŁD 296/19) which was appealed to the SAC again (see case files with a ref. No. I FSK 1875/19 – which is one of the cases under analysis). It should be noted that the challenged decision was concerned with settlement of VAT for 2008. The taxpayer in case No. I SA/ŁD 296/19 was granted the right of legal aid in the form of full exemption from the court fee in the proceedings before administrative courts (whereas the fee for the cassation appeal No. I FSK 1875/19 was paid).

In the cassation appeal registered in the SAC on 13 April 2019 (with a ref. No. I FSK 755/19), which was filed against judgement of 14 November 2018 (ref. No. III SA/GL 556/18), the disputed value was PLN 2.5 million. The case was concerned with a chain of transactions, which was deemed to be the so-called VAT carousel. The administrative decision was issued in the first instance by the Head of the Tax Office in Cieszyn on 30 March 2017 and was concerned with settlement of VAT for the period between February and April 2014. There was a tax audit carried out in the company as regards correctness of settlement of Value Added Tax for February, March, and April 2014, and based on the discoveries made during the audit, the first-instance authority initiated tax proceedings. The Company took part in the so-called tax carousel and bought/sold zinc and lead while acting as the ultimate buyer (i.e., the broker) that provided intra-Community supply of steel products and declared an excess of input tax over output tax to be returned to their bank account. According to the tax administration, the taxpayer actually settled input tax from invoices issued by fictitious companies involved in earlier transactions, which was increased by the Value Added Tax on profit margins added by subsequent entities included in the supply chain. In cooperation with other tax administration bodies in the country and in the European Union and based on responses obtained from entities involved in the supply chain earlier, the first-instance authority revealed entities involved in each transaction and defined the roles that these entities played in this scheme. The taxpayer was granted the right of legal aid in the form of exemption from the court fee in the proceedings before administrative courts in part (in the first instance) and in total (in the second instance).

In the cassation appeal registered in the SAC on 6 May 2019 (with a ref. No. I FSK 825/19), which was filed against judgement of 26 July 2017 (ref. No. I SA/KR 1458/16), the disputed value was PLN 2.5 million. The case involved the use of invoices that do not reflect actual economic transactions (the so-called blank invoices). The administrative decision was issued in the first instance by the Head of the Tax Audit Office in Lublin on 31 May 2016 and was concerned with settlement of VAT for the period between the year 2010 and June 2011. The authority's findings showed that the taxpayer conducted business activities related to the sales of spare parts of computer equipment and rendered construction services. The taxpayer was supposedly purchasing electronic equipment from companies that the authority believed to have been used in the scheme of trading in blank invoices. "In fact, they had no means to ensure supplies of computer equipment of such considerable value. Moreover, they did not conduct actual business activity and their operation was limited to issuing fictitious invoices upon request of various economic entities". These companies operated as a group of entities managed by one person and issued blank invoices to one another in different configurations. In order to have the purported sales declared in the invoices backed by purchase invoices, third parties convinced by this person set up businesses to issue purchase invoices to these companies. It was also discovered that these companies did not have the goods that were supposed to be sold and no evidence of transport of the goods to the companies was found. The taxpayer was granted the right of legal aid in the form of full exemption from the court fee in the proceedings before administrative courts in both instances.

In the cassation appeal registered in the SAC on 6 March 2019 (with a ref. No. I FSK 415/19), which was filed against judgement of 6 November 2018 (ref. No. III SA/WA 88/18), the disputed value was PLN 2.2 million. The case ought to be considered unusual due to the fact that the appellant was a local government unit (i.e., the city). The case was concerned with the possibility of deducting input tax as a result of purchase of goods and services in connection with implementation of a construction investment by the city. The administrative decision was issued in the first instance by the Head of the Tax Office in Legionowo on 29 May 2017 and was concerned with settlement of VAT for 2009. The court fee was paid in the course of proceedings before the administrative courts of both instances.

In the cassation appeal registered in the SAC on 23 May 2019 (with a ref. No. I FSK 435/19), which was filed against judgement of 17 October 2018 (ref. No. I SA/GD 658/18), the disputed value was PLN 2 million. The administrative decision was issued in the first instance by the Head of the Pomeranian Tax and Customs Office on 7 July 2017 and was concerned with settlement of VAT for April 2012. In the VAT-7 return filed for April 2012, the taxpayer declared, among others, the output tax arising from a VAT invoice documenting sale of "automatic welding and storage structures and gantry cranes assembly line – two pieces, metal sheet rollers MCB 3070 WT DAVI." The first-instance authority claimed that the invoice in question did not document actual sales, but it was the so-called blank invoice, thus the output tax on this invoice should not be included in the declaration. The court fee was paid in the course of proceedings before the administrative courts of both instances.

In the cassation appeal registered in the SAC on 23 October 2019 (with a ref. No. I FSK 2005/19), which was filed against judgement of 22 May 2019 (ref. No. I SA/BD 54/19), the disputed value was PLN 1.5 million. The case was concerned with a chain of transactions, which was deemed to be the so-called VAT carousel. The administrative decision was issued in the first instance by the Head of the First Tax Office in Bydgoszcz on 4 June 2018 and was concerned with settlement of VAT for the period between September and October 2014. The authority proclaimed that the purchase and sales transactions documented by the disputed invoices were both fictitious. The taxpayer had carried out neither the purchase nor the sales of the electronic equipment listed in the invoices. In fact, the supposed suppliers had never actually delivered the goods, and their business activity was limited to merely pretending to trade in electronic equipment and placing VAT invoices on the market; those invoices were fictitious in the strict sense of the word. All purchase and sales transactions carried out by the party between September and October 2014 were part of a tax carousel. The taxpayer was granted the right of legal aid in the form of full exemption from the court fee in the proceedings before administrative courts in both instances.

In the cassation appeal registered in the SAC on 20 September 2019 (with a ref. No. I FSK 1815/19), which was filed against judgement of 14 March 2019 (ref. No. III SA/WA 1001/18), the disputed value was PLN 1.4 million. The case was concerned with a chain of transactions, which was deemed to be the so-called VAT carousel. The administrative decision was issued in the first instance by the Head of the Kuyavian-Pomeranian Tax and Customs Office in Toruń on 3 April 2017 and was concerned with settlement of VAT for the period between July and September 2014. On the basis of the collected evidence, the authority of the first instance concluded that the taxpayer failed to acquire the rights to reduce the output tax by the amount of input tax arising from invoices for fuel supplies, which was declared on the submitted VAT-7 returns, as well as understated the output tax for July 2014 arising from a sale document issued in a form of a fiscal receipt. In the justification, the Head of the Tax and Customs Office pointed out that the collected evidence showed that the companies the taxpayer had purchased fuel from as well as entities involved in earlier supplies in question had a formal status of an entrepreneur carrying out fuel trading, however, they had not actually been running business activity. The court fee was paid in the course of proceedings before the administrative courts of both instances.

In the cassation appeal registered in the SAC on 28 May 2019 (with a ref. No. I FSK 1005/19), which was filed against judgement of 22 June 2018 (ref. No. III SA/

WA 1517/17), the disputed value was PLN 1.3 million. The case was concerned with a chain of transactions, which was deemed to be the so-called VAT carousel. The administrative decision was issued at the first instance by the Head of the Tax Audit Office in Szczecin on 26 September 2016 and was concerned with settlement of VAT for the period between January and March 2014. Based on the collected evidence, the first-instance authority determined that the taxpayer recorded VAT invoices documenting supply of diesel fuel with company A as the seller. Moreover, the authority indicated that the evidence – collected, among others, from proceedings carried out by the Head of the Tax Audit Office in Łódź, the Head of the Tax Audit Office in Warsaw, and the Head of the Tax Audit Office in Rzeszów – confirmed that the domestic business entities that had participated in fuel trading were, among others, companies A and B. Company B was supposed to purchase fuel as part of intra-Community import of goods from the territories of the European Union to its country. In turn, company A intended to make further trade in these goods within this country plausible. The Head of the Tax Audit Office pointed out that the findings concerning the above-mentioned entities that participated in the supply chain of diesel fuel – that had eventually ended up at the taxpayer's – have led to a conclusion that these entities (at the previous stages of trading) only pretended to conduct business related to trading in liquid fuels by issuing VAT invoices that did not reflect the actual course of transactions between the entities. According to the first-instance authority, the complainant failed to exercise a tradesperson's due diligence in terms of selection of and cooperation with company A. Moreover, in the authority's view, the VAT invoices that the above-mentioned entity is listed on as the issuer are dishonest – that is, they do not document the actual course of fuel purchase transactions in the period from January to March 2014 – wherever the taxpayer demonstrated no other sources of fuel origin. The above conclusion has led the Head of the Tax Audit Office to believe that there are no grounds for deducting the tax on the above-mentioned VAT invoices and it did not actually arise at all at an earlier stage of trading. The taxpayer was granted the right of legal aid in the form of partial exemption from the court fee in the proceedings before administrative courts in both instances.

In the cassation appeal registered in the SAC on 11 December 2019 (with a ref. No. I FSK 2284/19), which was filed against judgement of 21 August 2019 (ref. No. I SA/GL 370/19), the disputed value was PLN 1.2 million. The case was concerned with a chain of transactions, which was deemed to be the so-called VAT carousel. The administrative decision was issued in the first instance by the Head of the Tax Office in Dąbrowa Górnicza on 8 July 2016 and was concerned with settlement of VAT for December 2010. The taxpayer submitted a VAT-7 return to the Tax Office in Dąbrowa Górnicza for December 2010, which declared an excess of input tax over the output tax amounting to PLN 1,189 thousand (including the amount of PLN 1,189 thousand to be returned to the taxpayer's bank account within 25 days). In the course of the tax audit, it was established that the taxpayer had neither yards, nor warehouses on the territory of Poland, nor any tangible assets. The company was merely an intermediary in trade in goods between Polish and Czech as well as Slovak contractors. The outcome of the audit was a declaration that the complainant incorrectly settled Value Added Tax in the VAT-7 return. A complaint was lodged against this decision to the RAC in Gliwice, which suspended the court proceedings (III SA/GL 851/17) pursuant to Article 124(1)(4) of the PbAC with a judgement of 19 December 2017. It was then subsequently resumed upon the request of the representative of the insolvency administrator based on the ruling of 25 April 2019. The court fee was paid in both instances of proceedings before the administrative court.

In the cassation appeal registered in the SAC on 27 December 2019 (with a ref. No. I FSK 2355/19), which was filed against judgement of 11 September 2019 (ref. No. I SA/BD 256/19), the disputed value was PLN 1.2 million. The court fee was paid in the course of proceedings before the administrative courts of both instances. As part of their activity, the taxpayer mainly carried out repairs and modernisation of sports facilities as well as participated in construction of sports facilities from scratch (among others, sports complexes referred to as "Orlik").

They also carried out minor renovation works in sports halls and on school pitches, which consisted in installation of electronic boards, pitch nets preventing the ball from getting out of the area – the backstops, and putting up basketball boards, etc. Pursuant to Article 34(2)(1) of the Act of 2 July 2004 on the Freedom of Business Activity,[18] the taxpayer's company was removed from the Central Registration and Information on Business (CEIDG) on 18 May 2016; the entrepreneur was legally banned from conducting business activity. The case under analysis was concerned with the use of invoices that did not reflect real economic transactions (the so-called blank invoices): The taxpayer deducted input tax from blank invoices.

It is worth noting the course of proceedings before the administrative authorities in this case. Firstly, the first-instance decision was issued on 23 October 2015, but the second-instance body revoked it and referred it back for reconsideration (on 18 March 2016). Secondly, the first-instance decision was issued on 24 February 2017, but it was revoked once again by the second-instance

18 Journal of Laws of 2004 No. 173, item 1807, as amended.

authority (on 14 November 2017). For the third time, the first-instance decision was issued by the Head of the Kuyavian-Pomeranian Tax and Customs Office in Toruń on 19 September 2018 and was upheld on 20 February 2019. The contested decision was concerned with settlement of VAT for the period between July and December 2010.

In the cassation appeal registered in the SAC on 5 September 2019 (with a ref. No. I FSK 1704/19), which was filed against judgement of 16 May 2019 (ref. No. I SA/GL 460/19), the disputed value was PLN 1.2 million. The case was concerned with a chain of transactions, which was deemed to be the so-called VAT carousel. The administrative decision was issued at the first instance by the Head of the Second Silesian Tax Office in Bielsko-Biała on 12 January 2018 and was concerned with settlement of VAT for the period between March and September 2016. The taxpayer submitted VAT-7 returns to the tax office for the period between March and September 2016. Subsequently, there were tax audits carried out at the entity. They led to the conclusion that settlement of Value Added Tax for the periods indicated in the VAT-7 returns is not consistent with the actual facts stemming from the reference documents. There was a list of invoices drawn up during the audit, which were issued by the taxpayer during the period in question and documented sales of silver granules to company B; the invoices were juxtaposed with the purchase invoices received from company A. Payment receipts were also compared by matching them with each purchase and sale invoice. The comparisons revealed the following findings: Firstly, the taxpayer's profit margin on the sale of silver granules amounted to 3.19 % in seven transactions, ranged from 2.64 % to 2.99 % in eight, and in two transactions amounted to 3.30 % and 4.38 %; secondly, the issue dates of invoices documenting sales and purchase of the silver granulates were the same, which means that they were issued on the same day, except in one case, when the sale invoice was issued on the following day; thirdly, payments for invoices flowed from the final customer, which was company B, through the taxpayer to company A and were made within one or two days. Simultaneously, the materials provided by the Regional Prosecutor's Office in Szczecin showed that in the course of the proceedings the prosecutor charged the persons acting through the companies identified in the supply chain with committing criminal and tax offences related to fictitious trade in silver granules, which has caused the state treasury to suffer immense reduction in Value Added Tax. The court fee was paid in the course of proceedings before the administrative courts of both instances.

In the cassation appeal registered in the SAC on 4 November 2019 (with a ref. No. I FSK 2075/19), which was filed against judgement of 30 January 2019 (ref. No. I SA/GD 989/19), the disputed value was PLN 1.1 million. The administrative decision was issued in the first instance by the Head of the Tax Office in Tczew on 31 August 2016 and was concerned with settlement of VAT for the period between October and December 2015. In the correction of the VAT-7K return for the fourth quarter of 2015, the taxpayer declared an excess of input tax over the output tax amounting to PLN 1.1 million to be returned to their bank account within 180 days. The authority refused to refund the tax and determined that the basis for the correction was a correcting invoice dated 13 September 2015 issued for the invoice dated 8 July 2008, which served the taxpayer to reduce the value of net sales by PLN 5 million and the output tax due at the rate of 22 % by PLN 1.1 million. The authority refused the taxpayer the right to adjust the output tax for the fourth quarter of 2015 by indicating that adjustment was relevant for the third quarter of 2008, which fell outside the prescribed period based on the date of the correction. The court fee was paid in both instances of proceedings before the administrative court.

In the cassation appeal registered in the SAC on 5 August 2019 (with a ref. No. I FSK 1495/19), which was filed against judgement of 31 January 2019 (ref. No. III SA/WA 742/18), the disputed value was PLN 1.1 million. The administrative decision was issued at the first instance by the Head of the Masovian Tax and Customs Audit Office (HTO) on 14 July 2017 and was concerned with settlement of VAT for the period between January 2013 and December 2014. The HTO explained that during the audited period the taxpayer was dealing with sales of ready-to-eat meals, such as fresh salads, sandwiches, soups, tarts, and desserts, which they had treated as catering services taxed with an 8 % VAT rate until they obtained a positive tax ruling from the Minister of Finance dated 11 December 2012.

After obtaining the above-mentioned tax ruling, the taxpayer applied a 5 % VAT rate deeming their services to be deliveries of meals. According to the HTO, this was illegal. The court fee was paid in the course of proceedings before the administrative courts of both instances.

4.5. Proportional Court Fee in Cases Regarding VAT (6110) as a Source of Budgetary Revenue

Moving on to analysis of the structure of revenue from court fees, it should be noted that the proportional fees both in cases concerning tax rulings and other (e.g., retained VAT refunds) are of negligible fiscal significance. In the sample under examination (taking into account cases in which legal aid was granted), fixed fees accounted for 2.5 % of the total of the fees collected by administrative courts (this proportion was the same in both instances).

Thus, the proportional fees collected in the cases where the disputed value was determined were of primary importance. In accordance with the distribution of the DVs discussed in Section 2, half of the revenues from the court fees came from the cases with DVs of over PLN 10 million (where the proportional fee in the first instance amounted to PLN 100 thousand).

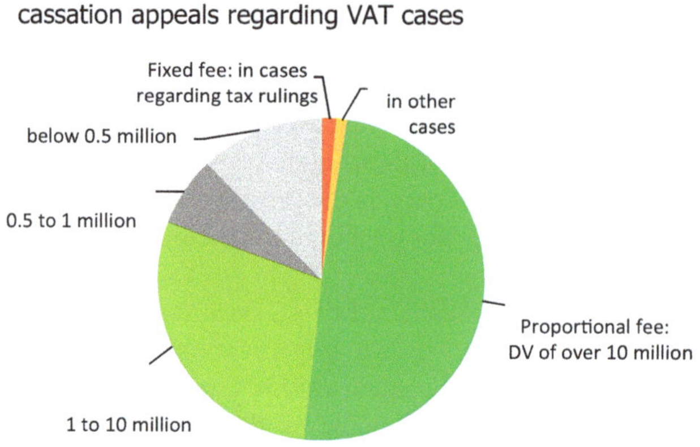

Figure 4.3. The share of each category of cases in the total amount of fees paid for cassation appeals regarding VAT cases

Source: own work.

However, this does not change the fact that these cases are the crucial contributors to the revenue from court fees generated by cases regarding VAT. In the sample under analysis, cases with a disputed value of over PLN 1 million represent nearly 80 % of the fees paid for cassation appeals (Figure 4.3).[19]

Summary

The study offers conclusions on three levels.

Firstly, it illustrates the role of administrative judiciary for the proper functioning of economic transactions, showing the scale of resolved disputes in terms of monetary value. It is thus justified to advocate that the disputed value be recorded in the statistical reporting system or in the Case Law and Case

19 The data account for the fees that were actually paid in and disregard the fees that were not paid because legal aid was granted.

Information Central Database. In view of the fact that the DV is clearly indicated in the appeal and, if there is a discrepancy in this respect, the DV is determined by the Court, its registration should not be overly burdensome.

Secondly, the study that has been conducted provides some indirect knowledge allowing to interpret the data presented in this chapter, which reflect the activities of tax authorities related to collecting VAT.

Thirdly, knowledge of the structure of revenue from court fees for complaints and cassation appeals rises a legitimate question as to the adequate value of the fixed fees set out in 2004. The amount of the fee collected for appeals against tax rulings is particularly noteworthy. This category of cases had not existed in practice at the time the amounts of court fees in administrative court proceedings were regulated (The basis for collecting a fixed fee of PLN 200 in the first instance is section 2(6) of the Regulation of the Council of Ministers on the Amounts of and Detailed Rules for Collecting Court Fees in Proceedings before Administrative Courts,[20] which is concerned with complaints not listed in the catalogue included in the Regulation). It is interesting to note the low fixed fee for complaints against decisions where the disputed value is known, for example, regarding VAT refunds.

20 Journal of Laws of 2003 No. 221, item 2193, as amended.

Bartosz Wojciechowski (University of Lodz)

Adam Olczyk (SGH Warsaw School of Economics)

5. Dispute over the Method of Interpreting Tax Law. Comparative Analysis of the Interpretative Strategy for Recognising the So-Called Difficult Cases in the Case Law of the Constitutional Tribunal and the Supreme Administrative Court

Abstract: The article addresses the issue of interpretive strategies in recognising difficult cases. The authors analyse the selected rulings of the Polish Constitutional Tribunal regarding: (1) taxation of mining excavations; (2) undisclosed sources of income (the 2013 ruling); (3) undisclosed sources of income (the 2014 ruling); (4) prescription of tax liabilities secured by a mortgage; and (5) definitions of the terms "construction" and "building" in real property tax. The authors analyse how the Polish administrative courts have changed the way they have ruled after the Constitutional Tribunal's rulings. Finally, the authors address the issue of functional interpretation of tax law, which is necessary in the world of "institutional pluralism". In their opinion, only comprehensive interpretation of tax law is adequate for an open, dynamic, and pluralistic legal system that includes not only domestic law, but also the European and international dimensions.

Keywords: Constitutional Court, tax law, institutional pluralism, functional interpretation of tax law, Polish administrative courts

Introduction

As far as interpretation of tax law is concerned, the dispute over the way it should be interpreted has nowadays been more pronounced than in any other areas of law. This dispute seems impossible to resolve because both sides are partly right; it is a conflict between the representatives of positivist theories and the representatives of iusnaturalism. The fundamental question is concerned with the concept of the law and its limits, but the answer is inextricably linked to the way the law is interpreted. Therefore, the dispute over interpretation of the law has a philosophical or a doctrinal dimension, but it is particularly important that it also – or perhaps above all – has a practical side. Thus, it involves differences in terms of comprehension of the law, in the way its limits are understood, and in how the essence of each legal institution is explained. And so, it becomes of vital importance to determine what arguments and rules are acceptable and legitimate, taking into account their correctness, rationality, and ultimately acceptability for the interpretation community serving as a platform for formulating them. Importantly, the nature of the dispute is not that of an antinomy; although it may so happen that one interpretative outcome will turn out contradictory to another.

In somewhat simplified terms, we can speak of a formalistic approach dominated by advocating for reference to textual interpretation of tax law, which is ultimately and irrevocably expressed through evocation of the principle of *in dubio pro tributario* (meaning resolving doubts in favour of the taxpayer). We can also agree upon distinguishing a second attitude that we have called an interpretative strategy in the title. Its nature is that of a discourse, its character is inclusive, and interpretation with that approach uses the textual interpretation of tax law merely as a starting point, which is the first chronological step in the whole process. This means that the textual interpretation is not conclusive and indisputable. On the contrary, the wording of a legal act or regulation that is subject to interpretation is only the point of departure and the process of interpretation is based on the principle of *interpretatio cessat in claris* (meaning interpretation ceases when everything is clear). Such an interpretation takes place through the use of every permissible method of interpretation and so of various types of legal reasoning, linguistic rules, functional or systemic interpretation as well as arguments and forms of legal discourse. The aim of such a comprehensive interpretation is to focus on achieving the objectives of the law, including the European law as an autonomous legal order.

The autonomy of tax law is a kind of a compromise between the principles of coherence as well as completeness of the system of law that encompasses tax law and the independence of tax law within that system, mainly in relation to other areas of the law, which also fall within the category of the system of public law *sensu largo*. This means that the process of interpretation necessarily involves taking into consideration the specific understanding of a concept or institution not only within the branch of tax law, but even in the context of the tax type.

In the European context, the functional interpretation referring to the *ratio legis* of a regulation is, therefore, based on two assumptions: firstly, of normative autonomy – meaning that the EU law defines validity of the laws – and, secondly, of completeness – meaning that it is possible to resolve any legal issue that arises in the area of jurisdiction of the EU law.

When discussing the internal legal systems of the Member States, the Court of Justice often refers to the general principles of law, which are common to all of them. That way, the Court gains a broader normative basis for adjudication of a case, increases the legitimacy of its judgements through their social acceptance in the Member States, and contributes to their enforcement in cooperation with the national courts.

We believe that such two interpretative strategies are noticeable in the approach to interpretation of tax law favoured by the Constitutional Tribunal and the Supreme Administrative Court. Interestingly, these strategies have changed over time in a way that caused both these courts to alter their approach to the methods of interpretation of tax law. Historically, the case law of the SAC has often contained statements giving priority to the textual interpretation of tax law (cf., judgement of 14 December 2000, FSA 2/00, ONSA 2001, No. 2, item 49, and of 4 June 2001, FPK 6/01, Commercial Law 2001, No. 7–8, item 57). The systemic and functional methods of interpretation were only applied within the limits set out by the textual interpretation (see the second of the cited judgements). A similar stance was expressed in the Resolution of the SAC of 20 March 2000 (FPS 14/99, ONSA 2000, No. 3, item 92), which states that "textual interpretation (…) is not only the starting point for any interpretation of the law but also defines its limits within the possible meaning of the words contained in the legal text." Such an approach can nowadays be considered anachronistic in the case law of the SAC as functional interpretation has assumed significance as exemplified with the case law presented below. The Constitutional Tribunal, in turn, advocated the adoption of a holistic interpretation model and called for a hermeneutic or multifaceted analysis of a legal text. In view of the above, linguistic analysis was enriched with an interpretation referring to constitutional and moral arguments as well as with deep functional and systematic analysis (cf., among others, judgement of 11 May 2004, K 4/03, OTK-A2004/5/41). That comprehensive, holistic approach had later transformed, and the courts somewhat changed places as regards the adopted interpretative strategy. Therefore, it is worth presenting a few argumentative disputes that will reflect the adopted way of legal reasoning and which are specific milestones in the Polish case law regarding interpretation of tax law.

5.1. Taxation of Mining Excavations

5.1.1. Legal Problem

The judgement of the Constitutional Tribunal on mining excavations of 13 September 2011, ref. No. P 33/09,[1] is still one of the most important points of

1 Official Collection of Case Law of the Constitutional Tribunal (OTK ZU) No. 7/A/2011, item 71.

reference – for the tax authorities, the taxpayers, and the administrative courts – when it comes to dealing with a problem of insufficiently clear legal regulation and deriving tax obligations from it; so, in a situation where the court's judgement and the adopted interpretative strategy assume particular importance. In the Central Database of Case Law of Administrative Courts[2], there are 4.4 thousand judgements where the administrative courts evoked this judgement;[3] it has also been repeatedly evoked in the rulings of the Constitutional Tribunal. This judgement was interpretative in character, which means that specific meaning of a legal provision was ruled to be in conformity or in non-conformity with the Constitution of the Republic of Poland.[4] Although the operative part of the judgement stated that the reviewed provision of the tax act is consistent with the Constitution of the Republic of Poland (in particular, with Article 217 in conjunction with Article 84 and Article 2), however, only provided that it is understood in a specific way that is beneficial for the taxpayers and so in a way that does not apply to underground mining excavations.

There are at least two important legal problems with this case. The first is direct classification of an underground mining excavation within the framework of property tax, however, it is of lesser importance in the context of present considerations. The second revolves around the principle *nulla poena sine lege certa*, specifically that the tax regulations must be defined in an act of law, and the principle of correct legislation. Both of these problems intertwine since doubts regarding classification of a mining excavation resulted from insufficient precision of the provisions of the law. What is important: Owing to their level of generality, the considerations presented in the judgement as regards the desired level of precision of legal regulation in specific areas of the law go far beyond problems with definitions within the framework of property tax and remain adequate for a broader number of cases. As such, they also seem worthy of analysis.

5.1.2. Case Law of Administrative Courts Prior to the Judgement of the Constitutional Tribunal

In the practice preceding issuance of the judgement in question, tax authorities and administrative courts had to deal with imprecision of the law, which

2 http://orzeczenia.nsa.gov.pl/ (accessed on: 5/11/2022).

3 As of 5 November 2022.

4 Cf. T. Woś, *Wyroki interpretacyjne i zakresowe w orzecznictwie Trybunału Konstytucyjnego*, „Studia Iuridica Lublinensia" 2016, t. Komentarz, Warszawa 3, p. 985.

otherwise should have allowed proper classification of mining excavations. The tax authorities maintained that a mining excavation and the equipment located on its premises, which serves the excavation, constitute a building that along with the equipment form a technical and a functional whole. This stance was often adopted by the authorities regardless of the resolution of seven judges of the SAC of 2 July

2001, ref. No. FPS 2/01, which stated the contrary: "An underground mining excavation is not subject to property tax because it is not any of the taxable items listed in Article 3(1) of the Act of 12 January 1991 on Local Taxes and Fees" (Journal of Laws No. 9, item 31, as amended). The resolution of the SAC, however, had only seemingly solved the problem as the provisions on local taxes and fees were amended after its adoption (as of 1 January 2003). The scope of the meaning of the term "building" was extended, which provided a premise for development of case law that was different than before and once again unfavourable for taxpayers.[5] Therefore, the amendment to the law has caused the existing discrepancies to widen and doubts to proliferate.[6] At the heart of the problem, there was still a question of what a building is and how this concept should be interpreted in the context of taxation and in the light of the provisions of other acts of law.

5.1.3. Judgement of the Constitutional Tribunal

Eventually, there was a judgement passed in respect of this matter by the Constitutional Tribunal, which contained important interpretative guidelines as to the possibility of claiming that "a regulation does not conform with the Constitution due to its ambiguity or imprecision". According to the Tribunal, this is the case in the following situations:

(1) When resolution of doubts is not possible with the application of the principles of exegesis of a legal text accepted within the legal culture;
(2) When application of the above principles does not allow to eliminate existing doubts without the need for the public authority to take essentially arbitrary decisions (as "In such a case, we may be dealing not

5 For example, in the SAC's judgements of 3 February 2006, ref. No. II FSK 656/05, of 15 January 2015, ref. No. II FSK 1114/09, or in the final judgement of the RAC in Wrocław of 16 May 2007, ref. No. I SA/Wr 1596/06.

6 More on this topic: P. Banasik, *Wyrobisko górnicze nie podlega podatkowi od nieruchomości. Glosa do wyroku TK z dnia 13 września 2011 r.*, „Przegląd Podatkowy" 2011, No. 12, pp. 34–35.

only with a violation of the principle of correct legislation, but also of the principle of division of power expressed in Article 10 of the Constitution of the Republic of Poland since, ultimately, the substance of the binding regulation in such a case is not decided by the authorities empowered to formulate the law but by the authorities empowered to apply it.").

(3) When difficulties in removing doubts, especially from the point of view of the addressees of a regulation, turn out to be grossly excessive, which cannot be justified by the complexity of the matter subject to regulation.

The Tribunal also pointed out that the ambiguity of a legal status must be assessed differently on the grounds of different branches of the law. One should,

first and foremost, make a distinction between private law (such as civil law, family law or commercial law) and public law (such as administrative law, tax law, and criminal law mentioned by the Tribunal). As far as public law is concerned, greater degree of unambiguous precision is required.

In the statement of reasons to its ruling, the Tribunal confirmed the existence of serious, objective difficulties related to taxation of underground mining excavations and the facilities and equipment located on their premises but simultaneously concluded that they could be eliminated. The Tribunal claimed that in order to achieve this aim, it is necessary to adequately apply the principles of interpretation adopted in the Polish legal culture, especially the principles of vertical systemic interpretation advocating the technique of interpreting the law in accordance with the Constitution and the functional principles. It was also concluded that adoption of these principles would ensure consistency of the decision in a given case with the Constitution of the Republic of Poland.

In the final passages of the statement of reasons, the Tribunal advised that "pursuant to the constitutional requirements, unclear tax regulations must not be interpreted to the detriment of the taxpayer, and consequently, if ultimately such regulations turn out to be polysemous, then in accordance with the principle *in dubio pro tributario*, the appropriate solution is to take into account the interest of the entity obliged to pay taxes." It was also stressed that "analogous application of imprecise provisions of tax law" and "extending application of unambiguous tax rules" is unacceptable when it contributes to increasing tax liability.

5.1.4. Case Law after the Judgement of the Constitutional Tribunal

Due to issuance of the judgement presented above, the tax authorities as well as administrative courts have obtained important guidelines that should be taken into consideration in the process of applying the law. The judgement emphasised the need to interpret tax law in a specific way that is favourable to the taxpayer.

This ruling has not only resolved the issue of taxation of mining excavations with property tax, but it has also clarified how the concept of a "building" should be interpreted as well as showed the direction that should be taken when analysing other concepts related to property tax. It might also be useful to highlight the practical importance of the relationship between the Act on Local Taxes and Fees and construction law, which is described by the Tribunal.

The Tribunal's judgement was frequently invoked in many cases attracting the attention of administrative courts, including those that have led to the establishment of certain lines of case law. Some of these disputes have resulted in resolutions taken by the Supreme Administrative Court with a composition of seven judges. The following such cases can be enumerated:

- Taxation of telecommunications cable lines placed in the cable ducting system;[7]
- Taxation of wind farms in 2017;[8]
- Taxation of a temporary construction work (as regards whether it can be treated as a construction for the purposes of property tax);[9]
- Taxation of garages that are separately owned but located in a multi-family residential building;[10]
- Classification of a telecommunications container as a temporary construction work within the category of buildings or constructions;[11]
- Classification of mining roof supports as retaining structures;[12]

---

7 For example judgements of the SAC: of 27 May 2010, ref. No. II FSK 1674/09, II FSK 1673/09; of 13 April 2011, ref. No. II FSK 144/10; of 5 October 2010, ref. No. II FSK 1240/10; of 14 June 2016, ref. No. II FSK 2651/15; of 19 December 2017, ref. No. II FSK 3361/15.

8 Examples of judgements: RAC in Rzeszów of 29 December 2017, ref. No. I SA/Rz 689/17; RAC in Bydgoszcz of 20 December 2017, ref. No. I SA/Bd 926/17, I SA/Bd 927/17, I SA/Bd 928/17, I SA/Bd 929/17; RAC in Poznań of 20 December 2017, ref. No. I SA/Po 995/17, I SA/Po 517/17, I SA/Po 518/17. Ultimately, the adopted line of case law was the one consistent with the opinion expressed in the judgement of the seven judges of the Supreme Administrative Court of 22 October 2018, ref. No. II FSK 2983/17.

9 Discrepancies in this respect served as basis for issuing a resolution of seven Judges of the SAC of 3 February 2014, ref. No. II FPS 11/13.

10 Resolution of seven Judges of the SAC of 27 February 2012, ref. No. II FPS 4/11.

11 The Constitutional Tribunal addressed this issue in the judgement of 13 December 2017, ref. No. SK 48/15 (OTK-A ZU 2018, item 2), which is elaborated on further in this publication.

12 Examples of judgements of the SAC: of 24 June 2016, ref. No. II FSK 1444/14; of 16 February 2017, ref. No. II FSK 285/15; of 9 March 2017, ref. No. II FSK 385/15.

- Classification of car washes;[13]
- Taxation of port infrastructure.[14]

This judgement is also sometimes invoked to supplement the argument regarding the role and significance of the principle *in dubio pro tributario* in the Polish legal order.[15]

5.2. Undisclosed Sources of Income – The First Judgement

5.2.1. Legal Problem

Although judgements of the Constitutional Tribunal concerning undisclosed sources of income[16] (i.e., the judgement of 18 July 2013, ref. No. SK 18/09,[17] hereinafter also referred to as the "first judgement", and the judgement of 29 July 2019, ref. No. P49/13[18], also referred to as the "second judgement") addressed several issues that were reviewed in terms of compliance with the constitutional standards, further deliberations herein will be focused on one issue only: violation of the principle of correct legislation. This problem was in fact the main focus of the Tribunal (and a large portion of the statement of reasons was devoted to it). Out of all the shortcomings of the above-mentioned provisions, it was the insufficient regulation of undisclosed income that was the most serious one; non-compliance with the constitutional standards was mainly attributed to the fact that the legislator treated the issue in an overly general fashion.

---

13 Judgements of the SAC of 7 September 2016, ref. No. II FSK 2131/15, II FSK 2806/14, II FSK 663/15, and the judgement of the SAC of 20 September 2017, ref. No. II FSK 1052/17, based on the judgements presented above.

14 Cf. the judgement of seven judges of the SAC of 7 July 2014, ref. No. II FPS 2/14, which refuses taking a resolution on this matter; especially the case law cited therein.

15 Judgement of the SAC of 8 May 2014, ref. No. II FSK 1274/12 and of 14 September 2016, ref. No. II FSK 2700/14.

16 Article 20(3) of the PIT Act referred to "income that cannot be backed by the disclosed sources or originates from undisclosed sources", which for the sake of simplification is hereinafter referred to collectively as the "undisclosed sources of income."

17 Official Collection of Case Law of the Constitutional Tribunal (OTK ZU) No. 6/A/ 2013, item 80.

18 OTK ZU 2014/7A/79, item 79.

5.2.2. Case Law of Administrative Courts before the Judgement of the Constitutional Tribunal

It should be noted that assessment of the regulation on undisclosed sources of income in terms of its generality was not at the heart of the disputes recognised by administrative courts before the Tribunal passed its judgement. Prior to the first judgement, neither the administrative authorities nor the courts probed the idea that the challenged provisions might be flawed due to the legislator's "exceptionally ambiguous formulation of the concept of income that cannot be backed by the disclosed sources or originates from undisclosed sources" (Article 20(3) of the PIT Act) and the resultant lack of clear determination of the rules concerning the time limit for the establishment of tax liability as regards tax on undisclosed income (see Article 68(4) of the TO in conjunction with Article 20(3) of the PIT Act).[19] This finds confirmation in the first judgement. The Tribunal has pointed out several times that the administrative authorities and administrative courts, which had to deal with the general shape of this legal institution, have ultimately developed certain views and legal constructions on their own in order to resolve the deficiencies of this regulation.[20]

Among such solutions that should be highlighted, there are views regarding the practical necessity to determine who bears the burden of proof in cases involving undisclosed sources of income. The issue was moulded by case law into a belief that the tax authority is obliged to, first and foremost, determine the amount of expenses that a taxpayer has incurred and the value of assets they have accumulated.[21] If there is an excess, the burden of proof is transferred onto

---

19 Judgement of 18 July 2013, ref. No. SK 18/09.

20 The Tribunal pointed out, inter alia, that "in fact, the legal provisions in question only form the frame of the institution [in question] because their substance has actually been shaped in practice, which inevitably must give rise to serious objections from the point of view of the principle of the democratic rule of law."

21 Such a view was expressed, among others, by the President of the SAC in a letter of 19 November 2012 filed before the Constitutional Tribunal within the framework of proceedings concerning undisclosed sources of income, which contained "Information on the administrative courts' application of regulations governing taxation of income that cannot be backed by the disclosed sources or originates from undisclosed sources." A similar view was offered in the letter of 25 October 2010, No. DD2/033/21 0/DZI/1 O/BMI9-12787, submitted by the Minister of Finance: https://ipo.trybunal.gov.pl/ipo/dok?dok=F1834434053%2FSK_18_09_MF_2010_10_25_nu_ADO.pdf dok?dok= F1834434053 %2FSK_18_09_MF_2010_10_25_nu_ADO.pdf (accessed on: 5/11/2022).

the taxpayer pursuant to a widely accepted practice (in evidence proceedings) of applying the general principle that "the burden of proof rests on the one who derives legal effects from a given fact".[22] What is more, there was a prevalent view that taxpayers are required to prove information on the sources of income and not only make them appear probable. Let us get ahead of further deliberations and agree with the Constitutional Tribunal that such an interpretation has not resulted from literal interpretation of the provisions of the law. Nor was it contradicting them. It was an extensive interpretation that the administrative courts had to adopt in the absence of relevant regulations in the act of law. Besides, the issue was not really provoking much controversy. Obviously, it is not unambiguous either; one can reasonably inquire why should obligations regarding the burden of proof in cases of undisclosed sources of income deserve differentiated treatment, if the legislator has not laid down any such requirement. Indeed, the legislator has in no way signalled that such different conditions of assessment should apply. The interpretation followed by administrative courts in this regard arose form the assumption that the character of the proceedings in cases involving undisclosed sources of income is an extraordinary one, which is not always expressly stated. The statements that have repeatedly made their way into the case law revolved around the fact it is the taxpayer who "knows best" what their actual and legal situation is; it is the taxpayer who has the most thorough knowledge on the sources of their income.[23]

Additionally, there is the issue of the consequences following from the principle *ei incumbit probatio, qui dicit, non qui negat* (i.e., the burden of proof rests on the one who claims, not on the one who denies); although it was not articulated by the authorities or the courts, it was evident from all the stances adopted in these cases. Indeed, tax authorities usually demonstrated in the first place that the taxpayer's expenses exceeded their income. If the taxpayer had not challenged this finding (or their attempts to do so had been unsuccessful), and at the same time had not declared sources of income that would explain the difference in question, it was then assumed that, in fact, it was not the authority that was "claiming" something. Once the authority effectively denied that income was backed by its disclosed sources, the parties to the proceedings "changed"

---

22 Such a phrase appears in as many as 257 judgements of administrative courts made before 18 July 2013, that is, before the first judgement was passed.

23 In a discussion on matters related to undisclosed sources of income, the terms "income" and "revenue" are used interchangeably. Cf. M. Jarzębska, *Dochody nieujawnione jako przedmiot opodatkowania podatkiem dochodowym od osób fizycznych*, „Zeszyty Naukowe PWSZ w Płocku. Nauki Ekonomiczne" 2016, Vol. XXIV, pp. 199–222.

places. There were two levels of this process: The first was concerned with the difference between expenditure and income, and the second – with indication of the source of income. In the first case, the burden of proof rested on the authority, in the second case – on the taxpayer. It was assumed that in an attempt to undermine the primary finding of the authority (that income or part of it has not been disclosed by the taxpayer, which means it is undisclosed income) the taxpayer assumes the role of the party that "claims" (that the income has, in fact, been disclosed). And since the taxpayer claims that, then the obligation to prove (and indicate the source of income) rests on the taxpayer – which leads back to the basic objections of the Tribunal.

It is worth nothing the unique character of the departure from textual interpretation in favour of functional interpretation in the cases under examination; it has not resulted from the ambition of issuing proactive judgements but was dictated by the necessity of supplementing what the legislator had failed to put forward when it manifested itself in the facts that were then audited and actually required a solution. The flaw of the practice followed by the administrative courts was that it was unfavourable for the taxpayer and, according to the Tribunal, when resorting to functional interpretation of tax law, one cannot adopt a solution that is unfavourable for the taxpayer.

5.2.3. Judgement of the Constitutional Tribunal

Such practice has been critically evaluated by the Constitutional Tribunal. In the statement of reasons to the first judgement, there are several places where the problematic issues related to taxation of undisclosed sources of income are deliberated upon. The Tribunal addressed, among other things, subsequent constructions shaped by the courts' case law,[24] claiming that the solutions adopted in practice have not arisen from the provisions of tax law but "have resulted from its functional interpretation." It was also noted that this interpretation was repeatedly followed to the detriment of the taxpayer, even though the principle *in dubio pro tributario* – which is the rule of functional interpretation of tax regulations based on the Constitution – demands that in the event of ambiguity

---

24 For example, the issue of "the taxpayer invoking revenues for which the tax liability has already prescribed" or regarding the question whether „the expenditure incurred by the taxpayer in a given tax year and the value of assets they accumulated in that year must be backed by assets originating form taxable or non-taxable revenue, regardless of whether the assets indicated last were accumulated in the same tax year or in previous years."

of a legal provision, which is impossible to eliminate, a legal norm be derived from it that takes into account the interests of the taxpayer."[25]

The Constitutional Tribunal made critical remarks in the judgement in question directed at the legislator as well as the tax authorities and the administrative courts. The conclusions were as follows: (1) The legal regulation was flawed as, firstly, it was too general and, secondly, it was inconsistent; moreover, (2) the courts' and the authorities' interpretation of these incorrect provisions has led to "further substantial deterioration of the faults." This was cased by the fact that the courts have adopted an interpretation that was unfavourable for the taxpayers.

5.2.4. Case Law after the Judgement of the Constitutional Tribunal

After the first judgement was passed, the case law of administrative courts remained basically uniform – at least as regards cases concerning the period when Article 20(3) of the PIT Act[26] was applicable in the wording that was derogated. In any case, it seems that following issuance of this judgement, the courts were left little freedom of adjudication: The Constitutional Tribunal clearly stated that the regulation is non-compliant with the Constitution of the Republic of Poland and – apart from Article 68(4) of the TO[27] (whose loss of validity was postponed in time) – the provisions indicated in the judgement were removed from the legal order on the day the judgement was passed. Such a situation could hardly raise any serious doubts of interpretation. However, it is worth noting that four judgements of the SAC express a stance that is different from the one that the statements of reasons to the Tribunal's judgement *prima facie* prompted. In the judgements of 17 October 2013 (ref. No. II FSK 2413/11, II FSK 2322/11, II FSK 2598/11, II FSK 2426/11), it was concluded that proceedings regarding undisclosed sources of income could only be

initiated and carried out until publication of the judgement of the Constitutional Tribunal. This interpretation was made on the basis of a passage

25 In the judgement under consideration, the Constitutional Tribunal did not clarify the matter further and so did not undertake to explain what provisions of the Constitution of the Republic of Poland the principle *in dubio pro tributario* arises from and what is its relationship with the functional interpretation. It should be added, however, that in earlier passages of the judgement, such explanation was liked to the judgement of the Constitutional Tribunal of 13 September 2011, ref. No. P 33/09.

26 Act of 26 July 1991 on Personal Income Tax (Journal of Laws 2000 No. 14, item 176, as amended).

27 Act of 29 August 1997 on the Tax Ordinance (Journal of Laws of 2015, item 613, as amended).

of the first judgement[28] and interpretation of Article 190(3) of the Constitution of the Republic of Poland. Undoubtedly, it conflicted with the practice followed so far and the vast majority of views expressed in the relevant literature. It has also not been approved by the subsequent compositions of the SAC. Although it may appear that such an interpretation was dictated by functional considerations (as the SAC mentions that in view of the Minister of Finance "the judgement of the Tribunal may produce effects involving financial outlays not provided for in the Budget Act"), such reasons are impossible to find in the statements of reasons to the judgements in question. *Ad vocem*, it can be noted that in these judgements the SAC followed the scheme that it was reproached for by the Constitutional Tribunal: In view of the ambiguity of the provisions of Article 190(3) of the Constitution of the Republic of Poland – and the indications of the Constitutional Tribunal as to further proceedings – an interpretation of the provisions was adopted, which was not favourable for the taxpayers.

However, as noted above, this stance was an isolated case. In subsequent judgements, the SAC claimed that the unconstitutionality of the provision had existed at the time the tax authority made its decision, and the judgement of the Constitutional Tribunal only confirmed this.[29] Therefore, there could be no doubt that the Tribunal's judgement substantiated reinstatement of the proceedings and subsequently repeal of the decision.[30]

5.3. Undisclosed Sources of Income – The Second Judgement

5.3.1. Judgement of the Constitutional Tribunal

In the present case, description of the legal problem (section 1) and the case law of the administrative courts before the judgement of the Tribunal (Section

28 The passage reads: "(…) the possibility to carry out proceedings regarding tax on undisclosed income on the basis of: 1) Article 20(3) of the PIT Act – in the wording in force between 1 January 1998 and 31 December 2006 – will be precluded when the present judgement is published in the Official Journal of Laws."

29 Cf., e.g., judgements of the SAC of 29 October 2013, ref. No.: II FSK 3180/12, II FSK 2513/13, II FSK 2514/13, II FSK 2517/12, II FSK 1071/12, II FSK 1073/12, II FSK 1074/12, II FSK 1075/12, II FSK 2821/12, II FSK 1748/13, II FSK 1072/12, II FSK 577/12, II FSK 2886/12, II FSK 1216/12 or of 30 October 2013, ref. No. II FSK 155/12.

30 Cf., e.g., judgement of the SAC of 29 November 2013, ref. No. II FSK 2315/12; of 29 July 2014, ref. No. II FSK 3008/13, ref. No. II FSK 3009/13, ref. No. II FSK 3007/13, ref. No. II FSK 3010/13, or of 1 October 2014, ref. No. II FSK 3799/13.

2) can be omitted because it coincides with the delineation of the first judgement presented

earlier. The second judgement was passed because Article 20(3) of the PIT Act was given a different wording at the beginning of 2007. However, the difference was negligible[31] and unrelated to the fundamental objections that the Constitutional Tribunal raised against this regulation in the first judgement: The provisions were too general, unclear, and imprecise when it comes to important matters.

It might seem that in view of the circumstances – since (as stated in the second judgement) the amendment has not had a significant impact on the assessment of the constitutionality of the applicable solutions – the Court's judgement should have simply been a repetition of the claims already made earlier by the Tribunal. Alternatively, the Tribunal might have confined itself to pointing to the first judgement and expressing an opinion that they maintain the stance taken up therein. Assuming, of course, that the Tribunal's case law is consistent.

Indeed, the second judgement of the Constitutional Tribunal repeated the opinion that the regulation concerning undisclosed sources of income remains unconstitutional. Additionally, however, the statement of reasons stirred up controversy (which was elaborated on in the relevant literature and duly noted in the case law) as regards removal of the provisions intended to prevent the taxpayers from hiding income (as well as the economic consequences of their actions) from the legal order. It was taken into account that when ruling again, the Tribunal was dealing with a provision that was still applicable. Declaration of unconstitutionality of a non-applicable regulation is obviously the basis for the resumption of proceedings as well as (as the judgements of administrative

31 The wording of the provision, which was covered by the first judgement, was as follows: "The amount of revenue that cannot be backed by the disclosed sources or originates from undisclosed sources is determined on the basis of expenditure incurred by the taxpayer in a tax year and the value of assets they accumulated in that year, if the expenditure and value are not backed by the assets accumulated within the tax year and in previous years, which are backed by the taxable or tax-free income." Whereas the wording of the provision reviewed within the framework of the second judgement of the Constitutional Tribunal was as follows: "The amount of revenue that cannot be backed by the disclosed sources or originates from undisclosed sources is determined on the basis of expenditure incurred by the taxpayer in a tax year and the value of assets they accumulated in that year, if the expenditure and value are not backed by the assets that are backed by tax-free income or income taxed earlier and were accumulated prior to incurring the expenditure or accumulating the assets in question."

courts passed after the first judgement have shown) abolition of the decisions taken on its basis. On the other hand, a judgement invalidating a provision of the law that has so far been applicable compels to take into account that immediate elimination of a given provision from the legal order will result in the emergence of a "legal vacuum": A situation where it will be impossible to find a legal regulation applicable to certain facts (even if clearly disapproved of, such as the case with hiding sources of income), which would adequately govern the circumstances.

Hence, in the second judgement, the Tribunal not only repeated the view expressed in the first judgement, which stated unconstitutionality of Article 20(3) of the PIT Act, but also added Section 5 entitled "Effects of the Judgement". The Tribunal proclaimed that since the effective date of invalidation of Article 20(3) of the PIT Act was postponed (based on Article 190(3) of the Constitution of the Republic of Poland), "it will still be possible to carry out proceedings on tax on undisclosed income pursuant to that legal provision." The Tribunal's arguments were justified with reasons that were functional in character.

> It was argued that "(…) it is unacceptable that some taxpayers evade their obligation but at the same time enjoy public benefits financed from taxes paid by other taxpayers. This would be tantamount to granting unjustified privilege to the taxpayer that is dishonest towards the taxpayer who reliably declares income and pays the amount of tax reflecting the actual value of their income. The fact that the challenged provision is applicable mainly to the dishonest taxpayers justifies the administrative authorities and courts taking action to minimize the negative financial consequences for the state and, thus, for all the citizens, which would result from tax evasion."

Therefore, as a result of recognising the severity of the economic and social consequences[32] of the ambiguity of the wording of Article 190(3) of the Constitution of the Republic of Poland, the Constitutional Tribunal recommended adopting an interpretation that not only followed from a functional approach but which – most importantly – was also detrimental to the taxpayer. Such a view

---

32 In a dissenting opinion on the second judgement, Judge Małgorzata Pyziak-Szafnicka states: "The practical consequences of the Tribunal's abolition – achieved with the judgements No. SK 18/09 and P 49/13 – are likely to prove momentous. The financial effects for the state budget – although easier to calculate – are of lesser importance. The profound significance should be attributed to the social impact in terms of shaping the awareness and attitude of the citizens towards the obligations imposed on them by the state; though this effect lends itself to no calculations. Compelling everyone equally to satisfy them in a consistent fashion seems to be the foundation of a democratic rule of law."

was in opposition to the very fundamental reason why the regulation in question had been declared unconstitutional.

5.3.2. Case Law after the Judgement of the Constitutional Tribunal

Until uniform adjudication practice of the SAC has developed, the case law of administrative courts had been divergent. Usually, the divergent lines of case law were unfolding depending on which regional administrative court passed judgements. It is worth mentioning the judgements of the Regional Administrative Courts in Rzeszów[33],

in Białystok[34], in Olsztyn,[35] and in Poznań.[36] They stressed, first of all, that Article 20(3) of the PIT Act should not be applied, because it had lost the presumption of constitutionality and that such an interpretation is advocated by the need to protect the rights of the individual as well as by procedural economy.[37] However, the SAC did not share this view and explicitly adopted an interpretation that was unfavourable for the taxpayers and allowed the possibility to continue carrying out proceedings, despite the fact that the regulations had been declared unconstitutional.[38] The second judgement could also serve as no effective basis for the reinstatement of the proceedings.[39] It should be noted that

---

33 Judgements with ref. No. I SA/Rz 250/14, I SA/Rz 482/14, I SA/Rz 483/14, I SA/Rz 756/14, I SA/Rz 324/14, I SA/ Rz 732/14, I SA/Rz 755/14.

34 Judgements with ref. No. I SA/ Bk 433/14, I SA/Bk 434/14, I SA/Bk 435/14, I SA/Bk 436/14.

35 Judgements with ref. No. I SA/Ol 699/14, I SA/Ol 737/14, I SA/Ol 747/14, I SA/Ol 760/14, I SA/Ol 787/14, I SA/ Ol 734/14, I SA/Ol 735/14, I SA/Ol 626/14, I SA/Ol 545/14, I SA/Ol 547/14.

36 Judgements with ref. No. I SA/Po 786/14, I SA/Po 453/14, I SA/Po 807/14, I SA/Po 733/14, I SA/Po 836/13, I SA/ Po 739/14, I SA/Po 433/14.

37 Judgement of the SAC of 19 June 2015, ref. No. II FSK 1109/15.

38 For example, judgements of the SAC with ref. No.: II FSK 528/15, II FSK 529/15, II FSK 598/15, II FSK 599/15, II FSK 31/15, II FSK 349/15, II FSK 350/15, II FSK 597/15, II FSK 600/15, II FSK 625/15, II FSK 596/15, II FSK 102/15, II FSK 188/15, II FSK 189/15, II FSK 70/15, II FSK 486/15, II FSK 532/15, II FSK 601/15, II FSK 103/15, II FSK 186/15, II FSK 187/15, II FSK 560/15, II FSK 645, II FSK 646/15, II FSK 471/15, II FSK 665/15, II FSK 666/15, II FSK 683/15, II FSK 801/15, II FSK 472/15, II FSK 626/15, II FSK 627/15, II FSK 201/15, II FSK 309/15.

39 As explained, among others, in the judgement of the SAC of 5 June 2019, "a judgement with a deferred effect – as a rule – does not produce consequences in the sphere of individual cases based on a constitutionally disqualified rule, if the legislator issues legal provisions replacing the ones found unconstitutional in a timely manner" – which happened in the case in question; the legislator passed relevant provisions within

these administrative courts' judgements often additionally invoked arguments emphasising the usefulness of the adopted method of reconstruction of legal norms. It was mentioned, for example, that the regulation plays both a fiscal and a preventive role, and the fact that it is applicable also serves to "discourage taxpayers from evading taxation."[40]

5.4. Prescription of Mortgage-Secured Tax Liabilities

5.4.1. Legal Problem

The wording of Article 70(6) of the Tax Ordinance, which was applicable between 1 January 1998 and 31 December 2002, stipulated that: "Tax liabilities secured by a mortgage do not prescribe, however, following expiry of a prescription period, tax arrears can only be recovered from the assets the mortgage

has been raised on." This legal provision had served as basis for the decisions made by the tax authorities and courts for years and excited no particular controversy. The Article had been applied along with the Article 33(2) in conjunction with Article 33(1) of the Tax Ordinance, which made the applicability of the above-mentioned means of securing a tax claim dependent on the existence of a "reasonable concern" for default on the tax liability.

A constitutional complaint challenged the validity of both of these regulations.[41] As for the prescription, it was stressed that the above-mentioned legal provision differentiates the rights of the taxpayers "in terms of the possibility of benefiting from expiry of a tax liability." In the second case, there were objections as to awarding the tax authorities too extensive freedom when deciding on securing tax receivables.

---

the required time limit. A similar view was presented by the SAC in the following judgements: of 15 February 2019, ref. No. II FSK 383/17, of 19 February 2019, ref. No. II FSK 1117/18, of 12 March 2019, ref. No. II FSK 810/17 and II FSK 812/17, and of 2 April 2019, ref. No. II FSK 3927/17.

40 For example, in the SAC's judgements of 13 November 2014, ref. No. II FSK 2680/14, II FSK 2621/14, II FSK 2620/14, II FSK 2608/14; of 14 November 2014, ref. No. II FSK 2683/14, II FSK 2681/14, or of 19 November 2014, ref. No. II FSK 2611/14, II FSK 2598/14, II FSK 2612/14.

41 Judgement of the Constitutional Tribunal of 8 October 2013, ref. No. SK 40/12 (OTK ZU No. 7/A/2013, item 97).

5.4.2. Case Law before the Judgement of the Constitutional Tribunal

The wording of the provision stipulating that mortgage-secured tax liabilities do not prescribe cast no major doubts (although the arguments substantiating the constitutional complaint were previously deliberated upon by administrative courts in several judgements[42]). Courts had to deal with judging what circumstances justify having reasonable concern for default on tax liability quite frequently (and, by the way, the issue remains relevant).

5.4.3. Judgement of the Constitutional Tribunal

The Constitutional Tribunal dismissed the allegation against the institution of securing liabilities and the condition of "reasonable concern", which it involves, and declared that this regulation meets the constitutional requirements.

The Tribunal, however, proclaimed the legal provision stipulating that tax liabilities secured by a mortgage do not prescribe to be incompatible with the Constitution of the Republic of Poland (pursuant to Article 64(2)). One of the main arguments indicated in the statement of reasons to this part of the judgement was that the regulation in question differentiates "the time limit of taxpayers' liability significantly depending on an arbitrary and accidental criterion, which is possession of assets allowing for the establishment of collateral in the form of a compulsory mortgage or lack it." The court explained further that it sees no "reason why it is the property owners that should be held liable for tax receivables for life." Moreover, according to the Tribunal, "if taxpayers' liabilities are secured with a compulsory mortgage during tax audit, Article 70(6) of the

42 For example, in the judgement of the RAC in Gdańsk of 6 March 2008, ref. No. I SA/Gd 1028/07 upheld by the judgement of the SAC of 25 March 2009, ref. No. II FSK 1309/08, the court explained: "Equality in terms of imposing taxation does not, in fact, prevent the legislator from differentiating the legal situation of the taxpayers. The principle of equality requires, first of all, that the same tax consequences follow from the same tax events, which means that different tax consequences ensue from different tax events. The principle of equality in terms of taxation does not preclude having what is dissimilar as regards taxation taxed according to the existing differences and thus differently. (…) Therefore, since the legislator provides that if tax liability is secured with a mortgage or a fiscal pledge, the tax liability does not prescribe, and potentially any taxpayer may own assets that a mortgage or pledge can be made against, the Tribunal's view is that the provision in question does not violate the constitutional principle of equality." Nevertheless, the SAC issued a judgement on 26 April 2012 stating that "interpretation of the provision of Article 70(6) of the TO contrary to its literal wording (…) and in line with a teleological point of view is unacceptable."

Tax Ordinance in the wording under examination causes prescription to become a sham institution devoid of substance, which (…) is absolutely unacceptable (…)." The Tribunal also pointed out that since the legislator introduced the institution of prescription of tax liabilities into the Polish legal order, they should define its applicability in a way that would respect the principles of universality and equality. This passage can be deciphered in the context of earlier passages of the statement of reasons where the Tribunal negatively assessed the existence of "lifetime tax liability", which is unlimited in time. Since prescription in tax law has been deemed "valuable" (as such a regulation has been introduced), then unjustifiably precluding the use of this institution for a certain group of entities (in particular, property owners) conflicts with the requirements of equality.

5.4.4. Case Law after the Judgement of the Constitutional Tribunal

After the judgement was passed, the case law of administrative courts was free from problems related to the legal consequences of finding a legal provision unconstitutional while it was still valid (until 31 December 2002). This provision was removed from the legal order, and the general rule regarding prescriptions was to be applied instead of it (as recommendations in this respect were voiced directly in the Tribunal's judgement in Section 5.2.).

The source of actual doubts of the administrative courts – after the Tribunal's judgement – was the question about the effect the judgement might have on Article 70(8) of the Tax Ordinance introduced later. This provision contained an analogous, slightly modified regulation; however, the essence of the provision remained the same: It provides that liabilities secured with a mortgage, or a fiscal pledge do not prescribe.

The case law of administrative courts took the side of the taxpayers in this case – although not without exceptions.[43] A vast number of judgements stated that the Tribunal's reservations as to the unconstitutionality of Article 70(6) of the Tax Ordinance should be upheld in the case of Article 70(8) of this Act as well, despite the lack of a judgement of the Tribunal in this regard.[44] The administrative courts argued that – first of all – such conclusions arise from the statement of reasons to the judgement of the Tribunal (which referred to Article 70(8) by arguing, inter alia, that although it was not subject to review, "the same

43 For example, judgement of the SAC of 30 October 2013, ref. No. I FSK 1667/12.
44 The cases are registered under the following reference numbers: P 6/16 and K 10/16.

constitutional reservations obviously apply to it as well").[45] There was also a view expressed in the case law that "based on the principle of direct application of the Constitution pursuant to Article 8(2) of the Constitution, the administrative court may refuse to apply a provision of the law, which is the basis for making a decision in a case, when this provision is manifestly inconsistent with the Constitution" – and according to the SAC that was exactly the case.[46]

It is worth noting that in the absence of the legislator's action – even despite clear guidelines of the Tribunal as to the necessity to remove Article 70(8) of the Tax Ordinance from the legal order and since the possibility of its application by administrative courts was questioned – the taxpayers began to apply for remission of tax arrears secured in that way and the courts ruled in their favour taking into account the Tribunal's judgement.[47] By the way, it may be noted that there were opinions voiced that the long waiting time for the judgement of the Tribunal is related to the letter of the Prosecutor General,[48] which indicated that "if the legal provision of Article 70(8) of the Ordinance were removed from the legal order, there would be a danger of expiry of tax arrears secured by mortgages or a tax pledge amounting to about PLN 1.8 billion due to expiry of the prescription period."[49] As years go by, this amount increases further.

---

45 For example, among others, in the judgements of the SAC: of 13 December 2013, II FSK 1807/12; of 17 April 2014, II FSK 1197/12; of 18 July 2014, I FSK 1042/13; of 16 September 2014; I FSK 317/14; of 21 January 2015, II FSK 1764/14; of 22 May 2015, II FSK 316/14; of 17 September 2015, I FSK 949/14; of 20 October 2016, II FSK 2467/14; of 10 January 2017, II FSK 3552/14; of 9 February 2017, II FSK 3236/16.

46 Judgement of the SAC of 20 April 2017, ref. No. I FSK 1834/15.

47 For example, judgement of the SAC of 20 October 2016, ref. No. II FSK 2467/14; of 1 December 2017, ref. No. II FSK 3366/15; ref. No. II FSK 3295/15.

48 Ref. No. of the letter is PK VIII TK 48.2016.

49 M. Majkowska, *Czy zobowiązania podatkowe zabezpieczone hipoteką się przedawniają? TK milczy, organy zawieszają postępowania*, „Gazeta Prawna", 9.03.2020, https://podatki.gazetaprawna.pl/artykuly/1458236,zobowiazania-podatkowe-przedawnienie-hipoteka-trybunal-konstytucyjny.html, zobo-wiazania-podatkowe-przedawnienie-hipoteka-trybunal-konstytucyjny.html (accessed on: 5.11.2022).

5.5. Construction, Building: – Definitions within the Framework of Property Tax

5.5.1. Legal Problem

The absence of sufficiently clear definitions on the grounds of property tax had been giving rise to discrepancies between the stance adopted in the case law of administrative courts and the one ultimately expressed by the Constitutional Tribunal (in the judgement of 13 December 2017, ref. No. SK 48/15). The problem focused on the possibility of deeming a construction site that meets the criteria for being a building pursuant to Article 1a(1)(1) of the Act on Local Taxes and Fees to be a building.[50] The view advocating that such a classification is possible (as stated in the Tribunal's judgement) was supported by two arguments: textual and teleological ones.

The first – linguistic – argument illustrates that since it is not precluded in the Act that a building cannot be a construction (although it is stipulated that a construction cannot be a building), it is thus legitimate to make such a classification – and recognise certain buildings as constructions. This is because there is no symmetrical exclusion of a building from the category of constructions.

The second – teleological – argument is linked to the first one. If it is acknowledged that a building can sometimes be a construction, the premises concerning the function of a given site need to be taken into account, for example, its purpose, furnishings, and the manner or possibility of potential use. That way, functional reasons (such as the attributes of a site) allow to make an appropriate classification in terms of taxation.

The opinions of the tax authorities, the taxpayers, and the administrative courts on this matter were often supported by references to the conclusions arising from of the judgement on mining excavations (P 33/09). Thus, a question arises, among others, whether the provisions of the Act on Local Taxes and Fees can be considered sufficiently precise to allow deriving property tax obligations from them.

50 The Act on Local Taxes and Fees (Journal of Laws of 2006 No. 121, item 844, as amended).

5.5.2. Case Law before the Judgement of the Constitutional Tribunal

Administrative courts have developed an almost uniform line of case law in this respect, which allows for such a classification.[51] Though there are some exceptions, they are clearly in the minority.[52] The Constitutional Tribunal even proclaimed that the fact that several judgements have not shared the prevalent legal view "does not undermine the validity of a claim about uniformity in the practice of applying the contested regulations."

It can be added that the consequences of the opinion adopted by the administrative courts have often guided assessment of the correctness of the proceedings carried out by tax authorities. For example, the authority's failure to take action to verify the function of a site in order to classify it correctly could signify breach of procedural rules.[53]

5.5.3. Judgement of the Constitutional Tribunal

The Tribunal's recognition that there is a uniform practice of interpreting the said regulation served as the basis for finding Article 1a(1)(2) of the Act on Local Taxes and Fees incompatible with the principle of particular specificity of tax regulations (which is derived from Article 84 in conjunction with Article 217, in conjunction with Article 64(3) of the Constitution of the Republic of Poland) – as regards classifying a construction site as a building, if it meets the criteria for being a building (pursuant to Article 1a(1)(1) of the Act on Local Taxes and Fees).

Three reasons underlie the Tribunal's view: (1) the linguistic argument has not been accepted; (2) the teleological argument has not been agreed with;

51 One can mention, for example, the following judgements of the SAC: of 2 February 2010, ref. No. II FSK 1485/08; of 2 February 2010, ref. No. II FSK 1559/08; of 2 February 2010, ref. No. II FSK 1577/08; of 2 February 2010, ref. No. II FSK 1578/08; of 2 February 2010, ref. No. II FSK 1579/08; of 2 February 2010, ref. No. II FSK 1592/08; of 2 February 2010, ref. No. II FSK 1621/08; of 2 February 2010, ref. No. II FSK 1622/08; of 2 February 2010, ref. No. II FSK 1623/23; of 18 December 2013, ref. No. II FSK 213/12; of 18 October 2016, file no. II FSK 1740/16; of 23 November 2016, ref. No. II FSK 1739/16. A comprehensive list of these judgement is provided in the judgement of the Constitutional Tribunal, which is subject to deliberation.

52 For example, the following judgements of the SAC: of 23 June 2016, ref. No. II FSK 1808/14; of 23 June 2016, ref. No. II FSK 1996/14; of 8 December 2016, ref. No. II FSK 3153/14; of 25 January 2017, ref. No. II FSK 3759/14.

53 See, for example, the SAC's judgement of 23 November 2016, ref. No. II FSK 1739/16.

(3) the view is concerned with the relationship between the principle *in dubio pro tributario* and functional interpretation.

In response to the linguistic argument, the Tribunal argued that in a situation where set A is excluded from set B, set B must be excluded from A; there is symmetry of exclusion in such a case. In response to the teleological argument, the Tribunal stated that taking into account the function of a given site is an extensive interpretation; there is no such prerequisite in the provisions of the law and it cannot be added, especially since it results in a "functional re-interpretation of the tax regulation to the detriment of the appellant."

The Tribunal also expressed its view on the rank of the principle *in dubio pro tributario* as far as interpretation of tax law is concerned. The Tribunal, first of all, pointed out that it has an "unquestionable constitutional basis" and, second of all, stressed that it is recommended to understand it in objective terms, which means that "it is applied relatively to the doubts regarding given tax regulation, which arise in the context of the rules of interpretation adopted in the legal culture." Following a brief description of the three directives of (textual, systemic, and functional) interpretation, which are prevalent in the Polish legal doctrine, the Tribunal stated that their application "results in – as if by principle – elimination of any ambiguities that burden a legal text and thus allows for the reconstruction of a legal norm as an unambiguous statement." Consequently, the Tribunal disagreed with the view presented in the case law that the principle *in dubio pro tributario* is only followed subsequently after the above mentioned three directives have been taken into account. The Tribunal also explained that the principle in question "as a rule of interpretation is [...] a directive of functional interpretation which – in the process of interpreting tax regulations – precludes other rationales referring to the values or objectives attributed to the legislator."

5.5.4. Case Law after the Judgement of the Constitutional Tribunal

Elaboration on the case law of the administrative judiciary following the judgement of the Tribunal under consideration goes beyond the scope of this study, which covers the period up to the end of 2017.[54] It can be noted, however, that this judgement is a certain insignia of the existence of the administrative

54 In 2017, there were six judgements of regional administrative courts made, which invoked judgement No. SK 48/15. Whereas in the judgements of the administrative courts after 2017, this judgement was often used as a point of reference, especially in cases where the subject-matter of a dispute involved the need to make general legal determinations regarding definitions within the framework of property tax.

courts' practice of functional interpretation in the period under examination; such interpretation is triggered by the imperfections of the literal approach – which is a key issue from the point of view of the court's decision-making process and the use of an appropriate interpretative strategy. This issue has become the focus of the case law already at the time when there were doubts as to taxation of mining excavations. The Tribunal's view on the directive of functional interpretation was then clarified, especially in the context of a public dispute with the views expressed by administrative courts. It was then consistently explained that the Tribunal always builds on the same assumption that imprecise regulation of tax law cannot be interpreted to the detriment of the taxpayer. As one can see, the view ultimately expressed in the Tribunal's judgements in this regard is not so much at odds with the view often voiced by the administrative courts, but there is some tension between the two.

Summary

The above analysis clearly shows that the dispute over the interpretative strategies classically revolves around the role of each context of interpretation. Likely, no one would contradict the conclusion that adoption of the rules of systemic or functional interpretation – where an unambiguous meaning of a concept is inferred on the basis of the rules of textual interpretation – is not an obligation of the interpreter but is only intended to revise the obtained result. The case is different when the rules of textual interpretation are insufficient to achieve this unambiguous result because such circumstances will necessitate the use of the other rules, which may result in correction of or change in the meaning of the legal provision subject to interpretation.

In the case of a comprehensive interpretation, apart from the legal text itself, the functional rule referring to the legislator's objectives, cultural conditions or the axiological aspects assumes great importance. It follows from the above that textual interpretation must be confronted with the result of systemic interpretation and functional analysis in order to determine whether there are no exceptional cases undermining the linguistic meaning of the provision of the law. The views of the Constitutional Tribunal and the Supreme Administrative Court differ in this respect.

In our opinion, one should take a critical look at the judgement of the Constitutional Tribunal of 13 December 2017, ref. No. SK 48/15 (OTK ZU 2/A/2018), which points out that "After careful textual interpretation and potentially rejection of the interpretative options that do not meet systemic requirements, in the event that the interpreter: (1) has obtained an unambiguous tax regulation, they are not allowed to modify the obtained interpretative result based on functional arguments, including teleological ones, if that would lead to deterioration of the legal circumstances of the taxpayer or another entity obliged to pay public levies; or (2) has not obtained an unambiguous tax regulation, out of the possible interpretative results they must chose the result most favourable for the taxpayer or another entity obliged to pay public levies, taking into account their legal circumstances". At the same time, in the judgement under analysis, the Tribunal noted that "it is impossible *in abstracto* to draw a boundary between simple and special ambiguity of a legal status, especially that such a boundary is a bit different depending on the branch of law and the matter that is subject to regulation. In general, doubts of interpretation in private law (such as civil, family, and commercial law) can be tolerated to a greater extent than in public law; as for the latter, there must be a clear distinction among administrative law, tax law, and criminal law, because the required level of precision increases with each of these branches of the law in the order as listed. This is a consequence of the different scope of freedom of interpretation admissible in each branch of the law, arising, inter alia, from the fact that each of them permits the use of functional rules of interpretation to resolve doubts to a varying degree."

We believe that it is not possible to stick to the literal, narrow interpretation of tax law, but it is necessary to interpret it properly in a wider functional and social context.[55] It should be stressed that when interpreting tax law very often, if not always, one will be dealing with the imprecision of regulation of an institution or legal concept. This is a consequence of the fact that it is a branch of the law, which is closely linked to the economy, the EU law, and social as well as cultural contexts.

Of course, interpretation of the law must respect judicial accountability and does not imply discretion of the judges based on their axiological or political preferences. This is because judges are bound by the need to take into account textual interpretation, which should always be the starting point for the interpretation. However, the interpretation process should take into consideration the legislative history of a legal norm, its EU context, and the circumstances arising from the comparative analysis of the legal orders of the Member States. In addition, when the court issues a judgement, it should respect

---

55 Por. B. Wojciechowski, *Stosowanie prawa podatkowego przez sądy administracyjne w sytuacji interpretacyjnego pluralizmu instytucjonalnego i otwartej tekstowości prawa*, „Państwo i Prawo" 2019, No. 12, pp. 58–72.

the content of the judgements passed earlier, especially with regard to consistency of a line of case law. Indeed, there is an interpretative chain in the process of applying the law,[56] which compels to seek answers in the case law passed so far since nothing happens in a conceptual void or a terminological vacuum. On the contrary, the endless process of writing a story about the law and about the way it is understood unfolds in front of our eyes. The law is a living organism that responds to changing social, cultural, and economic circumstances, especially in terms of its interpretation. Without this awareness, we would have to deal with something artificial and anachronistic, which would thus be exposed to righteous criticism and require constant changes in order to make matters more precise, which, of course, is not possible all the time due to the multitude of disputable cases, their complexity, and individualisation.

Only comprehensive interpretation is suitable for an open, dynamic, and pluralistic legal system that covers not only the national but also the European or international context. Paradoxically, stricter adherence to functional interpretation (based on intentional and teleological arguments) better serves the purpose of ensuring that values such as coherence, uniformity, and legal certainty are respected than complete reliance on textual arguments, which often correspond neither to the intention of the legislator nor to the social and economic reality that surrounds us. The overlap of these non-linguistic contexts may reveal the actual and desired content of the legal provision that is subject

56 S. Fish, *Is There a Text in This Class? The Authority of Interpretive Communities, Cambridge*, London 1980, s. 13–14, 171–172, 322. "Interpretive communities are made up of those who share interpretive strategies not for reading (in the conventional sense) but for writing texts, for constituting their properties and assigning their intentions. In other words, these strategies exist prior to the act of reading and therefore determine the shape of what is read rather than, as is usually assumed, the other way around. If it is an article of faith in a particular community that there are a variety of texts, its members will boast a repertoire of strategies for making them. And if a community believes in the existence of only one text, then the single strategy its members will employ will be forever writing it. The first community will accuse the members of the second of being reductive, and they in turn will call their accusers superficial. The assumption in each community will be that the other is not correctly perceiving the 'true text,' but the truth will be that each perceives the text (or texts) its interpretive strategies demand and call into being". (Fish 1980, 171)

to interpretation;[57] whereas giving primacy to the linguistic context is a mistake. Following the principle *interpretatio cessat in claris* does not imply competition among the different contexts of interpretation but rather an obligation to apply comprehensive interpretation encompassing all available types of arguments and rules of interpretation. To sum up, it seems that the strategy adopted by the Supreme Administrative Court better meets these requirements and it is worth accepting this Court's understanding of the principle *in dubio pro tributario*, which advocates that only after all the interpretative directives have been followed – through the use of textual interpretation verified and adjusted by the rules and guidelines characteristic of functional or systemic interpretation – the impossibility of removing doubts must lead to a decision that is favourable for the taxpayer.

57 Cf. A. Bielska-Brodziak, *Śladami prawodawcy faktycznego. Materiały legislacyjne jako narzędzie wykładni prawa*, Warszawa 2017, p. 304 et seq.

Dominik J. Gajewski (SGH Warsaw School of Economics)

Kamil Joński (SGH Warsaw School of Economics)

6. Regulatory Impact Assessment (RIA) as a Source Revealing the Legislative Objective in the Interpretation of Tax Law

Abstract: The chapter attempts to explore – on a theoretical and empirical level – the Regulatory Impact Assessment (RIA) as a potential contribution to interpretation of tax law. The RIA, which was introduced in 2001 and substantially reformed in 2013, outlines the expected fiscal, economic, and social impacts of the legislative proposals submitted to the Parliament by the Council of Ministers. It has been designed as a tool to improve the process of public policymaking and is likely to convey information that is relevant for interpretation of the law; indeed, tax law seems to be the branch that is most in need of such information. The evolution of the RIA as well as its required content are examined, and the Administrative Court verdicts citing the RIAs are identified and analysed.

Keywords: Tax cases, interpretation of the law, judicial argumentation, Regulatory Impact Assessment, public policy formulation

Introduction

In the previous chapter, which describes a dispute about the interpretation of tax law, B. Wojciechowski and A. Olczyk contrast the formalistic approach[1] relying on textual interpretation with the approach they call an interpretative strategy based on the principle *interpretatio cessat in claris*.

If the latter approach is adopted – especially considering the reality of the modern multimetric system of the law[2] – the functional and teleological interpretation assume immense significance. According to L. Leszczyński, application of an argument referring to the purpose will be more extensive in

---

1 It is worth mentioning the term "most locally applicable rule", cf. F. Schauer, *Formalism*, „Yale Law Journal" 1988, Vol. 97, No. 4, p. 521.

2 Cf. E. Łętowska, *Multicentryczność współczesnego systemu prawa i jej konsekwencje*, „Państwo i Prawo" 2005, z. 4, p. 3 et seq.; for more on the implications of the multicentricity paradigm, see: M. Zirk-Sadowski, M. Golecki, B. Wojciechowski, *Multicentrism as an emerging paradigm in legal theory*, Peter Lang, Frankfurt am Main 2009.

those branches of administrative law, which are clearly oriented at implementing a specific policy of guiding or organising social life.[3] Tax law can be included among them.

In practice, advancement of teleological arguments requires that the interpreter determine the legislative objective. Such an objective might be sought after in multiple places, however, the legal text itself is deemed to be fundamental, in particular the principles of law expressed within it. Nevertheless, this does not mean that the legislative objective cannot be reconstructed on the basis of sources other than the legislation itself, and legislative materials (or history) are particularly noteworthy in this case.[4]

Analysing the types of legislative materials produced in Poland, A. Bielska-Brodziak emphasises the role of assessment of the anticipated social and economic effects, which is called Regulatory Impact Assessment (hereinafter the RIA) that "should be paid attention to from the perspective of interpretative needs."[5]

In essence, the RIA is a tool for implementing the principle of the so-called evidence-based policy making, which means making informed decisions as regards the public policy on the basis of information that is as comprehensive as possible and taking into account all relevant aspects of an issue (i.e., analytical data).[6] Thus, it is a mechanism that allows the achievements of the Law & Economics (L&E)[7] to influence the results of the law-making process. If information available in the RIA is then used for the purposes of teleological argumentation, it may potentially extend the impact of this type of economic analysis from the law-making process onto the process of its application.

On the other hand, A. Bielska-Brodziak herself points out two groups of arguments that undermine the credibility of legislative materials as a source of

---

3 L. Leszczyński, *Wykładnia celowościowo-funkcjonalna przepisów prawa administracyjnego*, in: L. Leszczyński, M. Zirk-Sadowski, B. Wojciechowski, *Wykładnia w prawie administracyjnym, System Prawa Administracyjnego*, C.H. Beck, Warszawa 2015, p. 311.

4 *Ibidem*, pp. 294–300.

5 A. Bielska-Brodziak, *Budowa i treść uzasadnienia projektu*, w: *Śladami prawodawcy faktycznego*, Wolters Kluwer, Warszawa 2017.

6 The „Lepsze Regulacje 2015" [Better Regulation 2015] Programme, Annex to Resolution No. 13/2013 of the Council of Ministers of 22 January 2013, p. 3.

7 See more about this subject: K. Metelska-Szaniawska, J. Bełdowski, *Ekonomiczna analiza prawa (Law & Economics) – wprowadzenie*, w: R. Cooter, T. Ulen, *Ekonomiczna analiza prawa*, C.H. Beck, Warszawa 2011, p. XX.

information in the process of legal interpretation. The first group is concerned with internal inconsistency (as "due to their conflicting contents, legislative materials are less clear than the text that they are supposed to help interpret") and the second with vulnerability to manipulation ("both during the legislative process and at the stage when legislative materials are used.")[8]

This chapter addresses the issue of referring to information contained in RIAs in the process of interpretation of tax law by the administrative courts.

6.1. RIA in the Polish Law-Making Process

In accordance with Article 118(1) and (2) of the Constitution of the Republic of Poland, the legislative initiative is granted to the Members of Parliament, the Senate (which is the upper house of the Parliament), the President of the Republic of Poland, the Council of Ministers, and to a group of at least 100 thousand citizens entitled to vote for the Sejm (which is the lower house of the Parliament). Although the Constitution provides for no hierarchy that would favour the Council of Ministers as the primary source of legislative initiative, the long years of practice give no reason to doubt that its role as the initiator of legislative work is crucial.[9]

This role of the Council of Ministers manifests itself in the establishment of relevant institutions, especially the Government Legislation Centre (GLC),[10] and an increasing degree of regulation of the so-called Government Legislative Process in the subsequent versions of the Bylaws of the Council of Ministers (hereinafter: the Bylaws).[11]

8 A. Bielska-Brodziak, *Niewiarygodność materiałów legislacyjnych*, w: *Śladami prawodawcy faktycznego*, Wolters Kluwer, Warszawa 2017.

9 Cf. empirical data in: K. Joński, W. Rogowski, *Legislative inflation in Poland: bird's eye view on three decades after the the1989 breakthrough*, "The Journal of Legislative Studies" 2022, DOI: 10.1080/13572334.2022.2052465

10 Act of 24 July 1999 Amending the Act on the Departments of Government Administration and Some Other Acts (Journal of Laws No. 70, item 778).

11 Cf.: Resolution No. 13 of the Council of Ministers of 25 February 1997. Bylaws of the Council of Ministers (Monitor Polski 1997 No. 15, item 144, as amended); Resolution No. 49 of the Council of Ministers of 19 March 2002. Bylaws of the Council of Ministers (Monitor Polski 2002 No. 13, item 221, as amended); Resolution No. 190 of the Council of Ministers of 29 October 2013. Bylaws of the Council of Ministers (i.e., Monitor Polski 2022, item 348).

One of the steps in this process was introduction of the RIA to the Bylaws in September 2001,[12] which, on the one hand, can be viewed as a more detailed implementation of the requirement of Article 118(3) of the Constitution[13] for government submissions and, on the other, as an instrument of control of the government's legislative agenda; it is unlikely that its introduction is unrelated to the scandal over the so-called Bauc's Gap.[14] In its original version, the RIA was intended to contain a description as well as evaluation of the consequences anticipated to arise due to entry into force of a legal act, namely:

(a) The impact of the regulation, in particular on:
- budgetary and public sector revenues and expenditure;
- the labour market;
- the internal and external competitiveness of the economy;
- and the regional situation and development;

(b) The legal impact, including in particular limitation of discretion, simplification of the procedures in place, and enhancement of the internal coherence of the legal system.

The RIA was also intended to indicate the "sources of financing for the drafted solutions."

However, from the perspective of legal interpretation, it seems reasonable to conclude that the RIA in the form introduced into the Government Legislative Process in 2001 was moderately useful for unravelling the legislative objective. It rather served to control public expenditure on the legislative initiatives undertaken by each Ministry. In addition, empirical analysis of the early RIAs proved that "information on the costs and benefits of draft legal acts, which is available to the Ministries when they engage in law-making, is limited at best."[15]

---

12 Resolution No. 125 of the Council of Ministers of 4 September 2001 amending the Resolution – Bylaws of the Council of Ministers (Monitor Polski 2001, No. 33, item 547).

13 When the drafters submit a draft law to the Sejm, they present the financial consequences of its implementation.

14 See more about the scandal: *Prawdę mówiąc Bauc*, „Gazeta Wyborcza", 28.07.2001; D. Rosati, *Decyzje nie do uniknięcia*, „Rzeczpospolita", 4.09.2001.

15 K. Goetz, R. Zubek, *Stanowienie Prawa w Polsce. Reguły Legislacyjne a jakość ustawodawstwa, Sprawne Państwo – Program Ernst & Young*, Warszawa 2005, p. 29, https://www.inpris.pl/fileadmin/user_upload/documents/Biblioteka_PL/Stanowienie_Prawa_w_Polsce._Regu%C5%82y_Legislacyjne_a_jako%C5%9B%C4%87_ustawodawstwa.pdf (accessed on: 5.11.2022). Analyses of the RIAs drawn up in 2012,

The practice that was back then followed when formulating an RIA was also subject to criticism from the theoreticians and practitioners who offered far-reaching advice aimed at improving its quality.[16]

A fundamental change in this respect was brought about by the Council of Ministers' adoption of the program "Better Regulation 2015."[17] As the authors of this programme claimed: "the main goal of the programme is to ensure systemic and organisational solutions necessary for the making and evaluating the law based on analytical evidence, which would be aimed at solving real social and economic problems, including reduction of the costs of conducting business and enhancement of the competitiveness of the Polish economy. The solutions would address the whole regulatory cycle."[18] The starting point of such a cycle – which is illustrated with a relevant figure – was the "problem" that the adopted legal act was going to solve. The problem was subjected to analyses that culminated in an *ex-ante* document in the form of the RIA. After entry into force of a legal act, there was going to be an *ex-post* evaluation (RIA) that could indicate its shortcomings – other "problems" – which would need to be solved with a new legislative process, for example, amendments to the regulations. Thus, the "regulatory cycle" would be completed.

Adoption of such a perspective resulted in alternation of the scope of the RIA that in the form as of 2013 was ambitiously intended to be more than a tool for controlling the fiscal (or budgetary) impact of the government legislative initiatives.

According to Article 28(3) in conjunction with Article 102 of the 2013 Bylaws,[19] the RIA should also contain "identification of a problem to be solved"

---

which was a decade after its introduction but shortly before the reform related to the adoption of the "Better Regulation 2015" programme, are presented by: G. Kopińska. G. Makowski. P. Waglowski, M. Wiszowaty, *Tworzenie i konsultowanie rządowych projektów ustaw*, 2014, https://www.batory.org.pl/upload/files/Programy%20operacyjne/Odpowiedzialne%20Pan-stwo/Tworzenie_i_konsultowanie.pdf (accessed on: 5.11.2022).

16 W. Szpringer, W. Rogowski, *Ocena skutków regulacji. Poradnik OSR, doświadczenia, perspektywy*, C.H. Beck, Warszawa 2007.

17 Cf. Communication of the Minister of Economy of 12 April 2013 on the adoption by the Council of Ministers of a resolution on the adoption of a development programme entitled "Lepsze Regulacje 2015" [Better Regulation 2015] (Monitor Polski 2013, item 341).

18 Programme "Lepsze Regulacje 2015" [Better Regulation 2015], Annex to the Resolution No. 13/2013 of the Council of Ministers of 22 January 2013, p. 17.

19 Resolution No. 190 of the Council of Ministers of 29 October 2013. Bylaws of the Council of Ministers (M.P.2013.979); after the amendment of the Bylaws in 2016, the

and "determination of the purpose and nature of the intervention." This change was reflected, on the one hand, in the new RIA form (containing sections: 1. What problem is being solved? 2. The recommended solution, including planned intervention tools and the expected effect), which also included a section for describing evaluation of the functioning of the legal act being drafted (i.e., 12. How and when will the effects of the draft be evaluated and what measures will be used to this end?),[20] and, on the other hand, in preparation of detailed guidelines for the impact assessments and public consultations within the framework of the governmental legislative process.[21]

Reliable answers to such questions would undoubtedly be an invaluable source of information on the legislative objective, which could be employed for the purposes of teleological and functional interpretation. However, two reservations need to be voiced.

The first is concerned with the RIA's positioning within the legislative process. In line with the regulation of the impact assessment in the Bylaws of the Council of Ministers, this document is limited to the stage of the governmental legislative process. Therefore, the changes introduced at the stage of parliamentary work, which are often crucial for the final shape of the solutions, including in tax law, are not, in principle, subject to assessment (see, e.g., introduction of the universal obligation to use SAF-T.[22])

The second reservation is concerned with the reliability of the impact assessment process itself and the RIA that documents it. It is worth referring at this point to the telling phrase "policy-based evidence making"[23] that can be encountered in the relevant literature. The Supreme Audit Office's controls

---

provision under analysis was included in its entirety in section 28(3), cf. (M.P.2016.1006, consolidated text).

20 Form template cf. https://www.gov.pl/web/premier/ocena-wplywu-w-rzadowym-procesie-legislacyj-nym (accessed on: 5/11/2022).

21 https://rcl.gov.pl/legislacja/wytyczne-do-przeprowadzania-oceny-wplywu-oraz-konsultacji-publicznych--w-ramach-rzadowego-procesu-legislacyjnego/ (accessed on: 5/11/2022).

22 The legislative process is described in further detail from the perspective of the cost-benefit analyses, in: D.J. Gajewski et al., *Tendencje w polityce podatkowej w krajach Europy Środkowo-Wschodniej: obowiązki podatkowe przedsiębiorców*, w: M. Strojny (ed.), *Raport SGH i Forum Ekonomicznego 2020*, Oficyna Wydawnicza SGH, Warszawa 2020, pp. 493–495.

23 J. Torriti, *Impact Assessment and the Liberalization of the EU Energy Markets: Evidence-Based Policy-Making or Policy-Based Evidence-Making?*, "JCMS: Journal of Common Market Studies" 2010, Vol. 48, No. 4, pp. 1065–1081.

unveil the existence of this problem under the Polish conditions: "Analysis of 20 reviewed legislative processes indicates that the IA is not generally perceived as an instrument for perfecting the law supporting the policymakers in decision-making

as regards regulatory solutions. In cases where the political dimension prevails, an impact assessment may consist mainly in fulfilment of a formal requirement. (...) in the case of the next six [legislative processes], impact assessment activities were essentially to seek and present information on the previously adopted particular solutions and ready draft laws derived from earlier decisions taken by the Heads of the Ministries. In consequence, the impact assessment has not fully served its intended purpose of being a tool supporting decision-making by providing as comprehensive information as possible about the options for solving a particular problem, because it was limited to only one of them (which had been proposed)."[24]

Such practices should be deemed particularly problematic from the point of view of formulating teleological arguments on the basis of RIAs. It seems, indeed, that the parts of the RIA concerning identification of the problem and definition of the purpose and nature of the intervention are particularly sensitive to situations where political decision-makers impose the form of legislative solutions before the analysis to be carried out as part of impact assessment even takes place. This appears to be the case with calculation of the costs and benefits of the proposed solutions to a smaller degree as that can be done accurately despite such a reversal of the order of actions.

6.2. Referring to RIAs in the Case Law of Administrative Courts in Tax Matters

In order to verify whether and, if so, how administrative courts use the information contained in the RIAs to uncover the legislative objective and in consequence to perform teleological and functional interpretation of tax law, the Case Law and Case Information Central Database (CBOIS) was probed.[25] The following query was used: RAC's judgements with symbol 611 made between 1 January 2001 and 30 June 2022. There were 55 judgements found, including 14 of the SAC, which

---

24 Supreme Audit Office, *Conducting Impact Assessment as Part of a Governmental Legislation Process*, 2017, No. 174/2017/P/16/094/LWA, https://www.nik.gov.pl/plik/id,16190, vp,18712.pdf (accessed on: 5/11/2022), p. 14.

25 https://orzeczenia.nsa.gov.pl (accessed on: 5/11/2022).

seems to be a modest number suggesting scant use of the arguments originating from RIAs for the purposes of interpretation (see Figure 6.1).

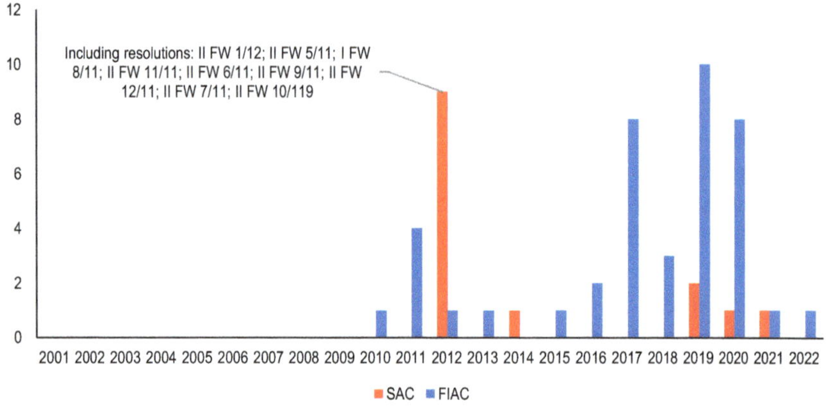

Figure 6.1. References to RIAs in the statements of reasons to administrative courts' judgements on tax matters (symbol 611) between January 2001 and June 2022
Source: Own study based on a query searched for in CBOIS.

It is interesting to note that there are no references to the information contained in RIAs in judgements passed before 2010, which may be attributed to the poor quality of the Assessments made at that time, as suggested by empirical research.[26]

The largest number of references to RIAs was found in the RAC's judgements passed between 2017 and 2020, which is a few years after implementation of the reform of the impact assessment process of 2013, when the sections for indicating teleological arguments were added to the RIA form. However, this number dropped sharply the following year.

Interestingly, it is more likely to find references to the information contained in RIAs in judgements passed by administrative courts of the first instance; they are hardly present in the judgements of the SAC. In this context, the year 2012

26 Cf. cited publications: K. Goetz, R. Zubek, Stanowienie Prawa w Polsce. Reguły Legislacyjne a jakość ustawodawstwa, Sprawne Państwo – Program Ernst &Young, Warszawa 2005; G. Kopińska. G. Makowski. P. Waglowski, M. Wiszowaty, *Tworzenie i konsultowanie rządowych projektów ustaw, Raport Fundacji Batorego*, Warszawa 2014.

appears to be intriguing; at that time, Division 2 of the SAC's Financial Chamber issued nine judgements resolving disputes over jurisdiction and referred to the RIA in the relevant statements of reason.

6.3. Argumentation of the Administrative Courts Based on Information from the RIA

Below, there is an in-depth analysis of some passages from the statements of reasons to the judgements of the RAC and the SAC, which were selected earlier during the study, paying special attention to the type of arguments derived with the use of information contained in the RIA. Considering the intention to most fully reflect the way the administrative courts employed the information contained in the RIA and the way they derived specific teleological arguments from that information, a decision was made to cite the relevant passages of the statements of reason *in extenso*. That way, we will verify the hypothesis whether this information serves to decipher the legislative objective for the purposes of teleological and functional interpretation. In addition, detailed analysis of the specific information employed by the courts will allow to verify the extent to which the reform of the impact assessment process of 2013 (in particular, extension of the scope of the RIA to identify a problem and determine the purpose and nature of the intervention) has contributed to greater usefulness of the RIA in the process of interpretation of the law.

Analysis of examples of instances where the administrative court referred to the RIA should start with a group of judgements of the RAC in Lublin;[27] they were concerned with examination of the admissibility of the interference of the so-called Gambling Act with the principle of freedom of economic activity. The RAC carried out a test of proportionality, taking into consideration the RIA (as of before the reform of 2013) as a source of information on the legislator's objective. The RAC concluded that "conditions have been met that border on interference with the freedom of economic activity and the right of ownership. Interference of the legislator in these spheres in accordance with Article 31(3) in conjunction with Article 22 in conjunction with Article 64(3) of the Constitution took place: (1) in the form of an act of law; the Act of 19 November 2009 on Gambling (repealing the previously applicable Act of 29 July 1992 on Games and Mutual Betting); (2) which introduced new regulations within the regulatory freedom of the legislator oriented – as is apparent from the justification to the draft

27 Judgement of 2011/07/13 (I SA/Lu 147/11) and I SA/Lu 148/11; I SA/Lu 89/11.

law and the impact assessment of the regulation – directly at the achievement of the social objective of reinforcing protection of the society and the rule of law from the effects of gambling, along with the expected gradual reduction of tax revenues resulting from expiry of permits and reduction in the number of active slot machines, despite simultaneous change in the flat tax rate; all that falls within the catalogue of values listed in Article 31(3) of the Constitution, which are essential for the evaluation of the existence of public interest in limitation of the constitutional rights and freedoms; (3) while the essence

of that freedom and that right has not been hurt with entry into force of the new act of law, since – as already indicated above – business activity in terms of organising the so-called low-prize gaming on slot machines has not ceased or been prevented from continuing on the basis of decisions made in line with the previously applicable law; neither has the introduction of a higher flat rate tax infringed on the substance of the right of ownership because the nature of the rate, although limiting the level of profit achieved by the game organiser (compared to the previous rate), is not that of a confiscation and does not result in any kind of "expropriation" of the entrepreneur. When confronting the objective of the new regulation (within the scope of the analysis), which is determined by the public interest of protection of the society and the rule of law against the effects of gambling, with the freedom of business activity and the right of ownership, it is impossible – in the context of the proportionality test – to ignore the fact that the said freedom and right belong to the category of the so-called second generation rights that are easier to limit. Consequently, one cannot fail to acknowledge that the linguistic convention that the legislator has followed on the basis of the relevant provisions of the Constitution (i.e., Article 22 and Article 64(3)) provides for the possibility and admissibility of setting restrictions."

Another example of the use of the RIA (drawn up before the reform of 2013) in order to determine the legislator's objective – in the context of implementation of the EU law – is available in the judgements of the RAC in Warsaw.[28] Interestingly, the Court made use of both the proclamation of the legislator's objective and the estimates of the fiscal effects of the drafted provisions. „The amendment to the act, which consisted in repealing Article 6(9)(4) of the Act on Tax on Acts in Civil Law [ATACL] and introducing Article 9(11)(d) of the ATACL, was in fact not an infringement of the EU law (as the appellant claims), but, on the contrary, it actually aimed at ensuring compliance with the provisions of Article 13 of the Directive (and from this point of view, the character of the amendment was

28 Judgement of 2022/01/12 (III SA/Wa 998/21) and III SA/Wa 1038/19.

that of implementation of the EU law). (…) It is also worth emphasising that in the draft amendment to the ATACL, the drafter pointed out that 'ensuring compliance of the Polish regulations with the European Union law may cause slightly negative financial consequences for the municipal budgetary revenues' (see the draft of the act amending the Act on Tax on Acts in Civil Law (Print 748) attached to the letter of the Prime Minister of 7 July 2008 to the Marshal of the Sejm of the Republic of Poland; Regulatory Impact Assessment, section IV(1) entitled Impact of the Regulation on the Public Finance Sector, Including the State Budget and Local Government Budgets, (…)). The purpose of the legislative changes was to ensure compliance of the Polish regulations with the

EU law, and they were likely o produce negative financial consequences for the municipal budgetary revenues."

The Supreme Administrative Court also used the RIA in the form as of before the reform of 2013 to determine the legislator's objective. In the judgement of 5 February 2019 (I FSK 426/17), the Court argued that: "definition of the obligations regarding reporting and updating of registration data, which differentiate certain categories of entities in this respect, was introduced into the Act on Registration and Identification of Taxpayers and Payers [ARITP] on the basis of the Act of 29 July 2011 Amending the ARITP and Certain Other Acts (Journal of Laws No. 171, item 1016, as amended). As evident from the justification to the draft amending act (Print No. 4159 of the Sejm of the sixth term), one of the objectives of the introduced changes was to lift some of the statutory obligations of citizens towards tax administration; one of the expected savings and social benefits both on the side of the tax administration and in its surroundings was: Natural persons entered in the PESEL register [which is the Universal Electronic System for Registration of the Population], who do not run business activity and are not registered as taxpayers of Value Added Tax, are not obliged to submit, including by post, identification and update notifications (see section of the justification to the draft entitled 'Impact Assessment of the Legal Act.')"

The RIA in the form as of before the reform was also used by the SAC in 2012 to put forward teleological arguments in nine judgements resolving disputes over the jurisdiction of the authorities.[29] "The systematic take on the above-mentioned provisions of the amending act leads to the conclusion that the legislator's objective was to change the current practice of liquidation of

29 Resolution of 2012-06-21 (II FW 1/12) and II FW 5/11; II FW 8/11; II FW 11/11; II FW 6/11; II FW 9/11; II FW 12/11; II FW 7/11; II FW 10/11.

vehicles taken over pursuant to Article 130a(10) of the Act on Road Traffic by way of making the Starosta [i.e., the Head of the Poviat] the body competent to deal with such matters. This conclusion finds confirmation in reasons that the legislator took into account and which were voiced in the Regulatory Impact Assessment: 'The new task imposed on the Poviat [i.e., a county] will be financed with charges for the removal and storage of vehicles, which are the Poviat's own income. The maximum rates for such charges are set out in Article 130a(6a) of the draft. Based on the drafted provision stipulated in Article 130a(10)(g), the costs of liquidation proceedings (i.e., storage, valuation, sale or destruction of the vehicle) will also be borne by the person who owns the vehicle on the date of issue of the removal order or jointly and severally by the holder. The decision on payment of these costs will be issued by the Starosta. It should be noted that the draft also provides for subsidies to the Poviats from the National Fund for Environmental Protection and

Water Management for collection of end-of-life vehicles acquired by the Poviats through the forfeiture of property. Subsidies for this purpose provided to the Poviats will take the form of grants subject to conditions similar to the ones applicable to subsidies to Gminas [i.e., municipalities] for the collection of abandoned end-of-life vehicles. The Poviat will receive an amount proportional to the number of vehicles that – on the day of transfer of their ownership to the Poviat by way of forfeiture – were wrecks (and waste) handed over to the dismantling station and indicated in the application for subsidy. In addition, the Poviats will bear the costs arising from the relevant Starostas' Offices submitting applications to the courts in order to obtain a ruling of forfeiture of vehicles that have been abandoned and not recovered within the statutory time limit' (cf. the Print of the Sejm of the Republic of Poland of the sixth term, No. 2816, available at http://www.sejm.gov.pl). Therefore, the Court cannot share the Starosta' view that interpretation of the above-mentioned provisions of the amending act cannot lead to a conclusion as to which authority is competent to conduct proceedings regarding forfeiture of the above-mentioned vehicle."

As regards examples of the use of the RIAs in a new form for the purposes of teleological and functional interpretation, it is worth mentioning the judgements of the RAC in Warsaw.[30] "When interpreting the said provision (i.e., Article 17(1)(57)(g) of the Act), it cannot be overlooked that it refers to real property subject to taxation with a special tax on income described in Article 24b(1) of the Act. The nature of the subject-matter of taxation with income tax referred to in Article

30 Judgement of 2019/09/06 (III SA/Wa 2981/18) and III SA/Wa 1904/18.

24b(1) of the Act – which in this case is real property mentioned in Article 24b(1) – affects interpretation of Article 17(1)(57)(g) that refers to this subject-matter. So, Article 24b(1) of the Act imposes a special tax on income derived from ownership of a particular category of buildings, namely: 'commercial real property of significant value (e.g., shopping malls); see the Impact Assessment of the Legal Act (p. 2) which is an Annex to the draft Act Amending the Act on Personal Income Tax, the Act on Corporate Income Tax, and the Act on Flat-Rate Tax on Certain Incomes of Natural Persons (Print 1878) (…).' Undoubtedly, by singling out a group of buildings defined in Article 24b(1) – which the Article 17(1)(57)(g) subject to interpretation refers to – the legislator had in mind real property that has the (generic) potential to generate consistent income for its owner, in particular from their lease (and it should be emphasised that the legislator excluded, for example, office buildings used for the taxpayer's own needs from this category).

There was a special tax introduced for the group of buildings defined in such a way, which is 'tax on proceeds from ownership' due each month."

Another example of the use of the "new" RIA to reconstruct the legislative objective is the series of judgements of the RAC in Gliwice[31] and the RAC in Wrocław[32] regarding imposition of excise duty on electricity consumed in metallurgical processes. "According to the Court, taking into account the assumptions and objectives of the Energy Directive, which is exclusion from its scope (i.e., from taxation with excise duty) of energy products (including electricity) used in metallurgical processes, it should be assumed that the EU legislator applies special treatment to the specific conditions that the metallurgical industry operates in as it is inherently subject to particular global competition and, at the same time, it is crucial from the point of view of the security policy of each country. Therefore, the national legislator introduced the concept of a 'metallurgical process' into the Act on Excise Duty [AED] without limiting it by a definition, which could be too narrow considering the technological conditions and thus would limit the exemption from Article 30(7a)(3) of the AED. This stance finds confirmation in the justification to the draft Act of 24 July 2015 Amending the Act on Excise Duty and Certain Other Acts (Journal of Laws of

31 Judgement of 2017/03/23 (III SA/Gl 1589/16) and III SA/Gl 672/16 (Judgement of 2016/12/14) – the SAC did not, however, refer to the RIA while examining cassation appeals – cf. Judgement of 2020/08/28 (I GSK 724/17) and I GSK 342/17 (judgement of 2019/11/28) – analogous arguments were also presented in judgements III SA/Gl 1466/16 and III SA/Gl 745/16.

32 Judgement of 2019/05/17 (I SA/Wr 86/19).

2015, item 1479) – Print of the Sejm No. 3255 – which indicates (as in point 1 of the Regulatory Impact Assessment) that exemption of the energy used in metallurgical processes is aimed at equating the competitive position of enterprises operating in Poland with the one held by the enterprises in other EU countries, which do not bear such costs of electricity. It was noted that the introduced exemption applies to all taxpayers of excise duty that is imposed on electricity used in metallurgical processes. Whereas the EU tax exemption is intended to improve the competitiveness of the industry in comparison to the Asian companies."

Another example may be the judgement of the RAC in Gliwice[33] concerning the scope of exemption from real property tax in the case of railway infrastructure. "In Appendix No. 1 to the Act on Railway Transport [ART], the only buildings that are listed directly are the buildings where there are devices and installations enumerated in point 5, which coincides with the content of the justification to the amending draft clearly indicating that the amendment was aimed at adaptation to

the concepts used in the ART, and adjustment of the above exemption was proposed in order to make it analogous to the provisions on air transport by way of specifying that the exemption also applies to buildings (such as signalling centres). The Regulatory Impact Assessment shows that in the case of railway infrastructure managers, 'the scope of exemption from real property tax is extended onto signalling centres' (as per point 4 of the RIA), and that 'the exemption of signalling centres from real property tax in the case of regional railway infrastructure managers will enable their networks to apply correspondingly lower fees for the provision of railway infrastructure.' Therefore, the legislator's intention behind adding buildings was evidently to allow for exemption of signalling centres from real property tax and not every building, as deduced by the interpretative authority".

It is particularly interesting to note the judgements where the administrative court (or the party whose arguments the court describes in the statements of reasons to the judgement) infers the legislator's objectives on the basis of estimates of the impact of the drafted solutions on the public finance sector, which are presented in the RIA.

Review of such rulings should begin with the judgement of the RAC in Kraków;[34] the argument derived from fiscal estimates solely served an auxiliary

33 Judgement of 2017/12/01 (I SA/Wr 970/17).
34 Judgement of 2015/07/27 (I SA/Kr 902/15).

function. “The Court also notices that the part of the justification to the draft act (Print No. 2565 of the Sejm of the 8th term) concerning amendments to Article 3(5) of the Act on Local Taxes and Fees, which is referred to in some of the above judgements (that are favourable to the complainant), is not an obvious substantive change as argued by some administrative courts. It is, therefore, appropriate to cite the entire paragraph of the justification to the draft amending act, which states that ‘(…) Amendment of a provision consists in clarifying that in the case of separation of ownership of premises, the tax obligation in respect of tax on land and part of a building that are joint property within the meaning of Article 3(2) of the Act of 24 June 1994 on Ownership of Premises (Journal of Laws of 2000, No. 80, item 903, as amended) is imposed on the owners of premises to the extent corresponding to their share in joint property established pursuant to Article 3(3) of the Act on Ownership of Premises.’ The wording of the above-mentioned passage of the justification does not indicate that the drafted change was obviously substantive in character; rather, it indicates problems with interpretation of the provision arising from the previous (literal) wording. Furthermore, the drafters never mentioned in the Regulatory Impact Assessment that this change would increase budgetary revenues.”

The RAC in Szczecin[35] went much further than that when interpreting the estimates of the financial consequences: “In the justification to the draft Act on Public Roads and on the Amendment to Some Other Acts, it was clarified that this amendment aims at streamlining and simplifying certain procedures and concepts used in the Act, adapting the provisions of the Act on Public Roads to other legal provisions, including to the requirements of the Constitution of the Republic of Poland. And so:

- Article 1(3) of the justification to the draft indicates that amendment to Article 4 of the Act on Public Roads puts the glossary of definitions of terms used in the Act in order. One important change is distinguishing the term ‘road’ from the term ‘road lane.’ The term ‘road’ is to solely signify a building whereas the ‘road lane’ is to mean the land on which the building is located along with the facilities and equipment linked to it (such as construction sites and technical equipment used for managing, securing, and servicing traffic);
- Article 2 of the justification to the draft indicates that the amendment to the Act on Local Taxes and Fees [ALTF], that is, amendment to Article 2(3)(4), is concerned with alteration of the definition of the road and the road lane;

35 Judgement of 16 June 2011 (I SA/Sz 246/11); when hearing a cassation appeal, the SAC did not explicitly refer to that argument, cf. judgement of 2014/01/22 (II FSK 2384/11).

- In addition, the impact of this regulation was assessed in the justification to the draft amending act, and so it was assumed that there would be: 'No impact of the regulation on the state budgetary revenues and expenditure.'

In the light of the above explanation of the justification to the draft amending Article 2(3)(4) of the ALTF, the College rightly noted that the legislator's intention can be directly inferred from this amending act. Since the effect of this amendment is 'the absence of impact of the regulation on state budgetary revenues and expenditure,' then it is reasonable to believe that if the amendments to the act extended the scope *ratione materiae* of the tax exemptions, the effect would undoubtedly be some impact on state budgetary revenues; in this case it would be reduction in budgetary revenues of Gminas [i.e., municipalities]. Hence, it is justified to make use of teleological interpretation of the drafted amendment to the legal regulation, which takes into account the legislator's intention." It is particularly intriguing to note that the Court used the phrase "the effect of this amendment is" while referring, after all, to a forecast of the fiscal impact and not to an instruction or testimony of intent. The availability of data that estimates can be based on remains of significance in this context. What is more, forecasts are naturally burdened with some risk of error.

What is more, in the case law of administrative courts, conclusions on the legislative objective are sometimes drawn from information on the lack of impact in areas subjected to less thorough analysis than the impact on the public finance sector. The RAC in Gliwice[36] argued in its judgement: "In the context of interpretation of Article 15(6) of the VAT Act, it is necessary to note as well that assumption of the rights and obligations of Gminas based on an act of law cannot, in principle, disrupt competition. One public authority assumes the rights and obligations of another public authority. This was indicated in the Regulatory Impact Assessment (RIA) of the draft Act on the Metropolitan Union in the Silesian Voivodeship in the following statement: 'entry into force of the drafted regulations will affect neither the competitiveness of the economy and entrepreneurship, including operation of entrepreneurs, nor family, the citizens, and households.' Therefore, the very premise of the legislator was that neither the assumption of the obligations of member Gminas nor conclusion of agreements between them affects the competitiveness of the economy and entrepreneurship, including operation of entrepreneurs." The SAC shared this view in the judgement of 3 March 2021 (I FSK 830/20).

36 Judgement of 2020/02/04 (I SA/Gl 1533/19)

Summary

The introduction of an analytical tool in the form of the RIA within the framework of the governmental legislative process arouse hopes of enhancing the reasonableness behind implementation of public policies under the paradigm of evidence-based policymaking. However, the use of the RIA goes beyond improvement of law-making as it may shape the process of its application to some extent. This is due to the adoption of teleological and functional interpretation where the RIA – especially in the form that was moulded by the reform of the impact assessment process in 2013 – may play an important role as a source revealing the legislative objective.

It should be noted that after 2010 there could be judgements found in the case law of administrative courts, which made use of information contained in the RIAs in such a way. However, it seems justified to claim that such judgements are still scarce and the potential of the RIA is not fully exploited in this respect.

On the other hand, employment of the RIA in the interpretation process must take into account reflections on the purpose and role of this document in the law-making process as well as on the nature of the information presented in it. This is particularly the case with macroeconomic forecasts (e.g., of the impact on the public finance sector), which are produced for the purposes of ensuring fiscal stability of the state.

Roman Wiatrowski

7. The Impact of the Preliminary Ruling Procedure on the Consideration of Economic Reality by Administrative Courts in the Interpretation of Tax Law

Abstract: The primary purpose of the chapter was to examine what impact preliminary rulings have on the administrative courts' consideration of economic reality. In his discussion, the author shows that the use of the preliminary ruling procedure by administrative courts has contributed to the formation of a line of jurisprudence that takes into account changes in economic reality in the interpretation of tax laws. The author showed that the consideration of economic reality in the interpretation of tax laws has occurred to the greatest extent in the goods and services tax. The chapter shows that the preliminary ruling procedure has contributed to filling an important gap that existed in the Polish jurisprudence of administrative courts to the extent that the need to take into account economic reality was not previously recognised. The line of jurisprudence formed in this way made it easier for taxpayers to conduct business, perform their tax obligations, and increased their security in connection with participation in transactions that could be considered an abuse of tax law. The preliminary questions of Polish administrative courts have contributed to the unification of jurisprudence in Poland and other European Union countries.

Keywords: administrative courts, preliminary questions, economic reality, tax law interpretation, value added tax, unification of jurisprudence.

Introduction

The previous two chapters referred to the interpretation of laws applied by administrative courts. This chapter, too, is related to statutory interpretation, but in relation to tax law as shaped by the application of the preliminary ruling procedure by administrative courts. In particular, it will consider how the preliminary ruling procedure has contributed to taking economic reality into account in the process of this interpretation.

In the jurisprudential practice of the application of the preliminary ruling procedure, CJEU rulings resulting from preliminary questions can affect the line of jurisprudence of national courts in numerous ways. Rulings of the CJEU in tax cases are milestones in the unification of the tax jurisprudence of administrative courts. Indeed, the fundamental aim of the preliminary ruling procedure is the uniform interpretation of EU law throughout the European Union, and most of the CJEU rulings that have been issued as a result of the activation of the preliminary ruling procedure by Polish administrative courts have had a wide impact on future national case law[1]. The preliminary ruling procedure not only contributed to the unification of jurisprudence, but in some cases resulted in a change in the previous line of jurisprudence. The change in the line of jurisprudence was influenced by the preliminary question concerning the relief for bad debts in value added tax[2]. In response to the preliminary question, the CJEU held that Article 90 of Council Directive 2006/112/EC of 28 November 2006 on the common system of value added tax (hereinafter also: Directive 112)[3] to be interpreted as precluding the reduction of the taxable amount for value added tax from being subject to the condition that, on the date of the supply of goods or services and also on the day preceding the date of submission of the adjustment to the tax declaration seeking to benefit from that reduction, the debtor is registered for VAT and is not in the course of insolvency proceedings or in the course of liquidation, and the creditor is still registered for VAT on the day preceding the date of submission of the adjustment to the tax declaration[4]. By virtue of the aforementioned judgement, the formal requirements stipulated in the VAT Act for benefiting from the bad debt relief (registration of the creditor as a VAT taxpayer as at the day preceding the day of filing the return and registration of the debtor as a VAT taxpayer and the absence of liquidation or bankruptcy proceedings against him) were removed from the legal order and taxpayers gained the right to claim this relief, directly on the basis of Art. 90(1) of Directive 112, which, in the Court's view, was sufficiently precise and unconditional to allow national courts to shape the legal position of individuals on its basis[5].

---

1 R. Wiatrowski, *Wykładnia prounijna Naczelnego Sądu Administracyjnego w zakresie przepisów dotyczących podatku od towarów i usług [Pro-Union Interpretation of the Supreme Administrative Court on Value Added Tax Regulations]*, Warsaw 2021, p. 427.

2 Order of the Supreme Administrative Court of 6 December 2018, file ref. I FSK 2261/15.

3 Official Journal of the EU L series of 2006. No. 347/1, as amended.

4 Judgment of the CJEU of 15 October 2020, in Case, C – 335/19, E. sp. z o.o. sp. k., ECLI:EU:C:2020:829.

5 By the Act of 11 August 2021. (Journal of Laws 2021.1626) amended the above-mentioned Act of 11 March 2004 on Value Added Tax (Journal of Laws 2021, item 685, 694, 802, 1163, 1243 and 1598) with effect from 1 October 2021.

In some cases, preliminary ruling practice has shaped new institutions that had no basis in EU law by filling gaps in EU law. An example is the institution of good faith. For the first time, the Court drew attention to this institution in connection with preliminary questions which concerned, inter alia, the question "whether the exclusion from the VAT system of transactions involving a person acting in good faith, but which constitute elements of a 'carousel' type of fraud perpetrated by third parties, is contrary to the general principles of proportionality, equal treatment or legal certainty?"[6]. Later, the Court answered questions from the European courts concerning whether, where a supply is made to a taxable person who did not know and could not have known (remained in good faith) that the transaction was being used for the purposes of a fraud committed by the seller, Art. 17 of the Sixth Directive must be interpreted as precluding a provision of national law under which the invalidity of a contract of sale resulting from a provision of national civil law under which the contract is incurably void as contrary to public policy on account of an unlawful caution on the part of the vendor results in the loss of the right to deduct VAT paid by that taxable person[7].

Subsequently, the Court considered the institution of good faith in the following areas: the right to deduct VAT, the exemption for intra-Community supplies of goods, the exemption for supplies of goods exported outside the European Union, joint and several liability and the correction of the tax shown on the invoice[8].

In Poland, too, the Administrative Courts have been presented with preliminary questions, an element of which was the institution of good faith. These concerned whether a taxpayer was entitled to deduct input tax in connection with the acquisition of goods if the transaction did not reflect actual economic events in terms of subjectivity[9]. In contrast, a question of preliminary ruling in national case law had important consequences, which concerned

6 Judgment of 12 January 2006 in Joined Cases C354/03-, C355/03 -and C484/03 – Optigen and Others, ECLI:EU:C:2006:16.

7 CJEU judgment of 6 July 2006 in Joined Cases C439/04 -and C440/04 -Kittel and Recolta Recycling, ECLI:EU:C:2006:446, para. 25.

8 D. Dominik-Ogińska, *Dobra wiara w podatku od wartości dodanej w orzecznictwie Trybunału Sprawiedliwości Unii Europejskiej [Good Faith in Value Added Tax in the Jurisprudence of the Court of Justice of the European Union (1)]*, 'Przegląd Prawa Podatkowego' 2013, no. 7, p. 29.

9 Decision of the Provincial Administrative Court in Łódź of 12 December 2012, file ref. SA/Łd 1140/12 and order of the Supreme Administrative Court of 6 March 2014, file ref. I FSK 516/13.

the national practice of considering in every case that there was no supply of goods and consequently refusing to take advantage of the exemption from value added tax (VAT) if the goods in question were exported outside the territory of the European Union and, after the export, the tax authorities found that the purchaser of the goods was not the person shown on the invoice issued by the taxable person, but another undetermined person[10]. In answering this question, the Court referred to good faith stating, inter alia, that the VAT exemption provided for in Article 146(1)(a) and (b) of that directive must be refused if the failure to identify the actual customer makes it impossible to establish that the transaction in question is a supply of goods within the meaning of that provision or if it is established that the taxable person knew or ought to have known that the transaction in question was linked to a fraud committed to the detriment of the common system of VAT[11].

The preliminary questions concerning *taxation* concern those areas of tax law whose regulations have been harmonised. Due *to* the enactment of Directive 2006/112 and the directives regulating excise duties, it is in the field of these taxes that most of the CJEU rulings have been issued.[12] To a lesser extent, the preliminary questions have had an impact on shaping the line of jurisprudence in other taxes. In addition to Article 113 TFEU[13] which concerns the harmonisation of legislation relating to turnover *taxes*, excise duties and other indirect taxes to the extent that such harmonisation is necessary to ensure the establishment and functioning of the internal market and to avoid distortions of competition, the legal basis for the harmonisation of tax legislation is also Article 114 TFEU, *under* which measures are adopted *for* the approximation of the laws, regulations and administrative provisions of the Member States which have as their object the establishment and functioning of the internal market. The scope of Article 114 TFEU is broad enough to allow *for the* enactment of acts of EU law relating

---

10 Order of the Supreme Administrative Court of 19 June 2018, file ref. I FSK 126/18.

11 Judgment of the CJEU of 17 October 2019, in Case C-653/18 *Unitel*, ECLI:EU:C:2019:876.

12 D. Mączyński, *Chapter III Wpływ orzeczeń Trybunału Sprawiedliwości Unii Europejskiej na stanowienie przepisów dotyczących pozostałych danin publicznych [w:] Wpływ orzecznictwa Trybunału Sprawiedliwości Unii Europejskiej na stanowienie polskiego prawa podatkowego [Influence of the Rulings of the Court of Justice of the European Union on the Establishment of Provisions Concerning other Public Taxes [in:] Influence of the Case Law of the Court of Justice of the European Union on the Establishment of Polish Tax Law]*, Warsaw 2021, p. 193.

13 Treaty on the Functioning of the European Union (OJ 2004. No. 90, item 864/2, consolidated version: OJ EU 2016. C 202, p. 47).

also to the tax sphere. Individual provisions of the TFEU, in particular Article 21 TFEU (formerly Article 18 TEC), Article 29 TFEU (formerly Article 24 TEC), Articles 30–32 TFEU (formerly Articles 25–27 TEC), Art. 34–37 TFEU (formerly Articles 28–31 TEC), Article 45 TFEU (formerly Article 39 TEC), Articles 49–55 TFEU (formerly Articles 43–48 TEC), Article 56 TFEU (formerly Article 49 TEC), Article 63 TFEU (formerly Article 56 TEC) and Article 65 TFEU (formerly Article 58 TEC)[14] .

Therefore, in the field of income taxes, it is possible to point to questions to the CJEU whose subject matter was issues of interpretation of the provisions of the TFEU (TEC). The subject of the question was, inter alia, whether the norms arising from Article 12, first indent, and Article 39(1) and (2) TFEU should be interpreted in such a way that they oppose the national provision adopted in Article 27b of the Act of 26 July 1991. of the Law of 26 July 1991 on income tax payable by natural persons[15] limiting the right to reduce income tax by the amount of compulsory health insurance premiums paid exclusively under national legislation in a situation where a resident pays compulsory health insurance premiums in another Member State on income taxed in Poland?[16].

In practice, the preliminary ruling procedure affects a wide range of tax law. The subject of the questions referred for a preliminary ruling remains not only issues concerning the interpretation of substantive law provisions, but also those which concern formal issues relating to tax proceedings. In particular, the Court has had to bend to the question concerning the right to interest. The Supreme Administrative Court referred to the CJEU a preliminary question concerning the compliance of Art. 78 par. 5 para. 1 and 2 of the Tax Ordinance[17] (which significantly restricts the right to interest on overpayments resulting from CJEU judgments) with EU law. This case concerns the right to interest on overpayments for investment funds from third countries[18].

In one of the most recent questions for a preliminary ruling, an administrative court asked the CJEU about the compatibility with EU law of a national

---

14 D. Mączyński, *Chapter III Wpływ orzeczeń Trybunału…[Influence of the Rulings of the Court…]*, p.194.

15 Consolidated text in Dz. U. of 2000, No. 14, item 176, as amended.

16 Decision of the Provincial Administrative Court in Wrocław of 3 October 2007, file ref. I SA/Wr 971/07.

17 Act of 29 August 1997. Tax Ordinance (consolidated text Dz.U. of 2012, item 749 as amended).

18 Order of the Supreme Administrative Court of 15 March 2022., file ref. II FSK 1602/ 19.

regulation and the practice based thereon, according to which a natural person [a member of the management board of a legal person], who may be jointly and severally liable for the VAT tax liabilities of a legal person with all of its private assets, is denied the right to participate actively in proceedings aimed at determining the legal person's aforementioned tax liability in the form of a final decision of the tax authority. At the same time, the question to the CJEU stipulates that such a person, in separate proceedings aimed at determining the joint and several liability of the said natural person for the VAT tax liabilities of the legal person, is deprived of an adequate means to effectively challenge previously made findings and assessments as to the existence or amount of the tax liability of the legal person[19]. A prominent issue raised in the preliminary questions of the European courts is the question of prescription[20]. As regards Polish administrative courts, it is worth noting the question of the compliance with the principles of equivalence and effectiveness, in the light of Article 4(3) of the TEU, of national legislation allowing for the dismissal of a request for a refund of overpaid VAT where that request was submitted by a taxpayer after the expiry of the five-year limitation period, despite the fact that the Court ruled after the expiry of that period that the VAT payment which was the subject of that refund request was not due[21]. In response to that question, the CJEU held that the principles of equivalence and effectiveness must, in the light of Article 4(3) TEU, be interpreted as not precluding national legislation such as that which allows the rejection of a claim for repayment of overpaid VAT where that claim was submitted by the taxable person after the expiry of the five-year limitation period, even though it is apparent from a Judgment of the Court, delivered after the expiry of that period, that the VAT payment which was the subject of that claim for repayment was not due[22] .

19 Decision of the Provincial Administrative Court in Wrocław of 25.01.2024, file ref. I SA/Wr 4/23.

20 e.g. judgments of the CJEU: of 21 March 2018, in Case C -533/16, ECLI:EU:C:2018:204; of 26 April 2018, in Case C -81/17, Zabrus Siret, ECLI:EU:C:2018:283, paragraph 30; of 8 September 2015, in Case C -105/14, Ivo Taricco, ECLI:EU:C:2015:555, paragraph 27; of 5 December 2017, in Case C -42/17, M.A.S. and M.B., ECLI:EU:C:2017:936, paragraph 20.

21 Order of the Supreme Administrative Court of 19 May 2016, file ref. I FSK 224/15.

22 Judgment of the CJEU of 20 December 2017, in Case C -500/16, ECLI:EU:C:2017:996.

7.1. The Economic Impact of the Preliminary Ruling Procedure

For the present study, however, the relevant questions are those preliminary questions from the Polish administrative courts which have had little positive impact on the economy.

In national jurisprudence and in national literature, such a concept has emerged, which is referred to as economic interpretation. In the jurisprudence of the administrative courts, this concept was used for the first time as early as 2004.[23] Indeed, the jurisprudence of the administrative courts recognises the need for an economic analysis of taxation, as well as a sociological analysis considering socio-political and even ethical content[24]. It has been aptly noted in the literature that the jurisprudence has adopted two different conceptions of the understanding of the term. The first has been described as "anti-abusive", while the second has been described as "pro-economic"[25]. The former is understood as a doctrine to combat tax avoidance[26]. According to this view, economic interpretation is to be regarded as such a way of applying tax law which, by way of interpretation, seeks to deprive the taxpayer of the benefit he could have obtained if he had conducted permitted civil law acts. The courts, citing the doctrine, point out that "economic interpretation is related to the issue of the adequacy of economic trading activities and the forms in which they are performed, on the one hand, and the content of the economic phenomena to which these behaviours relate and the forms they express, on the other". It is also emphasised that the application of this type of interpretation is aimed at "eliminating possible tax advantages that the taxpayer could achieve by means

---

23 Judgment of the Provincial Administrative Court in Poznań of 9 December 2004, file ref. I SA/Po 2342/03.

24 Judgment of the Supreme Administrative Court of 14 December 2004, file ref. FSK 826/04.

25 N. Kociak, *Wykładnia gospodarcza w orzecznictwie sądów administracyjnych [Economic Interpretation in the Jurisprudence of Administrative Courts]*, PP 2018, no. 4, p. 43.

26 e.g. judgments of the Supreme Administrative Court of 14.12.2004: file ref. FSK 826/04 and FSK 827/04; judgment of the Supreme Administrative Court of 17.12.2009, file ref. I FSK 1382/08; judgment of the Provincial Administrative Court in Białystok of 25.01.2010, file ref. I SA/Bk 556/09, judgment of the Supreme Administrative Court of 18.03.2010, file ref. II FSK 1838/08; judgments of the Supreme Administrative Court of 21.04.2011: file ref. I FSK 487/10 and I FSK 488/10; judgment of the Provincial Administrative Court in Rzeszów of 9.05.2017, file ref. I SA/Rz 143/17.

of economic behaviours or applied forms of economic turnover, which are not prohibited by law, but due to their atypicality are not noticed by the legislator".

This first understanding of economic interpretation assumes the autonomy of tax law. The essence of this concept is the assumption that taxation is charged on certain factual states and not on legal actions (acts). Therefore, in some decisions of administrative courts, it is argued that although tax law concerns economic phenomena also regulated by civil law norms, from the point of view of taxation, it is the economic phenomenon itself (e.g., income, property, consumption) that is relevant, and not its legal qualification in other branches of law. In this context, economic interpretation consists in analysing the economic ratio legis of the law and finding the real object of the tax, the real economic situation that the legislator wanted to tax, hidden under the form of a specific legal structure[27]. The consequence of such interpretative assumptions is to allow for the possibility of questioning the effectiveness under tax law of those acts which are valid and effective in the sphere of private law. Such actions are given a separate tax-legal qualification[28].

This second way of perceiving the economic – "pro-economic" – interpretation is based on the assumption that the taxpayer acts and should act in a manner typical of entities engaged in economic activity, i.e., for example, it seeks to make a profit and not a loss[29] . The Supreme Administrative Court held that the economic interpretation allows for the assumption that, when acting in market conditions, a taxpayer must take actions that are rational from its point of view, based on economic analyses and calculations, in order to achieve the highest possible economic efficiency. In particular, these actions may consist in making certain savings, reducing costs and expenses, minimising losses from certain business segments, or eliminating unprofitable ventures. It is noted that if the taxpayer did not take such actions, it could fail to face competition and its business could become unprofitable and start generating losses. Thus, the source of revenue, which is the running of the business in its entirety, would be

---

27 E.g. the judgment of the Provincial Administrative Court in Lublin of 31 January 2018, file ref. I SA/Lu 941/17.

28 M. Kalinowski, *Granice legalności unikania opodatkowania w polskim systemie podatkowym [Limits of the Legality of Tax Avoidance in the Polish Tax System]*, Toruń 2001, pp. 130–143; P. Karwat, *Obejście prawa podatkowego, [Circumvention of Tax Law]*, Warsaw 2002, pp. 207–208 and 219; H. Litwińczuk, *Obejście prawa podatkowego w świetle doświadczeń międzynarodowych [Circumvention of tax law in the light of international experience]*, Przegląd Podatkowy 1999, no. 4, pp. 3–4.

29 Resolution of the Supreme Administrative Court of 25 June 2012, file ref. II FPS 2/12.

jeopardised. In this sense, the Supreme Administrative Court recognises that any such undertaking aimed at preventing such a situation from arising should be perceived as leading to the preservation or safeguarding of the source of revenue, and the costs related thereto as deductible costs[30] .

In addition to the rationality of the taxpayer's actions, the second assumption is that all taxpayers should be subject to an adequate tax burden. This burden is adequate when the taxpayer pays tax in an amount that corresponds to the general assumptions of tax construction, considering the allowances and exemptions to which he is entitled. This understanding of deductible costs, based on their economic substance, prevails in modern tax legislation[31].

The need to use economic interpretation in this pro-economic sense is justified by the fact that "economic processes are characterised by their inherent dynamics". Therefore, reasoned, and rational economic decisions are necessary, originally taken under specific conditions determining their content and consequences, including legal and tax consequences, due to changes in the conditions of the economic environment[32].

Increases in costs, reductions in demand, unfavourable changes in the economyfrom the perspective of the negative effects of these changes on tax revenue may (even must) result in their revision in the new conditions of place and time[33] are mentioned as environmental conditions to be taken into account in this understanding of economic interpretation.

Referring to economic interpretation, the administrative courts held, inter alia, that under tax law, the successor entity enters into all legal relations to which the acquired entity was a party, with such effect as if the successor had been a party to those legal relations from the beginning. Consequently, it has been held that the succession referred to in Article 93 § 2 of the Tax Ordinance[34] is subject

30 Resolution of the Supreme Administrative Court of 25 June 2012, file ref. II FPS 2/12.

31 E.g. judgment of the Provincial Administrative Court in Warsaw of 14 April 2023, file ref. III SA/Wa 2017/22.

32 Judgement of the Provincial Administrative Court in Kraków of 11 July 2007, file ref. I SA/Kr 1509/06; the resolution of the Supreme Administrative Court of 25 June 2012, file ref. II FPS 2/12.

33 Judgement of the Provincial Administrative Court in Kraków of 11 July 2007, file ref. I SA/Kr 1509/06; the resolution of the Supreme Administrative Court of 25 June 2012, file ref. II FPS 2/12.

34 Act of 29 August 1997. – Tax Ordinance (Journal of Laws of 2012, item 749 as amended).

to all rights and obligations provided for in the provisions of the tax law, and not only those rights which have been realised[35] .

The national practice of referring to economic interpretation in the sense that economic needs are taken into account is directly reflected in the jurisprudence of the CJEU. The Court has repeatedly seen the need to consider actual economic and commercial events as a fundamental criterion for the application of the common VAT system[36]. The development of such a position by the CJEU appears to be a manifestation of a purposive interpretation. The literature also distinguishes a type of purposive interpretation that aims to ensure the effet utile of Union law ("functional interpretation"). In this case, the method of purposive interpretation is closely linked to systemic interpretation. It manifests itself by examining the context of a Union provision in order to assess which of the possible interpretations contributes most to its effectiveness[37] . In contrast, as will be shown below, the interpretation of VAT rules requires that the economic sense of the tax be taken into account.

7.2. Limitations on the Use of the Preliminary Ruling Procedure for Pro-business Interpretation

In looking at how the submission of questions to the Court of Justice by the administrative courts has contributed to taking account of economic aspects in interpreting legislation, it is necessary to present not only some of the questions referred for a preliminary ruling and the positions taken by the Court of Justice on those questions, but also to indicate what effects the preliminary rulings have had on the line of decisions taken by the administrative courts. It is for the referring court or tribunal to take the ultimate decision on whether to apply the interpretation of provisions of European Union law given in the reference for a preliminary ruling in the case before it. It is for the referring court to draw specific conclusions from the preliminary ruling and, if necessary, to decide not to apply the provision of national law held to be incompatible with European

35 e.g. the judgment of the Provincial Administrative Court in Warsaw of 3 September 2015, file ref. VIII SA/Wa 1147/14.

36 Judgment of the CJEU of 7 October 2010 in Joined Cases C53/09 -and C55/09 -Loyalty Management UK and Baxi Group, ECLI:EU:C:2010:590, paragraphs 39, 40 and the case law cited therein.

37 K. Lenaerts, J. A. Gutiérrez-Fons, *Metody wykładni Trybunału Sprawiedliwości Unii Europejskiej [Methods of Interpretation of the Court of Justice of the European Union]*, Warszawa 2024, p. 127.

Union law[38]. The role of national courts in the application of a question referred for a preliminary ruling varies and depends on a number of factors, in particular the facts of the case. Of significant importance in the implementation of a CJEU decision are the indications contained in the preliminary ruling itself. The Court often gives precise indications as to how the court should proceed. Examples of this are the judgments of the Court in the field of value added tax, where the Court indicated to the national courts what specific elements can prove the exercise of an economic activity[39], or how to examine whether there has been an infringement of the principle of competitiveness[40].

The extent to which national courts are bound by the preliminary rulings of the CJEU is also relevant for assessing the impact of the questions referred for a preliminary ruling on the ultimate scope of pro-business interpretation. Although there is no explicit basis indicating that national courts are bound by CJEU judgments, the view that CJEU judgments are binding on national courts is derived directly from CJEU case law[41]. On this basis, it has been recognised in the literature that judgments of the CJEU are binding from the moment they are rendered, final and non-appealable by the national court which has made a preliminary reference[42]. Higher courts that hear appeals are also bound by judgments of the CJEU[43]. However, this bindingness is not unlimited, as the national court, applies the CJEU judgment only if and to the extent that the CJEU's position will be applicable to the main case before the national court[44] .

---

38 Recommendations to national courts on the submission of references for a preliminary ruling (OJ EU. C. 2019 No 380, p. 1), para 11; judgments of the CJEU of 7 October 2010, in Case C653/11 -Paul Newey, ECLI:EU:C:2010:590, paragraph 42 and the case law cited therein; judgment of 22 November 2018, in Case C295/17 -MEO – Serviços de Comunicações e Multimédia, EU:C:2018:942, paragraph 43.

39 E.g. Judgments of the CJ: in Joined Cases C-180/10 and C-181/10, Słaby, Kuć, ECLI:EU:C:2011:589, paragraphs 37–41; of 20 June 2013, in Case C-219/12, Urfahr, ECLI:EU:C:2013:413, paragraph 22.

40 Judgment of the CJ of 9 November 2017 in Case C499/16, AZ, ECLI:EU:C:2017:846 .

41 Judgment of the CJEU of 24 June 1969 in Case 29/68, Milchkontor, ECLI:EU:C:1969:27.

42 A. Skoczylas, Problem zachowania jednolitości orzecznictwa sądów administracyjnych, [in:] System Prawa Administracyjnego, t. 10, Sądowa kontrola administracji publicznej [The problem of preserving the uniformity of the jurisprudence of administrative courts, [in:] System Prawa Administracyjnego, vol. 10, Judicial control of public administration] R. Hauser, Z. Niewiadomski, A. Wróbel, (ed.), Warszawa 2016, p. 763 et seq.

43 Order of the CJEU of 5 March 1986 in Case 69/85, Wünsche Handelsgesellschaft, ECLI:EU:C:1986:104.

44 R. Wiatrowski, *Wykładnia prounijna… [Pro-EU Interpretation...]*, p. 427.

An example of a limitation of the effect of a preliminary ruling can be found in the judgment of the Supreme Administrative Court, which limited the scope of application of the CJEU judgment in Case C-499/16, *AZ*[45]. The Court instructed the court to examine whether pastry and biscuit products with a shelf life of less than 45 days, but which, in the eyes of the consumer, are similar to pastry and biscuit products with a minimum shelf life of more than 45 days, such as those produced by AZ, and which are mutually substitutable, are present on the national market. However, the Supreme Administrative Court, referring to the principle of procedural autonomy, held that the obligation arising from the CJEU judgment to examine the competitiveness of the goods should be transferred to the tax authorities in tax proceedings, the subject of which is the assessment of the tax liability and not the granting of an individual interpretation[46]. The Supreme Administrative Court also referred to procedural autonomy when applying the Aviva judgment[47]. The inapplicability of the principle of legitimate expectations to completed and commenced states was explained by the Supreme Administrative Court by the subject matter of the case. The subject of the court's review was an individual interpretation in which the company described a future event that did not relate to a specific accounting period in which the exemption was applied[48] .

The effects of the application of CJEU rulings resulting from questions referred for a preliminary ruling may be limited not only by procedural autonomy but also by the principle of legitimate expectations or the prohibition of rulings *contra legem*[49].

7.3. The Special Importance of the Preliminary Ruling Procedure for the Interpretation of Tax Legislation

In Polish jurisprudence practice, questions for preliminary rulings are referred primarily in tax matters, in the field of value added tax. In 2023, the Polish administrative courts submitted four questions for preliminary rulings which

45 Judgment of the CJEU of 9 November 2017 in Case C499/16-, AZ, ECLI:EU:C:2017:846.

46 Judgment of the Supreme Administrative Court of 25 January 2018, case no. I FSK 1155/15, similarly in the judgment of the Supreme Administrative Court of 7 February 2018, case no. I FSK 1662/15.

47 CJEU judgment of 21 September 2017, in Case C-605/15, Aviva, ECLI:EU:C:2017:718.

48 Judgment of the Supreme Administrative Court of 15 March 2018, file ref. I FSK 953/ 15.

49 R. Wiatrowski, *Wykładnia prounijna… [Pro-EU Interpretation...]*, pp. 430–431.

concerned taxes. Three questions were related to value added tax[50], one question was related to real estate tax[51], In 2022, Polish administrative courts submitted eight questions for preliminary rulings in the field of taxes, of which 5 decisions were referred by the adjudicating panels of the Supreme Administrative Court, 2 decisions – by the Provincial Administrative Court in Wrocław and 1 decision – by the Provincial Administrative Court in Gliwice. Five of these cases concerned the tax on goods and services[52]. One case was related to income tax[53], tax ordinance[54] and excise tax[55].

Also, in the light of the total number of referrals to the CJEU from all tax cases, questions from tax cases have a significant position. According to statistics from the Court of Justice, in 2022 the Court received 546 preliminary references, including 61 tax cases[56]. In 2021, there were respectively 567 preliminary ruling questions overall and in 2020 – 557 overall. In terms of the scale of references for a preliminary ruling, countries such as Germany, Italy and Bulgaria remain at the top of the "geographical" classification of references for a preliminary ruling (98, 63 and 43 references to the Court in 2022 respectively). This is followed by Spain and Poland, whose courts referred 41 and 39 references to the Court in the same year. Austria, with its 34 references for a preliminary ruling, remained fairly similar to the previous year (37 references in 2021). The Dutch, Romanian and Belgian courts, with 28, 29 and 30 requests respectively, are in constant dialogue with the Court. There has also been a significant increase in the number

---

50 Orders: Supreme Administrative Court of 18 January 2023; file ref. I FSK 923/19; Provincial Administrative Court in Wrocław of 28 December 2023, file ref. I Sa/Wr 92/23; Supreme Administrative Court of 16 June 2023, file ref. I FSK 535/20.

51 Order of the Supreme Administrative Court of 19 April 2023, file ref. III FSK 3/22.

52 Orders: Provincial Administrative Court in Wrocław of 28 January 2022, file ref. I SA/Wr 208/21, Supreme Administrative Court of 23 February 2022, file ref. I FSK 1712/18, Supreme Administrative Court of 26 May 2022, file ref. I FSK 1212/18, Supreme Administrative Court of 23 June 2022, file ref. I FSK 1225/18, Provincial Administrative Court in Wrocław of 22 September 2022, file ref. I SA/Wr 73/22.

53 Decision of the Provincial Administrative Court in Gliwice of 28 November 2022, file ref. I SA/Gl 942/22.

54 Order of the Supreme Administrative Court of 15 March 2022, file ref. II FSK 1602/19.

55 Order of the Supreme Administrative Court of 28 December 2022, file ref. I GSK 380/19.

56 https://curia.europa.eu/jcms/upload/docs/application/pdf/2023-03/stats_cour_2022_pl.pdf.

of references for preliminary rulings submitted by Portuguese courts, with 28 requests to the Court in 2022 (compared to 20 in 2021).

When discussing the impact of questions referred for a preliminary ruling on the shaping of pro-economic interpretation, the effectiveness of domestic questions referred for a preliminary ruling cannot be overlooked. In the Polish practice of referring questions for a preliminary ruling in the field of tax law, the Court has refused to answer only one question for a preliminary ruling, holding that the factual circumstances took place before the accession of the Republic of Poland to the European Union[57].

Thus, the impact of the preliminary ruling procedure on the jurisprudence of the national courts is of relevance primarily in tax matters and, in particular, in value added tax. At this point, it is appropriate to analyse those judgments which have made a particular contribution to shaping a pro-economic interpretation of national law. In this respect, those rulings relating to value added tax will also be of particular importance.

The preliminary ruling procedure has achieved its greatest effectiveness for pro-economic interpretation in the goods and services tax. Indeed, it cannot be ignored that value added tax is a tax on economic events[58]. Emphasising the economic sense of the goods and services tax, the Court notes that the VAT Directive establishes a common VAT system based, in particular, on a uniform definition of taxable transactions[59] . The concept of the economic nature of VAT was first raised by the Court when analysing the meaning of the definition of a supply of goods. Pursuant to Council Directive 2006/112/EC of 28 November 2006 on the common system of value added tax (OJ 2006 L series. No. 347/1 as amended; hereinafter: Directive 112; formerly the Sixth Directive), a supply of goods means the transfer of the right to dispose of goods as owner. Thus, the provision does not refer to the familiar concept of transfer of ownership under national civil law systems. The Court held that the supply of goods within the meaning of the directive is not limited to the civil law transfer of ownership.

57 Order of the CJ of 6 March 2007, in Case C-168/06, *Ceramika Paradyż*, ECLI:EU:C:2007:139.

58 A. Bartosiewicz, *Opodatkowanie świadczeń złożonych podatkiem od towarów i usług. W: Wykładnia i stosowanie prawa podatkowego. Węzłowe problemy [Taxation of Composite Benefits with Value Added Tax. In: Interpretation and Application of Tax Law. Knotty Problems]*, B. Brzeziński (ed.), Wolters Kluwer Polska, Warsaw. pp. 276–277.

59 Judgments of the CJEU: in Joined Cases C-354/03, C-355/03 and C-484/03 Optigen and Others, paragraph 36; in Case C-255/02 Halifax and Others, ECLI:EU:C:2006:121, paragraph 48; and in Case C-653/11 Paul Newey, paragraph 39.

The transfer of the economic right to dispose of the thing as owner is relevant, provided that it gives the purchaser in practice analogous rights to the transfer of title[60]. Also subsequently, the Court has repeatedly emphasised that the concept of "supply of goods" provided for in Article 5(1) of the Sixth Directive and Article 14(1) of Directive 112 does not refer to a transfer of ownership in the form provided for by the relevant national legislation, but includes any transaction of transfer of a thing by a party who authorises the other party to dispose of that thing as if he were its owner[61] .

In the Court's view, the concept of supply is objective in nature and that it applies irrespective of the purposes and results of the transactions concerned, there being no obligation on the part of the tax administration to carry out an investigation in order to ascertain the intentions of the taxable person concerned or to take into account the intentions of an economic operator other than that taxable person acting in the same supply chain[62]. The objective nature of the transaction does not exclude the need to take into account the economic sense of the actions taken by the parties to the transaction. Indeed, economic, and commercial reality is a fundamental criterion for the application of the common VAT system to be taken into account when classifying a transaction as a "chargeable transaction" within the meaning of the VAT Directive 112[63].

The need to take into account the economic nature of VAT has been noted in domestic case law, where the view is presented that when interpreting terms used

---

60 CJEU judgment of 8 February 1998, in Case C-320/88 Shipping and Forwarding Enterprise Safe, ECLI:EU:C:1990:61.

61 Judgment of the CJEU of 14 July 2005 in Case C-435/03 British American Tobacco and Newman Shipping, ECLI:EU:C:2005:464, paragraph 35; cited judgments: in Joined Cases C-354/03, C-355/03 and C-484/03 Optigen and Others, paragraph 39; in Case C-255/02 Halifax and Others, paragraph 51; judgments: 3 June 2010, in Case C-237/ 09 De Fruytier, ECLI:EU:C:2010:316, paragraph 24; 18 July 2013, in Case C-78/12 Evita-K, ECLI:EU:C:2013:486, paragraph 33; 21 November 2013, in Case C-494/12 Dixons Retail, ECLI:EU:C:2013:758, paragraph 20.

62 Judgments of the CJEU: in Joined Cases C-354/03, C-355/03 and C-484/03 Optigen and Others, paragraphs 44–46 and also paragraphs 51, 55; in Case C-255/02 Halifax and Others, paragraphs 56, 57; in Joined Cases C-439/04 and 440/04 Kittel and Recolta Recycling, ECLI:EU:C:2006:446, paragraphs 41–44; as well as the aforementioned judgment in Case C-653/11 Paul Newey, paragraph 41; in Case C-494/12 Dixons Retail, paragraph 21.

63 CJEU judgment in Case C653/11 -Paul Newey, paragraph 42 and case law cited therein; judgment of 22 November 2018, Case C295/17 -MEO – Serviços de Comunicações e Multimédia, EU:C:2018:942, paragraph 43.

in the VAT Act, it is the economic value and effects of a given taxable activity that is decisive, and not its definition in national civil law, which is, after all, different in each Member State[64]. In the following part of the study, those VAT institutions will be discussed in which the preliminary ruling procedure applied by Polish administrative courts has most effectively contributed to taking economic reality into account in interpreting tax law.

7.4. Pro-economic Interpretation in Relation to Comprehensive Benefits

The need to take into account the economic sense of the services provided, and supplies made for VAT purposes is derived by the Supreme Administrative Court in particular with regard to complex services.

It follows from CJEU jurisprudence that each activity should, in principle, be regarded as separate and independent for VAT purposes. At the same time, however, an activity consisting – in economic terms – of a single comprehensive supply should not be artificially separated so as not to impair the functionality of the VAT system. Therefore, in order to correctly assess a given service for VAT purposes, it is first necessary to look for the characteristics of the activity in question in order to determine whether the taxable person is supplying the consumer (understood as the average consumer) with several separate supplies or with a single composite supply[65].

The Court has taken the view that a single benefit is present when several of its elements should be considered constitutive of the principal benefit. At the same time, one or more services which constitute ancillary acts share the legal fate of the principal supply. The same is true if two or more supplies made by the taxable person to the consumer, understood as the average consumer, are so closely linked that they objectively constitute a single inseparable economic supply, the separation of which would be artificial. The Court stated in particular that: "*Where two or more supplies (or activities) made by a taxable person to a consumer, defined as the average consumer, are so closely linked that they objectively form, from an economic point of view, a single economic supply, separation of which would be artificial, all those supplies or activities constitute a single supply for the purposes of the application of value added tax*"[66].

---

64 Judgment of the Supreme Administrative Court of 26.03.2015, file ref. I FSK 2174/13.

65 Judgment of the CJEU of 25 February 1999,in Case C-349/96 CPP, ECLI:EU:C:1999:93.

66 Judgment of the CJEU of 27 October 2005,in Case C-41/04 Levob Verzekeringen BV, ECLI:EU:C:2005:649.

The relevant question in terms of composite benefits was whether the service of insurance could be considered as a separate service from the service of leasing. In particular, the Court considered that the service of insuring a leased asset and the leasing service are, in principle, separate and independent services for VAT purposes.[67] In the grounds for its judgment, the Court recalled its previous case law, which shows that in order to decide whether services are to be treated as separate or as inextricably linked to each other, it is determined by how they are viewed from an economic point of view. He recalled that not only should each transaction in principle be considered as separate and independent, but also that a transaction consisting of a single benefit in economic terms should not be artificially separated[68]. In order to determine whether the benefits constitute several independent benefits or a single benefit, it is necessary to look for elements specific to the transaction under consideration and to take into account the totality of the circumstances in which the transaction takes place.

The preliminary question on the taxation rules for benefits related to rental services also contributed to shaping the national line of jurisprudence on viewing benefits as either complex or separate.

In its analysis in the judgment of 16 April 2015, Wojskowa Agencja Mieszkaniowa in Warsaw, C42/14, the Court, as in the BGŻ Leasing case, referred to the transaction-specific elements[69] and also took into account the interests of the service recipients[70] .

The CJEU takes the view that, in the framework of the cooperation established under Article 267 TFEU, in order to determine whether a commercial transaction constitutes several independent supplies or a single supply for VAT purposes, the national court must determine the characteristic elements of the transaction concerned, taking into account the economic purpose of that transaction and the interest of the recipients of that supply, and making an overall and definitive assessment of the facts in that regard[71]. Thus, in order to determine whether

---

67 Judgment of the CJEU of 17 January 2013, in Case C- 224/11, BGŻ Leasing, EU:C:2013:15.

68 Judgment of the CJEU, in Case C- 224/11, BGŻ Leasing, para 31 and case law cited therein.

69 Judgment of the CJEU of 16 April 2015, in Case C42/14, Wojskowa Agencja Mieszkaniowa w Warszawie, EU:C:2015:229, para. 32.

70 Judgment of the CJEU, in Case C42/14, para 35, Wojskowa Agencja Mieszkaniowa w Warszawie.

71 Judgment of the CJEU of 18 October 2018, in Case C153/17, Volkswagen Financial Services (UK), EU:C:2018:845, paras 32, 33 and case law cited therein.

a transaction which involves multiple supplies constitutes a single transaction for VAT purposes, the Court takes into account the economic purpose of that transaction[72].

The Supreme Administrative Court, accepting the position of the CJEU, examines whether the specified services are so closely linked to each other that they form a single whole in economic terms. In this respect, it refers to the economic sense of the service provided by the taxpayer. In particular, the Supreme Administrative Court held that if the task of the taxpayer is to organise the investment and construction process and the sale of real estate, then the activities performed as part of the agreement on the management of the investment process constitute one inseparable whole taxed at a single VAT rate[73] .

7.5. The Importance of Pro-business Interpretation in Qualifying Events as Tax Abuse

The economic sense of transactions is often examined by administrative courts when reviewing whether, in certain factual situations, transactions can be seen as an abuse of tax law.

According to CJEU jurisprudence, it is inherent in the VAT mechanism that a fictitious acquisition transaction cannot give rise to any right to deduct that tax, since such a transaction cannot have any connection with transactions charged with output tax[74]. Accordingly, in the first instance, the denial of a taxpayer's right of deduction may be justified by the finding that the evidence of the actual performance of the transaction relied upon to justify the right of deduction has not been produced[75]. As regards the assessment of the evidence presented to establish the existence of a taxable transaction, this must be carried out by the national court in accordance with the evidentiary rules of national

72 Judgments of the CJEU of 19 November 2009, in Case C461/08, Don Bosco Onroerend Goed, EU:C:2009:722, paragraph 39; of 28 October 2010, in Case C-175/09, Axa UK, EU:C:2010:646, paragraph 23; of 27 September 2012, and in Case C392/11, Field Fisher Waterhouse, EU:C:2012:597, paragraph 23.

73 Judgment of the Supreme Administrative Court of 24 October 2023, reference I FSK 2201/18.

74 Judgment of the CJEU of 8 May 2019, in EN.SA., C712/17, EU:C:2019:374, paras 24, 25 and case law cited therein.

75 Judgment of the CJEU of 25 May 2023, in Case C – 114/22, paragraph 33, ECLI:EU:C:2023:430.

law, by making an overall assessment of all the elements and facts of the case[76]. Therefore, the Supreme Administrative Court in particular considered that invoices for the sale of goods or the provision of services should be regarded as empty, not generating a right to deduct input tax, if the transactions are devoid of economic sense (purpose)[77] or such sense is not present at all in the economic activity carried out by the taxpayer[78]. The economic sense is also emphasised when qualifying a transaction as a carousel fraud. The jurisprudence emphasises that an essential element of carousel fraud is the economic senselessness of the participation in the transaction of many entities, most of which do not bring any tangible benefit, apart from merely driving away transactions involving so-called "missing traders" and entities that have to declare an intra-Community supply of goods and claim tax refunds[79].

Another area, in terms of abuse of rights, where the economic aspect should be considered crucial, remains sham transactions resulting in the denial of the right to deduct input tax. The case law of the Supreme Administrative Court has not identified such transactions only with situations that do not reflect an economic purpose. Against this background, in the jurisprudence as well as in the doctrine, different positions could be found regarding the assessment of the tax consequences of such an arrangement of civil-legal relations, which leads to the avoidance or reduction of taxation. According to some views, civil law agreements could not lead to tax avoidance or reduction of tax liabilities and limit the application of tax law[80]. According to others, the provisions of the tax law do not contain norms prohibiting or prescribing certain behaviour, but only norms defining the consequences of behaviour under this law[81].

---

76 Judgment of the CJEU of 6 September 2012, Mecsek-Gabona, C- 273/11, EU:C:2012:547, para 53; CJEU order of 9 January 2023, A.T.S. 2003, C- 289/22, EU:C:2023:26, para 46 and case law cited therein.

77 E.g. judgments of the Supreme Administrative Court: of 24 March 2020, file ref. I FSK 109/20; of 17 May 2023, file ref. I FSK 82/23, of 20 October 2022, file ref. I FSK 1347/18.

78 Judgment of the Supreme Administrative Court of 24 March 2023, file ref. I FSK 110/20.

79 Judgment of the Provincial Administrative Court in Warsaw of 30 March 2021, case file III SA/Wa 1575/20.

80 Cf. the judgment of the Supreme Administrative Court of 7 November 1991, ref. SA/Po 1198/91, OSP 1993 no. 10 item 204; A. Gomułowicz, *Relationship of civil law with tax law*, Przegląd Podatkowy 1996 no. 11 p. 3.

81 Judgment of the Supreme Administrative Court of 29 May 2002, ref. III SA 2602/00, POP 2003 no. 1, pp. 11–13 with gloss by B. Brzezinski, pp. 83–85.

In the light of the Court's case law, there can be no doubt that Article 88(3a)(4)(c) of the Value Added Tax Act of 11 March 2004[82] (hereinafter also referred to as the VAT Act), by its normative content, places emphasis on the need to prove the invalidity of the disputed transaction from the point of view of civil law, and not on the abuse of the tax law, which is relevant to depriving the taxpayer of the right to deduct, and is not reflected in the content of this regulation. A doubt therefore arose as to whether the normative construction of the national provision, referring only to the institution of nullity of the transaction in the light of the provisions of national civil law, constitutes a correct basis for excluding the right to deduct the tax associated with it. This issue, as a result of a preliminary question from the Supreme Administrative Court[83] was assessed by the CJEU in its judgment of 25 May 2023[84]. In that judgment, the Court stated that "Articles 167, 168(a), 178(a) and Art. 273 of Directive 112, in the light of the principles of fiscal neutrality and proportionality, must be interpreted as precluding national legislation under which a taxable person is deprived of the right to deduct input VAT on the sole ground that a taxable economic transaction is considered to be sham and invalid under national civil law, without it being necessary to show that the conditions for categorising that transaction as bogus under European Union law are fulfilled or, if the transaction in question has actually been carried out, that it is the result of VAT fraud or abuse of rights." This ruling related to trade marks. The Court held that the principle of the prohibition of abusive practices, applicable in the VAT field, prohibits only wholly artificial constructions detached from economic reality and created for the sole purpose of obtaining a tax advantage, the granting of which would be contrary to the objectives of Directive 112 (paragraph 46 of the grounds of the judgment and the case law cited therein).

It follows that the right to deduct may only be denied if the transaction constituted a fraud or sham transaction resulting in an abuse of the right. Only wholly artificial constructions detached from economic reality and created with the sole purpose of obtaining a tax advantage are considered by the Court to be sham transactions resulting in an abuse of the right. As a consequence of the CJEU's case law in case C-114/22, the most recent judgments of the Supreme Administrative Court state that, in the context of the tax on goods and services,

---

82 Journal of Laws of 2011. No. 177 item 1054 as amended.

83 Order of the Supreme Administrative Court of 23 November 2021, file ref. I FSK 2310/19.

84 Judgment of the CJEU, in case C-114/22.

an abuse of the right within the meaning of civil law should be understood as behaviour contrary to the economic and social purpose of the right to deduct tax expressed in the tax law, due to the fact that, despite the formal fulfilment of the prerequisite for the exercise of this right, it was formed essentially with the aim of obtaining a tax advantage, the granting of which would be contrary to the purpose of this norm[85] .

7.6. The Effect of the Contractual Provisions of the Parties to the Transaction on Tax Liabilities

It was worth checking whether the economic treatment of the transaction allows the content of the contractual provisions of the parties to the transaction to be taken into account in interpreting the tax law.

In business transactions, contracts between the parties play an important role. In them, the mutual rights and obligations of the parties to the transaction are shaped. It should be presumed that since contracts may shape the essential elements of the transaction, they may also affect certain elements of the tax obligation. However, in the earlier jurisprudence of the administrative courts, the principle has been formed that tax obligations cannot be modified by civil law contracts[86]. Thus, by a civil contract, concluded within the limits of freedom of contract in the sense of civil law, the essential elements of the tax obligation cannot be shaped. A tax obligation arises in the conditions defined by the law somewhat automatically, i.e., independently of the will and intention of the subjects subject to this obligation.

In particular, the Supreme Administrative Court decided to verify the extent to which contractual provisions may affect the formation of VAT rates in the case of the letting of immovable property. It therefore asked the Court whether the VAT Directive should be interpreted as meaning that, in circumstances such as those in the main proceedings, the letting of immovable property and the supply of services connected with that letting must be regarded as a single supply

85 Judgment of the Supreme Administrative Court of 7.11.2023, file ref. I FSK 40/20.

86 Judgments of the Supreme Administrative Court of: 12 July 2006 file ref. II FSK 995/05, 8 February 2013 file ref. I FSK 477/12 13 March 2014 file ref. I FSK 614/13, and judgments: Provincial Administrative Court in Warsaw of 19 December 2011, file ref. III SA/Wa 897/11, Provincial Administrative Court in Warsaw of 7 October 2015, file ref. III SA/Wa 4019/14, Provincial Administrative Court in Poznań of 6 November 2009, file ref. I SA/Po 479/09, Provincial Administrative Court in Wrocław of 29 May 2015, file ref. I SA/Wr 329/15.

wholly exempt from VAT or as several independent supplies assessed separately in terms of their VAT treatment[87]. As the Court pointed out, the referring court sought in particular to ascertain the relevance, in those circumstances, of the fact, first, that the tenancy agreement provides that the landlord is obliged to provide the services in question to the tenant even though, in principle, those services could, at least in part, be provided by a third party and, second, that the tenant's non-payment of additional charges for the tenancy gives the landlord the right to terminate the tenancy agreement[88].

In response to a question from the referring court, the Court found that, where the rented property appears objectively, from an economic point of view, to constitute a single unit with the accompanying services, the latter may be regarded as a single supply together with the rent. In the Court's view, this may be the case, in particular, with turnkey office leases, ready for use, together with the supply of utilities and certain other benefits, and with short-term leases of property, for example for holidays or for professional reasons, which are made available with these benefits without the possibility of separating them[89]. The Court has indicated how the contractual provisions of the parties will allow the provision of utilities to be treated as separate from the rental service. This will be the case if the tenant can choose the providers or uses of the goods or services in question, the benefits relating to those goods or services. In particular, if the tenant can decide on its consumption of water, electricity or heat, which can be ascertained by setting up individual meters and invoiced on that basis. As for services, such as cleaning of common parts of jointly owned properties, they may be considered separate from the rental if they can be arranged by each tenant individually or by tenants jointly and if, in all cases, the invoices issued to the tenant show the supply of these goods and services on items separate from the rental[90].

The Court also indicated which contractual provisions do not affect the perception of the benefits as separate. In particular, the fact that non-payment of additional rental charges enables the landlord to terminate the lease does not in any way prevent the benefits to which those charges relate from being regarded as separate benefits from the lease. Similarly, the fact that the tenant

87 Order of the Supreme Administrative Court of 22 October 2013, file ref. I FSK 1389/12.

88 Judgment of the CJEU in case C-42/14 Wojskowa Agencja Mieszkaniowa.

89 Judgment of the CJEU in Case C-42/14 Wojskowa Agencja Mieszkaniowa, para 42.

90 Judgment of the CJEU in Case C-42/14 Wojskowa Agencja Mieszkaniowa, paragraph 39.

has the option to obtain these benefits from an entity of his or her choice is not conclusive, since the possibility that the elements of one benefit will in other circumstances be provided separately is closely related to the idea of a single complex transaction[91].

In the Wojskowa Agencja Mieszkaniowa judgment, the CJEU made clear the need to take into account the provisions of the contracts when qualifying the acts. The Court considered it necessary to examine whether, on the basis of the contract, the tenant and the landlord primarily intend, respectively, to obtain and make available the lease of the property and only auxiliary intend, respectively, to obtain and provide other benefits, even if they are necessary for the use of the property[92].

The CJEU judgment in the case of Wojskowa Agencja Mieszkaniowa in Warsaw, C-42/14, is significant for European case law. By referring directly to the wording of the contract, the Court has developed a practice affecting the tax treatment of rental benefits and accompanying services.

In the light of the above judgment of the CJEU in the case of Wojskowa Agencja Mieszkaniowa in Warsaw, in the jurisprudence of Polish administrative courts the view has developed that the supply of water, electricity, heat and waste disposal should – as a rule – be regarded as separate and independent from contracts of lease of real estate (premises), which means that there are no grounds for concluding that these supplies fall within the concept of "provision of services connected with immovable property", as they do not have a direct (close) connection with the immovable property in question, due to the fact that immovable property is not a constitutive element of such – separate from the lease of immovable property – transactions. A different conclusion, in the opinion of the Supreme Administrative Court's view, could only be drawn if the elements of the supply, including those indicating the economic reasons for concluding the contract, were so closely linked to the lease of the premises (real estate) that they would objectively form only one indivisible economic supply, the separation of which would be artificial[93].

---

91 Judgment of the CJEU in Case C-42/14 Wojskowa Agencja Mieszkaniowa, paragraphs 40 and 41.

92 Judgment of the CJEU in Case C-42/14 Wojskowa Agencja Mieszkaniowa, paragraph 37.

93 E.g. Judgment of the Supreme Administrative Court of 14 March 2023, file ref. I FSK 205/20.

Case C -42-14 is not the only example in which the Supreme Administrative Court has asked the CJEU to verify what effect the contractual provisions that bind the parties together may have on tax liabilities.

The issue of the effect of contractual provisions on the moment of obligation was also reviewed in relation to construction services. The Tribunal was responding to a question from a national court relating to the point at which tax liability arises in respect of construction services. In this case, it was examining whether the moment when tax liability arises is affected by the fact that the parties to the transaction agreed that, in order for the payment of remuneration for the construction or construction/assembly works to be made, it was necessary for the contracting authority to express its acceptance of their performance in the protocol of acceptance of those works[94]. In the case before the referring court, the dispute concerned the point in time at which the construction services were performed and, in particular, whether, in view of the provisions found in the contracts it concluded, that point in time could only occur after acceptance of the works by the contracting authority, notwithstanding the fact that they had actually been performed earlier. The Court noted that although, in relation to the supply of construction or installation services, they are generally considered to be completed on the date of material completion of the works, economic and commercial reality is the basic criterion for the application of the common VAT system, which must be taken into account[95]. Due to contractual provisions reflecting the economic and commercial reality of the field in which the service is performed, the Court allowed for the possibility that the service would only be considered to be performed after the date of material completion of the service, following the fulfilment of certain conditions inherent in the service and critical to ensuring its completeness. In relation to construction services, this was of such significance that a supply of services is only taxed if there is a legal relationship between the provider and the recipient of the service in which reciprocal services are exchanged, as the payment received by the provider is a true reflection of the value for the separate service provided to the recipient of the service[96] . In the Court's view, in view of the contractual provisions which provide for the right of the contracting authority to verify the conformity of the construction or building work performed before it is accepted, and the service provider's obligation to make the necessary adjustments so that the result actually corresponds to what

94 Judgment of the CJEU of 2 May 2019, in Case C-224/18 Budimex, ECLI:EU:C:2019:347.

95 Judgment of the CJEU in Case C-224/18 Budimex, paragraph 27.

96 Judgment of the CJEU in Case C-224/18 Budimex, paragraphs 29 and 30.

was agreed, it may not be impossible to determine the taxable amount and the amount of tax due before the work is accepted by the contracting authority[97]. On the other hand, to the extent that it is not possible to determine the consideration payable by the recipient of the service prior to his acceptance of the construction or building services, the tax on those services may not become chargeable before that acceptance[98]. Ultimately, the CJEU concluded that, in these circumstances and to the extent that the acceptance of works was agreed in the contract for the provision of services – where such a condition reflects the norms and standards existing in the field in which the service is performed, which is subject to verification by the court of reference – this formality must be considered to be covered as such by the service and is therefore decisive for the conclusion that the service in question has actually been performed[99].

It follows from the above judgment of the Court in the Budimex case that, to the extent that the acceptance of works has been agreed in a contract for the provision of services – where such a condition reflects the norms and standards existing in the field in which the service is performed – it must be considered that this formality is, as such, covered by the service and that it is therefore decisive for considering that the service in question has actually been performed.

Thus, not only the relevant contractual provisions, but also the norms and standards existing in the field in which the service is performed, i.e., business practice, proved to be crucial. It is normal practice that construction and building services are performed on the basis of a previously concluded contract specifying, among other things, the scope of such a service, the conditions concerning its performance, the deadline for performance and the method of financial settlement. In these contracts, the contracting authority usually reserves the right to examine the correctness of the performance of the service before accepting it, which may result in the need for the contractor to perform additional actions to ensure that the contracted service is performed in accordance with the mutually agreed terms. The above characteristics of the services are reflected, inter alia, in the contractual provisions defining precisely the moment of "takeover" of the performed works (construction service) by the ordering party (purchaser of the service). According to commonly concluded contracts –, the works will be taken over by the ordering party when they are completed in accordance with the contract. In business practice, a so-called acceptance protocol (takeover

97 Judgment of the CJEU in Case C-224/18 Budimex, paragraph 31.
98 Judgment of the CJEU in Case C-224/18 Budimex, paragraph 34.
99 Judgment of the CJEU in Case C-224/18 Budimex, paragraph 35.

certificate for the works) is used. The time when the works are completed is then deemed to be the time when the "take-over certificate for the works" is issued or when it should have been issued. Only from this point onwards does the responsibility for the custody of the works pass to the client.

The preliminary question concerning the moment when tax obligation arises in the case of construction works[100] has significantly contributed to a change in the line of rulings of the Supreme Administrative Court. The Supreme Administrative Court's jurisprudence assumed that a construction service or a construction and installation service should be deemed to be performed at the moment of actual completion of construction works or a part thereof (in the case of a service that is partially accepted), performed in accordance with the project and principles of technical knowledge, notified by the contractor to their recipient, which moment should be distinguished from the drawing up and signing of a take-over protocol aimed at documenting and confirming the moment of actual completion of the works or a part thereof[101].

The current case law of the Supreme Administrative Court takes the view that a service may be deemed to have been performed upon acceptance of the works if such a condition has been provided for in a contract for the provision of construction and construction and installation services, where such a condition reflects the norms and standards existing in the field in which such a service is performed[102].

The Budimex ruling did not only result in a change of jurisprudence regarding the moment when tax liability arises. The Supreme Administrative Court held that the ruling may also be useful with regard to verification of the taxpayer's due diligence in selecting a contractor in the case of construction services for the performance of which the taxpayer intends to exercise the right to deduct input tax. As noted by the Court, taking into account the existence of the so-called good faith on the part of the tax deductor requires a determination that the norms and standards existing in the field to which the service relates have been observed. Thus, the tax authority, when assessing the so-called good faith

100 Order of the Supreme Administrative Court of 28 November 2017, file ref. I FSK 65/16.

101 Judgments of the Supreme Administrative Court of: 18 April 2013, file ref. I FSK 943/12; 6 July 2017, file ref. I FSK 2148/15.

102 Judgments of the Supreme Administrative Court of: 18 July 2019, file ref. I FSK 65/16; 10 October 2019, file ref. I FSK 1455/17.

of the taxpayer, may have regard to the standards relating to the specific field of economic activity[103].

On the one hand, the CJEU judgment in the *Budimex case continues the position taken in* CJEU *case* C-42/14, Wojskowa Agencja Mieszkaniowa, according to which contractual terms may be relevant in the qualification of activities for VAT purposes. However, on the other side of the *Budimex judgment, the Court explicitly made the consideration of contractual terms dependent on the economic practice in the relevant field of services. The differences between the above judgments can be explained in view of the fact that in the case* C-42/14, Wojskowa Agencja Mieszkaniowa, the Court was deciding the question of the level of rates in the case of rental and ancillary services. On the other hand, in Budimex, C-224/18, the CJEU ruled on the possibility of postponing the moment of tax liability in the case of construction services that require verification by the contracting authority. In the case of complex supplies, such as rental services, the transaction-specific elements are important. These lease-specific elements were taken into account by the CJEU, holding that it must be examined in particular whether, on the basis of the contract, the tenant and the landlord primarily intend, respectively, to obtain and make available the lease of the property and only auxiliary intend, respectively, to obtain and provide other services, even if they are necessary for the use of the property[104]. The dependence of the contractual terms on economic practice in the Budimex case, on the other hand, stems from the fact that the practice in the field of construction services may develop differently in different countries and may be influenced by the different standards of construction work adopted by the contracting parties in a given transaction.

Both the Budimex and Wojskowa Agencja Mieszkaniowa judgments have played an important role in shaping the jurisprudence of administrative courts about the need to take economic reality into account when interpreting value added tax regulations.

103 Judgment of the Supreme Administrative Court of 14 May 2021, reference I FSK 580/21.

104 R. Wiatrowski, *Gospodarczy cel zawarcia umowy jako kryterium oceny opodatkowania transakcji podatkiem od towarów i usług* [Economic Purpose of Concluding a Contract as a Criterion for Assessing the Taxation of a Transaction with Goods and Services Tax], "Analizy i Studia CASP", 2021, no. 1(11), pp. 35–49.

7.7. Economic Independence as a Premise for Qualifying Entities as Taxpayers

The use of the preliminary ruling procedure allowed the Supreme Administrative Court to form a position on which entities could be considered to be sufficiently independent to be considered as independent VAT taxpayers.

In particular, the Supreme Administrative Court raised doubts as to which organisational units of municipalities have sufficient autonomy to be regarded as independent VAT taxpayers. Initially, the literature on the subject as well as the jurisprudence permitted the view that not only municipalities, but also their local government units and budgetary establishments could be deemed to be separate VAT taxpayers[105].

The position of the Supreme Administrative Court changed substantially as a result of a resolution of the Supreme Administrative Court, which held that, under national law, a municipal budget unit is not a VAT taxpayer due to its lack of independence in conducting business activities. The Supreme Administrative Court noted that a municipality, as a basic unit of local self-government, has legal personality and is entitled to property and other property rights, while a municipal budget unit is an organisational unit without legal personality. Denying sufficient autonomy to a budgetary unit, the Supreme Administrative Court pointed, inter alia, to the following circumstances

- The establishment, remit, merger or abolition of such a unit is decided by the municipality,
- a municipal budget unit has no property of its own, but manages a certain part of the municipality's property that has been entrusted to it by the municipality,
- any activity that may be subject to VAT is carried out on behalf of and for the account of the municipality within the limit of the funds allocated to the entity by the municipality in the budget resolution for the year in question,
- the expenses of such a unit are paid directly from the municipal budget and the income is paid into the municipal account,
- the amount of expenditure of a municipal budgetary unit is therefore not related to the amount of income it has earned, which, moreover, it cannot dispose of,

105 S. Owczarczuk, Ewolucja statusu gminy jako podatnika z perspektywy 25 lat funkcjonowania podatku od towarów i usług w Polsce – wnioski de lege lata i postulaty de lege ferenda *[Evolution of the Status of a Municipality as a Taxpayer from the Perspective of 25 Years of the Functioning of the Goods and Services Tax in Poland – conclusions de lege lata and postulates de lege ferenda]*, ST 2020, no. 6, pp. 7–17.

- the budgetary unit is also not liable for damage caused by its activities, this liability is borne solely by the municipality.

However, the resolution I FPS 1/13 did not end the disputes concerning the perception of budgetary units as VAT taxpayers. The Supreme Administrative Court referred a question to the CJEU for a preliminary ruling on whether an organisational unit of a municipality may be regarded as a taxable person for VAT in a situation where it carries out activities in a capacity other than that of a public authority within the meaning of Article 13 of Directive 112, even though it does not meet the condition of autonomy (independence)?[106]. Ultimately, the CJEU determined that budget entities cannot be considered taxable persons for value added tax because they do not meet the criterion of autonomy provided for in Article 9(1) of Directive 112 The CJEU determined in its judgment in Case C-276/14[107] .

The judgment of the CJ in case C-276/14, Gmina Wrocław contributed to a significant change in the line of rulings of administrative courts concerning another local government unit, i.e., a budgetary establishment. Initially, the jurisprudence presented a view on the "impaired" VAT tax subjectivity of a local government budget establishment: sufficiently separate and independent to be a taxpayer in relation to the local government unit in terms of performing its own tasks (municipal services) for third parties[108]. The Supreme Administrative Court also expressed its position on the subjective separateness of budget establishments, on the grounds of VAT, in the justification of the resolution of 24 June 2013, I FPS 1/13, in which it was stated that the legal and tax subjectivity of local government budget establishments is constituted by a separate financial regime concerning these entities, different from that concerning municipal budget entities, and, moreover, the explicit identification of establishments as entities performing tasks of municipalities within the framework of municipal economy allows them to be recognised as taxpayers of the tax on goods and services.

The position of the Supreme Administrative Court with regard to budgetary establishments changed significantly after the judgment of the CJ in case C-276/

106 Order of the Supreme Administrative Court of 10 December 2013, file ref. I FSK 311/12.

107 Judgment of the CJEU of 29 September 2015, in Case C-276/14, Gmina Wrocław, ECLI:EU:C:2015:431.

108 Judgment of the Supreme Administrative Court of 18 October 2011, file ref. I FSK 1369/10.

14, Gmina Wrocław. The task of deciding whether a budgetary establishment is an independent VAT taxpayer was undertaken by the Supreme Administrative Court in the resolution of a seven-judge panel of 26 October 2015, I FPS 4/15[109]. It follows from the justification of the resolution that, having regard to the judgment of the CJ in Case C-276/14, Gmina Wrocław, when assessing whether a local government budgetary establishment is an independent entity, the Supreme Administrative Court examined whether a local government budgetary establishment is subordinated to a municipality when performing its tasks. In particular, it considered it important whether the local government budgetary establishment performs its activities in its own name, on its own account and on its own responsibility, and whether it bears the economic risk connected with the performance of its activities. With the above in mind, the Supreme Administrative Court stated that:

- a local government budgetary establishment has no legal personality, as it acts in the name of and on behalf of the entity that created it, and the head of the establishment acts single-handedly on the basis of a power of attorney;
- a self-government budgetary establishment carries out only the local authority's own tasks in the field of municipal management in the nature of public utility activities;
- the allocation of property to a local government budgetary establishment is of an organisational nature only; the property remains under the direct authority of the local government unit, which determines the rules for the management of the property allocated to the establishment;
- responsibility for the liabilities of the local government budgetary establishment is borne by the local government unit that created it; the local government unit also assumes the liabilities of the budgetary establishment in the event of its liquidation.

In view of the above, the Supreme Administrative Court stated that in the light of the criteria for independence of a taxpayer indicated in the judgment C-276/14, Gmina Wrocław, it cannot be assumed that a local government budgetary establishment performs economic activity in its own name, on its own account and on its own responsibility, and that it bears the economic risk connected with the conduct of economic activity. In the resolution, the Supreme Administrative Court took into account that in order to assess the independence of an entity as

109 Resolution of the Supreme Administrative Court of 26 October 2015, file ref. I FPS 4/15.

a VAT taxpayer, it should be considered important whether the person performs the activity in its own name, on its own account and on its own responsibility, and whether it bears the economic risk related to the conduct of the activity. In the Supreme Administrative Court's opinion, the insufficient independence of a budgetary establishment is evidenced by the fact that a local government budgetary establishment is established to perform the local government's own tasks in the area of municipal management, acting in this respect on its behalf, as a separate organisational unit, relying on the municipality's assets under permanent management, which means that these assets remain the property of this unit and are used to perform its statutory tasks – only for pragmatic reasons – through this establishment.

The Supreme Administrative Court also decided to verify whether spouses may arrange their mutual relations with each other so as to be separate VAT taxpayers within the framework of one agricultural holding. The Supreme Administrative Court decided to address the question whether Art. 9, 295 and 296 of the VAT Directive 112 must be interpreted as precluding the practice of a Member State which excludes the possibility of considering spouses who carry out agricultural activities on a single holding using matrimonial property as separate taxable persons for VAT, even where it is possible to separate the property which each spouse uses for the purposes of his or her own activity, with the consequence that under this practice, in circumstances where the spouses carry out agricultural activity under the flat-rate scheme for farmers, the election by one of the spouses to tax his or her activity under the general VAT rules causes the other spouse to lose his or her flat-rate farmer status[110]. The jurisprudence of the Supreme Administrative Court prior to the referral of the question excluded the possibility of considering spouses carrying out agricultural activity within the framework of one holding with the use of property covered by marital joint property as separate VAT taxpayers[111].

In answering the Supreme Administrative Court's question concerning the economic relations of spouses who run an agricultural holding covered by marital community of property, the Court interpreted Articles 9, 295 and 296 of Directive 112 as precluding a practice of a Member State which excludes the possibility of considering spouses who carry out an agricultural activity

110 Order of the Supreme Administrative Court of 22 July 2020, file ref. I FSK 2024/17.

111 Cf. the judgments of the Supreme Administrative Court of 29 May 2014, file ref. I FSK 757/13, of 27.10.2015, file ref. I FSK 546-550/14, of 5 July 2016, file ref. I FSK 181-183/15.

on a single holding using property covered by marital community of property as separate taxable persons for value added tax (VAT) where each of those spouses carries out an economic activity independently. On the other hand, the Court considers that those provisions do not preclude, in circumstances where the spouses carry out that agricultural activity under the flat-rate scheme for farmers, the fact that one spouse chooses to tax his or her activity under the normal VAT scheme from causing the other spouse to lose his or her flat-rate farmer status, if, after an examination of the specific situation, that effect proves necessary in order to counter the risk of fraud and abuse, which cannot be excluded by the presentation of appropriate evidence by the spouses, or if the exercise of that activity by those spouses in an independent manner, and so that each of them does so on the basis of the general VAT rules, does not give rise to administrative difficulties in comparison with the situation of coexistence on the part of the said spouses of two different statuses[112]. In this judgment, the CJEU drew attention to previous case law, which shows that a person who carries out an agricultural activity on a farm that he owns together with his spouse as part of a matrimonial community of property has the status of a taxable person when that activity is carried out in an independent manner, that is, on his own account and under his own responsibility, bearing the economic risk of carrying out his activity himself[113]. As an important indication that the spouses are engaged in separate independent economic activities, the Court pointed to the fact that the spouses separately manage the means of breeding, as the breeding is separate from an economic, financial and organisational point of view. In that regard, the Court concludes, at the same time, that the mere fact that those spouses carry out their activities as part of a single agricultural holding which they own in the context of a marital community of property is irrelevant[114]. In the case before the Court, however, the key fact was that one of the spouses carried out their activities under the general VAT rules, while the other spouse intends to remain under the flat-rate scheme for farmers. Therefore, the Tribunal set out to examine whether a Member State, in order to avoid the coexistence of two different statuses on the part of the spouses, could provide that the resignation of one spouse from the flat-rate scheme for farmers would result in the other spouse losing his or her status as a flat-rate farmer[115]. The Tribunal concludes that this requires an examination of whether, in the light of the specific situation,

112 Judgment of the CJEU of 22 March 2022, in Case C697/20-, W.G., ECLI:EU:C:2022:210.
113 Judgment of the CJEU in Case C697/20, paragraph 24.
114 Judgment of the CJEU in Case C697/20, para 25.
115 Judgment of the CJEU in case C697/20, para 30.

the loss of the other spouse's status as a flat-rate farmer is necessary to counter the risk of fraud and abuse, which cannot be ruled out by the spouses providing adequate evidence showing, in particular, that each of them carries out his or her activities independently[116].

As a result of the judgment in case C-697/20, there has been a change in the case law of the Supreme Administrative Court. According to the new jurisprudence, without the risk of abuse and fraud being established, it is not possible to deprive one of the spouses who jointly carry out agricultural activity on a single holding using property covered by matrimonial joint property, of the status of a flat-rate farmer, due to the fact that the other spouse is registered as a taxpayer accounting for VAT under the general rules. According to this case law, the determination of such a risk, and thus its elimination, should take place in the course of investigations, in the course of which, inter alia, the spouses may present relevant documents to be examined by the tax authorities of both instances, as well as these authorities will be able to undertake, on their own initiative, other necessary evidentiary actions[117].

The ruling in Case C-697/20 helped to shape the Supreme Administrative Court's position that each spouse carries out an independent economic activity from separate assets, despite the binding matrimonial community of law. In particular, the Supreme Administrative Court held that the transfer of an excavator-loader from the wife's business, where the item was shown as a fixed asset, to her husband's business, where it will constitute a registered fixed asset, should be deemed to be a supply of goods in the light of Article 7(1) and (2) of the VAT Act. As emphasised by the Supreme Administrative Court, the supply of goods emphasises the economic aspects of owning the goods like an owner, which in this case will be the case[118] .

---

116 Judgment of the CJEU in case C697/20, para 33.

117 Judgment of the Supreme Administrative Court of 8 September 2022, file ref. I FSK 2024/17; similar positions were also presented in other judgments of the Supreme Administrative Court: of 1 July 2022, file ref. I FSK 1006/18; of 13 July 2022, file ref. I FSK 888/20.

118 Judgment of the Supreme Administrative Court of 7 June 2023, file ref. I FSK 440/19.

7.8. Distinguish between Business and Private Property Management

Finally, it is worth pointing out that the preliminary ruling procedure of the Polish administrative courts has also helped to determine which entities carry out economic activities and which merely manage private assets.

The position of the Supreme Administrative Court was not in doubt to the extent that it was accepted that the condition for recognising that an entity is acting as a taxpayer of goods and services is to establish that it is acting as a producer, trader, service provider, logger of natural resources, farmer or as a freelancer[119]. However, the Supreme Administrative Court had doubts as to which factual circumstances demonstrate professional conduct.

In order to clarify these doubts, the Supreme Administrative Court issued a preliminary question concerning, inter alia, whether a natural person who carried out an agricultural activity on land acquired under a VAT exemption and converted into land designated for development as a result of a change in the zoning plan independent of that person's will should be regarded as a taxpayer of VAT when he sells that land[120]. The effect of the ruling in *C-180/10 and C-181/10*[121], has been to develop premises which make it possible to distinguish between activities relating to the mere exercise of the right of ownership and the exercise of an economic activity. In this respect, the case law on the trading of land and, in particular, building plots can be regarded as meaningful. The use of the preliminary ruling in Joined Cases C-180/10 and C-181/10[122] has made it possible to elaborate on the circumstances which prove organised activity on the subject of real estate trading. In particular, the Supreme Administrative Court included:

- the purchase of land for joint ownership by a person engaged in general construction and renovation and development services and in the development and sale of real estate,
- acquisition of land which, according to the local development plan, was located in a zone of land intended for economic activities,

119 Judgment by seven judges of the Supreme Administrative Court of 29 October 2007, file ref. I FPS 3/07.

120 Order of the Supreme Administrative Court of 9 March 2010, file ref. I FSK 2039/08.

121 CJ judgments: in Joined Cases C-180/10 and C-181/10, Słaby, Kuć.

122 CJ judgments: in Joined Cases C-180/10 and C-181/10, Słaby, Kuć.

- determination by decision of the conditions of development and land use for a project consisting in the construction of a residential and commercial complex and the separation of internal roads from the general area, which took place, inter alia, as a result of the applicant's efforts,
- providing the site with utilities: electricity, gas and water[123].

In another judgment, also citing the judgment cited, CJ *C-180/10 and C-181/10,* the Supreme Administrative Court stated that taking active steps in the area of real estate transactions involving means similar to those used by traders occurred in a situation where the taxpayer divided an agricultural property into 15 building plots, applied for development conditions for individual building plots, made public in the form of press advertisements information about holding building plots for sale, provided verbal information to the village mayor about the search for purchasers of building plots, took measures to supply the plot from the electricity grid, established for the benefit of each new owner an easement to cross the plot earmarked for an internal road over its entire length and width and to run all utilities to the plot through it, offered for sale several plots of land to choose from. The Supreme Administrative Court justified its approval of the views expressed in C-180/10 and C-181/10 by pointing out that the case law of the CJEU is of exceptional importance in the system of sources of EU law, and in particular pointed out that, guided, in addition to systemic and contextual arguments, by purposive and axiological arguments, i.e., the principle of conforming interpretation and the "spirit of the Treaty" – verbalises general principles of EU law[124]. The importance of the CJEU judgment in cases C-180/10 and C-181/10, is evidenced by the fact that the Supreme Administrative Court, when considering cassation appeals concerning the qualification of real estate trading as an economic activity, refers to this judgment every time. The theses contained in the CJEU judgment are the starting point in the judgments of the Supreme Administrative Court for the assessment of the facts of the cases presented to the Supreme Administrative Court.

The notion of carrying out economic activity related to real estate in the case law of the Supreme Administrative Court has not been limited solely to the supply of buildings or parts of buildings together with land and building plots requiring definition, but to all taxable activities which, carried out sporadically in

123 Judgment of the Supreme Administrative Court of 18 October 2011, file ref. I FSK 1536/10.

124 Judgment of the Supreme Administrative Court of 5 April 2017, reference I FSK 1423/15.

connection with commercial, service or production activities, are performed by a given entity[125]. The Supreme Administrative Court has, for example, held that the leasing of land constitutes an economic activity and as a service to lease real estate on one's own account, which is confirmed by the fact that the concluded lease contracts are continuous and are concluded for profit[126].

For this article, it is particularly relevant that the Supreme Administrative Court, using the position of the CJEU taken in Case C-180/10 and C-181/10, Słaby, Kuć, to define the prerequisites of economic activity, has paid particular attention to *economic reality. This is* because it identified those circumstances which are usually indicative of professional involvement.

So far, the activity of the administrative courts in launching the preliminary ruling procedure concerning the qualification of activity as the exercise of economic activity has not been exhausted. Recently, the administrative courts have referred further preliminary questions, the subject of which remains the definition of economic activity. In one of the cases, the Supreme Administrative Court asked whether a farmer who is a VAT taxpayer under the general rules, and who transfers ownership of a plot of land to the State Treasury, by way of expropriation in exchange for compensation in connection with its change of use for non-agricultural purposes, is a taxpayer obliged to account for VAT on that supply, solely on the grounds that the plot of land was used for the purposes of an agricultural activity subject to VAT[127]. In another question, the Provincial Administrative Court in Wrocław asked the CJEU, inter alia, whether a person who sells real estate, previously not used for business activity, is conducting a business activity independently, commissioning the preparation of the sale to a professional entrepreneur, who then, as the proxy of that person, undertakes a number of organised activities in order to divide and sell it for a higher price[128].

Summary

The chapter presents the impact of the preliminary rulings on the administrative courts' consideration of economic reality. The arguments therein make it possible

---

125 Judgment of the Supreme Administrative Court of 13 November 2012, file ref. I FSK 1805/11.

126 Judgment of the Supreme Administrative Court of 18 December 2014, reference I FSK 1991/13.

127 Order of the Supreme Administrative Court of 18 January 2023, file ref. I FSK 923/19.

128 Order of 28 December 2023, reference I SA/Wr 92/23.

to consider that the judgments of the CJEU in the field of value added tax have had a particular impact on pro-economic interpretation. This is due to the fact that the construction of this tax is economic in nature. It may be pointed out that the use of the preliminary ruling procedure allowed Polish administrative courts to shape the jurisprudence lines in the VAT on, inter alia, complex services, abuse of tax law, significance of contractual provisions of the parties and taxpayers of the VAT. It has also had an impact on the development of rationales to help distinguish between the management of private assets and economic activities. The launch of the preliminary ruling procedure has contributed to the formation of a pro-business line of jurisprudence of the Supreme Administrative Court. It is characterised by the fact that in interpreting the provisions of tax law, important elements of economic reality are taken into account. In this way, the preliminary ruling procedure has contributed to filling an important gap that existed in the Polish case law of administrative courts to the extent that the need to take economic reality into account was previously overlooked. The newly formed line of jurisprudence, due to its pro-economic interpretation, not only facilitated economic activity, but also made it easier to fulfil tax obligations. It has also contributed to increasing the security of those who unwittingly participate in transactions perceived as an abuse of tax law. Indeed, the result of the application of the preliminary ruling procedure is a jurisprudential practice that takes into account, in the good faith test, the economic specificities of the business transactions involved.

An analysis of the effects of the CJEU rulings in cases in which preliminary questions have been referred to the CJEU makes it possible to recognise that this procedure has contributed to taking into account the changing economic climate in the interpretation of tax law provisions by administrative courts and that, in certain circumstances, the contractual provisions of the parties to a transaction may be relevant for the determination of certain elements of tax liability.

Attention should be drawn to the activity of Polish administrative courts in submitting questions for a preliminary ruling, which is not inferior to that of other courts in the Member States. As a consequence, the use of the preliminary ruling procedure has contributed not only to the unification of the interpretation of national law in Poland, but also to the unification of its interpretation throughout the European Union.

Dominik J. Gajewski (SGH Warsaw School of Economics)

Conclusion

The present elaboration is a summary of a research project devoted to analysis of an important component of the institutional environment of the Polish economy, which is the administrative judiciary. The authors of the project, who are lawyers and economists that mostly have vast experience in the structures of the administrative judiciary, adopt an interdisciplinary perspective and use a variety of both qualitative and quantitative research methods: Starting from analysis of the normative text and the history of reforms of administrative courts, through statistical analyses, to examination of court judgements (i.e., big data research). By presenting the diverse aspects of operation of the administrative judicial system, the authors attempt to show them against the background of the economy that the entities interacting with the administrative authorities operate in; and such interactions in some cases take the form of disputes that are resolved by the court.

The analyses presented in this elaboration describe the process of transformation of the administrative judiciary, which displays improvement of its status and tendencies to expand its cognition along with the processes unfolding in the sphere of the law and the economy (e.g., Poland's accession to the European Union entailed judicial review of administrative decisions in matters related to the EU funds). At the same time, measures were taken to ensure efficiency of administrative courts and contact between the court and the citizen, which would rise up to the challenges of the present day (e.g., the level of computerisation which proved important at the time of the COVID-19 pandemic).

Analysis of the "demand" for judicial review of public administration – and so of the number of cases brought before the administrative courts – indicates that in the years 2004–2021 the number of complaints submitted to the RAC oscillated in the range between 60 and 80 thousand, which falls within the limits forecast by the authors of the concept of two-instance administrative courts. However, the significant scale of the observable changes captures attention; the factors that have considerably contributed to these changes are systemic amendments to the law (e.g., introduction of the institution of challengeable tax rulings and changes regarding the rules for organising games on slot machines) and fluctuations in the number of complaints regarding excise duty and social assistance (whose pattern prompts to reasonably hypothesize the existence of a correlation between these complaints and the cyclical fluctuations in the economy).

In the context of "supply", or rather of maintaining the capacity of the administrative court system to exercise the right to trial set out in Article 45 of the Constitution of the Republic of Poland, it should be pointed out that despite significant changes in the number of submitted complaints, the level of effectiveness of the administrative judiciary – treated as a system – is satisfactory. Even during the COVID-19 pandemic, following initial deterioration, the efficiency of the SAC and the RAC returned to its previous level (although largely due to the adopted *ad hoc* legislative solutions). However, all that was accompanied by a fundamental change in the way cases were handled; the courts were more inclined to consider a case at a closed session rather than at a hearing. Determining whether this change produced an impact on enforcement of the right to trail before the SAC and the RAC (as well as the social view of their functioning) would require separate in-depth research.

The use of quantitative analyses of a large group of individual judgements on cases concerning excise duty and VAT allowed us to trace the course of an administrative court dispute starting from the strictly economic domain (i.e., an event that has occurred within the framework of economic trade) through interaction of entities with public administration (i.e., issuing a tax decision) to the stage of a court dispute. The obtained results lead to two important conclusions.

Firstly, analysis of the time elapsed from the occurrence of economic events to the initiation of a dispute at the administrative court indicates that – as regards VAT cases – 5 years go by between the occurrence of economic events and the issue date of a decision that gets challenged at the RAC (half of the typical observations are in the 3–6 years range). The case is different with the structure of cases concerning excise duty.

Secondly, although examination of statistical data on the number of cases regarding excise duty, which were brought before the court in the years 2004–2021, justifies hypothesizing their correlation with cyclical fluctuations in the economy, its verification at the level of individual judgements (i.e., analysis of the structure of the cases in question) encourages scepticism in this regard. This result is an excellent illustration of the risks involved in arriving at hasty conclusions about the correlations between economic phenomena and the functioning of legal institutions based on aggregated statistical data. Such conclusions – when formulated for example for the purposes of draft reforms – should only have the status of a hypothesis that needs to be verified at the micro level (and development of databases, such as CBOIS, and big data techniques open up spectacular possibilities in this respect).

A more general conclusion, which can be drawn from analyses presented in Chapters three and four, is concerned with the somewhat "conditional" role that administrative courts play as a component of the institutional environment of the economy. When exercising control over the legitimacy of the activities of the public administration, they do not affect the situation of economic entities "by default". It is because a specific filter is needed in order to "trigger" judicial review and it is the strategic decisions (within the meaning of the game theory) made by private entities and the administrative authorities. In the context of tax cases arising from actual economic events, it means that, first, tax consequences of such an event must be challenged by the administrative authority, and, second, the taxpayer must file a complaint with the administrative court against the final decision of the authority. The outcome of this interaction is shaped by various factors emerging both on the side of the taxpayer and the authority (such as, e.g., goals set for it or circumstances affecting the time sequence of its actions). In other words, the role of the court as a component of the institutional environment of the economy crucially depends on the parties to the proceedings themselves, that is, the administrative authorities and the taxpayers.

It would be a cliché to say that besides the "quantitative" dimension of the functioning of the administrative judiciary (expressed with the number and structure of the cases as well as the effectiveness of their recognition), which has been analysed, the merits of how administrative court disputes are resolved is of key importance as well. And that, in turn, depends on the administrative judges' method of interpreting the law. Based on analysis of selected cases of a dialogue between the SAC and the Constitutional Tribunal as regards adjudication, the authors of Chapter 5 point out that paradoxically it is the stronger adherence to the functional interpretation (invoking intentional and teleological arguments) that better serves assurance that values such as cohesion, uniformity, and legal certainty are respected, rather than strict adherence to the textual arguments, which often correspond neither to the intention of the legislator nor to the social and economic reality that surrounds us.

Such an assertion validates research into a specific source of information about the legislative objective, namely the Regulatory Impact Assessment (RIA), which was introduced into the Polish law-making system in order to improve its rationality (including due to the use of economic analysis) within the paradigm of evidence-based policymaking. It turns out that there were judgements after 2010, which made use of the information contained in such documents.

However, it seems justified to claim that the potential of the RIA is not fully exploited in this respect.

In the last chapter it was shown that, thanks to the preliminary ruling procedure, the jurisprudence of administrative courts takes into account the economic reality in the process of interpreting the provisions of tax law. Due to the economic nature of the goods and services tax, the activity of the administrative courts in referring questions for a preliminary ruling is of particular importance in the process of interpreting provisions concerning precisely this tax. This has resulted not only in taking account of economic reality in interpreting VAT provisions, but has also contributed to the unification of jurisprudence on this tax in Poland and other European Union countries.

References

Adamiak B., *Model sądownictwa administracyjnego a funkcje sądownictwa administracyjnego* [Administrative Judicial Model versus Functions of Administrative Judiciary] in: *Polski model sądownictwa administracyjnego* [The Polish Model of Administrative Judiciary], J. Stelmasiak, J. Niczyporuk, S. Fundowicz (ed.), Lublin 2003.

Banasik P., Wyrobisko górnicze nie podlega podatkowi od nieruchomości [Mining Excavation is Not Subject to Real Property Tax]. Gloss to the Judgement of the Constitutional Tribunal of 13 September 2011, "Przegląd Podatkowy" 2011, No. 12.

Bartosiewicz A., Opodatkowanie świadczeń złożonych podatkiem od towarów i usług. W: Wykładnia i stosowanie prawa podatkowego. Węzłowe problemy [Taxation of composite benefits with value added tax. *In: Interpretation and application of tax law. Knotty problems]*, B. Brzeziński (ed.), Wolters Kluwer Polska, Warsaw.

Bielska-Brodziak A., Śladami prawodawcy faktycznego. *Materiały legislacyjne jako narzędzie wykładni prawa* [Following the Footsteps of the Actual Legislator. Legislative Materials as a Tool of Interpretation of the Law], Warsaw 2017.

Borkowski J., Jendrośka J., Orzechowski R., Zieliński A., Kodeks *postępowania administracyjnego. Komentarz* [Code of Administrative Procedure. Commentaries], Warsaw 1985.

Borkowski J., Kodyfikacja postępowania administracyjnego w Polsce [Codification of Administrative Procedure in Poland], "Studia Prawno-Ekonomiczne" 1983, Vol. XXX.

Borkowski J., Reforma polskiego sądownictwa administracyjnego [Reform of the Polish Administrative Judiciary], "Państwo i Prawo" 2002, No. 5.

Chruściak R., Prace parlamentarne nad konstytucyjnym i ustawowym uregulowaniem Naczelnego Sądu [Parliamentary Work on Constitutional and Statutory Regulation of the Supreme Administrative Court] in: *Sądownictwo administracyjne gwarantem wolności i praw obywatelskich 1980–2005* [Administrative Judiciary as the Guarantor of Civil Rights and Freedoms], J. Góral, R. Hauser, J. Trzciński (eds.), Warsaw 2005.

Dauter B., Kabat A., Niezgódka-Medek M., *Prawo o postępowaniu przed sądami administracyjnymi. Komentarz* [Law on Proceedings before Administrative Courts. Commentary], Warsaw 2016.

Dominik-Ogińska D., *Dobra wiara w podatku od wartości dodanej w orzecznictwie Trybunału Sprawiedliwości Unii Europejskiej [Good faith in value added tax in the jurisprudence of the Court of Justice of the European Union (1)*], "Przegląd Prawa Podatkowego" 2013, no. 7.

Fish S., *Is There a Text in This Class? The Authority of Interpretive Communities*, Cambridge, London 1980.

Gajewski D.J., Joński K., *Liczba skarg wnoszonych do wojewódzkich sądów administracyjnych a cyklicz-ne wahania gospodarki* [Number of Complaints Submitted to Regional Administrative Courts and Cyclical Fluctuations in the Economy], "ZNSA" 2020, No. 5.

Gajewski D.J., Joński K., *Country Note: Procedures of the Polish Tax Authorities and the VAT Gap: Evidence from Administrative Court Files*, "Intertax" 2020, Vol. 48, No. 11.

Gajewski D.J. et al., *Tendencje w polityce podatkowej w krajach Europy Środkowo-Wschodniej: obowiąz-ki podatkowe przedsiębiorców* [Trends in Tax Policy in Countries of Central and Eastern Europe: Tax Obligations of Entrepreneurs] in: *Raport SGH i Forum Ekonomicznego 2020* [Report of the Warsaw School of Economics and the Economic Forum of 2020], M. Strojny (ed.), Oficyna Wydawnicza SGH, Warsaw 2020.

Gajewski D.J. (ed.), *VAT Gap in Poland: Policy Problem and Policy Response*, Peter Lang 2024.

Garlicki L., *Polskie prawo konstytucyjne. Zarys wykładu* [Polish Constitutional Law. Outline of the Lecture], Warsaw 2009.

Gołębiowska A., Zientarski B., *Efektywność działania administracji publicznej w Polsce* [Effectiveness of Public Administration in Poland] in: *Prawo do dobrej administracji jako prawo podstawowe o randze konstytucyjnej* [Right to Good Administration as a Fundamental Right with a Constitutional Rank], Warsaw 2016.

Gomułowicz A., *Związek prawa cywilnego z prawem podatkowym* [Relationship of civil law with tax law], Przegląd Podatkowy 1996 no. 11.

Hauser R., Skoczylas A., Piątek W., Środki odwoławcze w postępowaniu sądowoadministracyjnym w świetle ustawy nowelizującej z dnia 9 kwietnia 2015 r. – analiza najistotniejszych zmian [Legal Remedies in Administrative Court Proceedings in the Context of the Amending Act of 9 April 2015. Analysis of the Most Important Changes] "Zeszyty Naukowe Sądownictwa Administracyjnego" 2015, No. 4.

Hauser R., Dziesięciolecie przekształceń ustrojowych Naczelnego Sądu Administracyjnego i jego orzecznictwa [Decade of Systemic Transformations of the Supreme Administrative Court and Its Case Law], "Samorząd Terytorialny" 2000, No. 1–2.

Hauser R., Kształtowanie się pozycji i ustroju Naczelnego Sądu Administracyjnego [Development of the Position and System of the Supreme Administrative Court], "Zeszyty Naukowe Sądownictwa Administracyjnego" 2010, No. 5–6, a jubilee edition for the 30th anniversary of the SAC 1980–2010.

Hauser R., *Rola przepisów procesowych w realizacji materialnego prawa administracyjnego* [Role of Procedural Rules in Implementation of Substantive Administrative Law] in: *Rola materialnego prawa administracyjnego a ochrona praw jednostki* [Role of Substantive Administrative Law versus Protection of the Rights of the Individual], Z. Leoński (ed.), Poznań 1998.

Hauser R., Sądownictwo administracyjne w przyszłej konstytucji [Administrative Judiciary in Future Constitution], "Ruch Prawniczy, Ekonomiczny i Socjologiczny" 1995, No. 2.

Iserzon E., Starościak J., *Prawo administracyjne w zarysie* [Outline of Administrative Law], Warsaw 1959.

Izdebski H., Sądownictwo administracyjne w Europie [Administrative Judiciary in Europe], "ZNSA" 2007, No. 4.

Jagielska M., *Skarga* [Complaint] in: *Prawo o postępowaniu przed sądami administracyjnymi. Komentarz* [Law on Proceedings before Administrative Courts. Commentary], R. Hauser, M. Wierzbowski (eds.), Warsaw 2013.

Jarzębska M., *Dochody nieujawnione jako przedmiot opodatkowania podatkiem dochodowym od osób fizycznych* [Undisclosed Income as Object of Taxation with Personal Income Tax], "Zeszyty Naukowe PWSZ w Płocku. Nauki Ekonomiczne" 2016, Vol. XXIV.

Jaśkowska M., Masternak M., Ochendowski E., *Postępowanie sądowoadministracyjne* [Administrative Court Proceedings], Warsaw 2004.

Jędrzejczyk Z., Kukuła K., Skrzypek J., *Badania operacyjne w przykładach i zadaniach* [Examples of Operational Research and Exercises], Wydawnictwo Naukowe PWN, Warsaw 2015.

Joński K., Rogowski W., *Legislative Inflation in Poland: Bird's Eye view on Three Decades after the 1989 Breakthrough*, "The Journal of Legislative Studies" 2022, DOI: 10.1080/13572334.2022.2052465

Kalinowski M., *Granice legalności unikania opodatkowania w polskim systemie podatkowym* [Limits of the Legality of Tax Avoidance in the Polish Tax System], Toruń 2001.

Kamiński M., Orzekanie merytoryczne sądów administracyjnych. Uwagi na tle szwajcarskiego, austriackiego i niemieckiego systemu prawnego [Substantive Case Law of Administrative Courts. Comments in the Context of the Swiss, Austrian, and German System of the Law] in: *Przyszłość sądownictwa administracyjnego w Polsce z uwzględnieniem tendencji europejskich* [Future of Administrative Judiciary in Poland, Including European Trends], "Biuletyn RPO" 2012, No. 75.

Karwat P., *Obejście prawa podatkowego* [Circumvention of Tax Law], Warsaw 2002.

Kijowski D., Płoskonka J., Prutis S., Srocki S., *Model ustrojowy sądownictwa administracyjnego. Raport Programu Reformy Administracji Publicznej* [Systemic Model of Administrative Judiciary. Report on the Programme of Reform of Public Administration], Warsaw 1999.

Kociak N., *Wykładnia gospodarcza w orzecznictwie sądów administracyjnych* [Economic Interpretation in the Jurisprudence of Administrative Courts], Przegląd Podatkowy 2018, no. 4.

Kolodko G., *Globalization and Catching-up: from Recession to Growth in Transition Economies*, "Communist and Post-Communist Studies" 2001, No. 34.

Konarski X., Sibiga G., Zastosowanie środków komunikacji elektronicznej w postępowaniu administra-cyjnym ogólnym po nowelizacji K.p.a. [Adoption of Electronic Means of Communication in General Administrative Proceedings Following Amendment to the Code of Administrative Procedure], "Monitor Prawniczy" 2006, No. 2.

Kowalski M., *Prawo pomocy w systemie ochrony praw człowieka* [Legal Assistance in the System of Protection of Human Rights], Warsaw 2013.

Kusiak-Winter R., Wartości i antywartości w prawie administracyjnym z perspektywy nauki administracji [Values and Anti-Values in Administrative Law; Perspective of Administrative Studies] in: *Antywartości w prawie administracyjnym* [Anti-Values in Administrative Law], A. Błaś (ed.), Warsaw 2016.

Kwietko-Bębnowski M., Informatyzacja sądów administracyjnych – próba oceny i poradnik praktyczny [Computerisation of Administrative Courts – Evaluation Attempt and Practical Guide], "Przegląd Podatkowy" 2020, No. 6.

Langrod J., *Zarys sądownictwa administracyjnego ze szczególnym uwzględnieniem sądownictwa admi-nistracyjnego w Polsce* [Outline of Administrative Judiciary: Including in Particular Administrative Judiciary in Poland], Warsaw 1925.

Leszczyński L., Wykładnia celowościowo-funkcjonalna przepisów prawa administracyjnego [Functional and Teleological Interpretation of the Provisions of Administrative Law] in: L. Leszczyński, M. Zirk-Sadowski, B. Wojciechowski, Wykładnia w prawie administracyjnym, System Prawa Administracyjnego [Interpretation of Administrative Law. System of Administrative Law], C.H. Beck, Warsaw 2015.

Lenaerts K., Gutiérrez-Fons J.A., *Metody wykładni Trybunału Sprawiedliwości Unii Europejskiej* [Methods of Interpretation of the Court of Justice of the European Union], Warszawa 2024.

Litwińczuk H., *Obejście prawa podatkowego w świetle doświadczeń międzynarodowych* [Circumvention of Tax Law in the Light of International Experience], "Przegląd Podatkowy" 1999, no. 4.

Lucas R., *Macroeconomic Priorities*, "American Economic Review" 2003, Vol. 93, No. 1, pp. 1–14.

Łętowska E., *Multicentryczność współczesnego systemu prawa i jej konsekwencje* [Multicentricity of the Modern System of Law and its Consequences], "Państwo i Prawo" 2005.

Mączyński D., *Chapter III Wpływ orzeczeń Trybunału Sprawiedliwości Unii Europejskiej na stanowienie przepisów dotyczących pozostałych danin publicznych [w:] Wpływ orzecznictwa Trybunału Sprawiedliwości Unii Europejskiej na stanowienie polskiego prawa podatkowego [Influence of the rulings of the Court of Justice of the European Union on the establishment of provisions concerning other public taxes [in:] Influence of the case law of the Court of Justice of the European Union on the establishment of Polish tax law]*, Warsaw 2021.

Metelska-Szaniawska K., Bełdowski J., *Ekonomiczna analiza prawa (Law &Economics) – wprowadzenie* [Economic Analysis of Law (Law & Economics) – Introduction] in: R. Coote, T. Ulen, *Ekonomiczna analiza prawa* [Economic Analysis of Law], C.H. Beck, Warsaw 2011.

Mudrecki A., *Główne problemy występujące w podatkach dochodowych na tle orzecznictwa sądów administracyjnych* [Main Problems in Income Taxes in the Context of Case Law of Administrative Courts] "Annales Universitatis Mariae Curie-Skłodowska" 2016, sectio H, vol. L1.

Niewiadomski Z., Zirk-Sadowski M., *Prawo wobec wyzwań epoki cyfryzacji* [Challenges of the Era of Digitalisation Facing the Law] in: *Cyfryzacja gospodarki i społeczeństwa – szanse i wyzwania dla sektorów infrastrukturalnych* [Digitalisation of the Economy and Society – Opportunities and Challenges Facing the Infrastructural Sectors], J. Gajewski, W. Paprocki, J. Pieregud (eds.), Gdańsk 2016.

Niewiadomski Z., *Wyzwania współczesności i ich wpływ na treść pojęcia „administracja publiczna"* [Contemporary Challenges and Their Impact on the Notion of "Public Administration"] in: *System prawa administracyjnego* [System of Administrative Law], Vol. 1, *Instytucje prawa administracyjnego* [Institutions of Administrative Law], R. Hauser, Z. Niewiadomski, A. Wróbel (eds.), Warsaw 2015.

North D.C., *Institutions, Ideology and Economic Performance*, "Cato Journal" 1992, Vol. 11, No. 3, Polish translation after: *Instytucje, ideologia a wyniki gospodarcze*, Forum Obywatelskiego Roz-woju, Warszawa 2007, https://for.org.pl/upload/File/Instytucje_%20ideologia_%20i_%20wyniki_%20gospodarcze1.pdf (accessed on: 5/11/2022).

Owczarczuk S., *Ewolucja statusu gminy jako podatnika z perspektywy 25 lat funkcjonowania podatku od towarów i usług w Polsce – wnioski de lege lata i postulaty de lege ferenda* [Evolution of the status of a municipality as a taxpayer from the perspective of 25 years of the functioning of the goods and services tax in Poland – conclusions de lege lata and postulates de lege ferenda], ST 2020, no. 6.

Piątek W., Skoczylas A., *Sądownictwo administracyjne po II wojnie światowej* [Administrative Judiciary after World War II] in: *Sądowa kontrola administracji publicznej* [Judicial Review of Public Administration], Vol. 10, R. Hauser, Z. Niewiadomski, A. Wróbel (eds.), Warsaw.

Pietrasz P., *Informatyzacja polskiego postępowania przed sądami administracyjnymi a jego zasady ogólne* [Computerisation of the Polish Administrative Court Proceedings and General Principles that Apply to It], Warsaw 2020.

Recommendations to national courts on the submission of references for a preliminary ruling (OJ EU. C. 2019, No. 380).

Schauer F., *Formalism*, "Yale Law Journal" 1988, Vol. 97, No. 4.

Skoczylas A., *Problem zachowania jednolitości orzecznictwa sądów administracyjnych*, [in:] *System Prawa Administracyjnego, t. 10, Sądowa kontrola administracji publicznej* [The problem of preserving the uniformity of the jurisprudence of administrative courts, [in:] System Prawa Administracyjnego, vol. 10, Judicial control of public administration] R. Hauser, Z. Niewiadomski, A. Wróbel (ed.), Warszawa 2016.

Świątkiewicz J., *Jak kształtowało się orzecznictwo Naczelnego Sądu Administracyjnego* [Evolution of the Case Law of the Supreme Administrative Court] in: *Sądownictwo administracyjne gwarantem wolności i praw obywatelskich 1980–2005* [Administrative Judiciary as a Guarantor of Civil Rights and Freedoms 1980–2005], J. Góral, R. Hauser, J. Trzciński (eds.), Warsaw 2005.

Torriti J., *Impact Assessment and the Liberalization of the EU Energy Markets: Evidence-Based Policy-Making or Policy-Based Evidence-Making?*, "JCMS: Journal of Common Market Studies", Vol. 48, No. 4.

Trzciński J., *Sądownictwo administracyjne jako gwarant ochrony wolności i praw jednostki* [Administrative Judiciary as a Guarantor of Protection of the Rights and Freedoms of the Individual] in: *Trzecia władza, sądy i trybunały w Polsce* [The Third Estate: Courts and Tribunals in Poland], A. Szmyt (ed.), Gdańsk 2008.

Waśko J., *Wszczynanie postępowań karnych skarbowych w trakcie postępowań kontrolnych – analiza praktyki wybranych urzędów kontroli skarbowej* [Initiation of Fiscal Criminal Proceedings During Audit Proceedings – Analysis of the Practice of the Selected Tax Audit Offices], "Przegląd Podatkowy" 2017, No. 2.

Wiatrowski R., *Gospodarczy cel zawarcia umowy jako kryterium oceny opodatkowania transakcji podatkiem od towarów i usług* [Economic Purpose of Concluding a Contract as a Criterion for Assessing the Taxation of a Transaction with Goods and Services Tax], "Analizy i Studia CASP" 2021, no. 1(11).

Wiatrowski R., *Wykładnia prounijna Naczelnego Sądu Administracyjnego w zakresie przepisów dotyczących podatku od towarów i usług* [Pro-Union Interpretation of the Supreme Administrative Court on Value Added Tax Regulations], Warsaw 2021.

Wiktorowska A., *Środki odwoławcze* [Legal Remedies] w: *Prawo o postępowaniu przed sądami administracyjnymi. Komentarz* [Law on Proceedings before Administrative Courts. Commentary], R. Hauser, M. Wierzbowski (eds.), Warsaw 2013.

Wild M. (ed.), Dziurda M., Rylski P., Sadomski J., *Ustawa o kosztach sądowych w sprawach cywilnych. Analiza funkcjonowania – wnioski* de lege ferenda [Act on Court Costs in Civil Cases. Analysis of the Functioning – Conclusions *de lege ferenda*], The Institute of Justice 2015.

Wiśniewski L., *Gwarancje praw i wolności człowieka i obywatela w przyszłej konstytucji* [Guarantees of Human and Civil Rights and Freedoms in Future Constitution] in: *Prawa, wolności i obowiązki człowieka i obywatela w nowej polskiej konstytucji* [Rights, Freedoms, and Duties of a Person and a Citizen in the New Polish Constitution], Poznań 1990.

Wojciechowski B., Stosowanie prawa podatkowego przez sądy administracyjne w sytuacji interpretacyjnego nego pluralizmu instytucjonalnego i otwartej tekstowości prawa [Application of Tax Law by Administrative Courts When Faced with Institutional Pluralism of Interpretation and Open Textuality of the Law], "Państwo i Prawo" 2019, No. 12.

Woś T., Knysiak-Molczyk H., Romańska M., *Postępowanie sądowoadministracyjne* [Administrative Court Proceedings], Warsaw 2017.

Woś T., Wyroki interpretacyjne i zakresowe w orzecznictwie Trybunału Konstytucyjnego [Interpretative and Limited Judgements in the Case Law of the Constitutional Tribunal], "Studia Iuridica Lublinensia" 2016, Vol. XXV, No. 3.

Zawadzki S., *Mój życiowy sukces: NSA* [My Life Success: the SAC] in: *XX lat Naczelnego Sądu Administracyjnego* [Twenty Years of the Supreme Administrative Court], Warsaw 2000.

Zimmermann J., *Z podstawowych zagadnień sądownictwa administracyjnego* [On the Basics of Administrative Judiciary] in: *Sądownictwo administracyjne gwarantem wolności i praw obywatelskich 1980–2005* [Administrative Judiciary as the Guarantor of Civil Rights and Freedoms 1980–2005], J. Góral, R. Hauser, J. Trzciński (eds.), Warsaw 2005.

Zirk-Sadowski M., Golecki M., Wojciechowski B., *Multicentrism as an Emerging Paradigm in Legal Theory*, Peter Lang, Frankfurt am Main 2009.

Zukowski R., *Stabilization and Recession in a Transitional Economy: The Case of Poland*, "World Development" 1993, Vol. 21, No. 7, pp. 1163–1178.

Internet Sources

A Mean Feat, The Economist, 9.01.2016, https://www.economist.com/finance-and-econo-mics/2016/01/09/a-mean-feat (accessed on: 22/08/2022).

CASE, *Study and Reports on the VAT Gap in the EU-28 Member States*, 2020, https://op.europa.eu/s/wNXJ (accessed on: 22/08/2022).

CEPEJ, *European Judicial Systems Efficiency and Quality of Justice*, Edition 2016 (2014 data), CEPEJ STUDIES, No. 23, https://rm.coe.int/european-judicial-systems-eficiency-and-quality-of--justice-cepej-stud/1680788228 (accessed on: 22/08/2022).

https://curia.europa.eu/jcms/upload/docs/application/pdf/2023-03/stats_cour_2022_pl.pdf.

Annual Information on the Activities of the National Revenue Information, https://www.kis.gov.pl/dzia-lalnosc/raporty-z-dzialalnosci (accessed on:22/08/2022).

Costello C. et al., *Economic Value of the Judiciary: A Pilot Study for Five Countries on Volume, Value and Duration of Large Commercial Cases*, 2020, https://www.encj.eu/node/563 (accessed on: 22/08/2022).

Galligan D., Matczak M., *Strategie orzekania sądowego, Raport opracowany w ramach programu Sprawne Państwo* [Strategies for Judicial Adjudication; Report Produced under the Efficient State Programme], Ernst & Young, Warsaw 2005, https://www.researchgate.net/profile/ Marcin-Matczak/publication/238704455_Strategie_orzekania_sadowego/links/0046352ed840402adf000000/Strategie-orzekania-sadowego.pdf (accessed on: 22/08/2022).

Goetz K., Zubek R., Stanowienie Prawa w Polsce. Reguły Legislacyjne a jakość ustawodawstwa, Raport opracowany w ramach programu Sprawne Państwo [Law-Making in Poland. Legislative Rules versus the Quality of Legislation; Report Produced under the Efficient State Programme], Ernst&Young, Warsaw 2005, https://www.inpris.pl/fileadmin/user_upload/documents/Biblioteka_PL/Stanowienie_Prawa_w_Polsce._Regu%C5%82y_Legislacyjne_a_jako%C5%9B%C4%87_ustawodawstwa.pdf (accessed on: 22/08/2022).

Kopińska G., Makowski G., Waglowski P., Wiszowaty M., *Tworzenie i konsultowanie rządowych projektów ustaw* [Development and Consultation of Government Draft Acts of Law], 2014, https://www.batory.org.pl/upload/files/Programy%20operacyjne/Odpo-wiedzialne%20Panstwo/Tworzenie_i_konsultowanie.pdf (accessed on: 22/08/2022).

Ladziński A. et al., *Instrumentalne wszczynanie postępowań karnych skarbowych w trakcie postępo-wań kontrolnych i podatkowych – analiza praktyki stosowania art. 70 § 6 pkt 1 Ordynacji Podatko-wej* [Instrumental Initiation of Fiscal Criminal Proceedings During Tax Audit Proceedings – Analysis of the Practice of Application of Article 70(6)(1) of Tax Ordinance], https://gww.pl/raport-instrumentalne-wszczynanie-postepowan-kar-2/.pdf (accessed on: 22/08/2022).

Majkowska M., Czy zobowiązania podatkowe zabezpieczone hipoteką się przedawniają? TK milczy, organy zawieszają postępowania [Do Mortgage-Secured Tax Liabilities Prescribe? The Constitutional Tribunal Falls Silent and the Authorities Suspend Proceedings], "Gazeta Prawna" 9/03/2020, https://podatki.gazetaprawna.pl/artykuly/1458236,zobowiazania-podatkowe-przedawnienie-hipoteka-trybunal-konstytucyjny.html (accessed on: 22/08/2022).

Supreme Audit Office, Impact Assessment as Part of Governmental Legislation Process, reg. No. 174/2017/P/16/094/LWA, 2017, https://www.nik.gov.pl/plik/id,16190, vp,18712. pdf (accessed on: 22/08/2022).

Opinion of 24 April 2020 on the Amendments Proposed by the Legislative Council to the Provisions of the Civil Procedure Code, https://www.gov.pl/web/radalegislacyjna/opinia-z-24-kwietnia-2020-r-na-temat-proponowanych-przez-rade-legislacyjna-zmian-w--przepisach-kodeksu-postepowania-cywilnego#_ftn29 (accessed on: 22/08/2022).

Letter of the Minister of Finance of 25 October 2010 to the Constitutional Tribunal (No. DD2/033/21 0/DZI/1 O/BMI9-12787), https://ipo.trybunal.gov.pl/ipo/dok?dok=F1834434053%2FSK_18_09_MF_2010_10_25_nu_ADO.pdf (accessed on: 22/08/2022).

"Lepsze Regulacje 2015" [Better Regulation 2015] Programme, Annex to the Resolution No. 13/2013 of the Council of Ministers of 22 January 2013, https://www.inpris.pl/fileadmin/user_upload/documents/Biblioteka_PL/Program_Lepsze_Regulacje_2015_01.pdf (accessed on: 22/08/2022).

The Judicial Review of Administrative Acts – Recommendation Rec (2004) 20 and Explanatory Memorandum (2005) https://book.coe.int/en/legal-instruments/3241-the-judicial-review--of-administrative-acts-recommendation-rec200420-and-explanatory-memorandum.html (accessed on: 22/08/2022).

Address of the Ombudsman to the Minister of Justice delivered on 2 June 2020 (No.: IV.510.21.2020.MC), https://bip.brpo.gov.pl/sites/default/files/Wystapienie%20do%20MS,%202.06.2020.pdf (accessed on: 22/08/2022).

Legal Acts

Treaty on the Functioning of the European Union (OJ 2004. No. 90, item 864/2, consolidated version: OJ 2016. C 202, p. 47).

Constitutional Act of 19 February 1947 on the Regime and Scope of Operation of the Supreme Authorities of the Republic of Poland (Journal of Laws No. 18, item 71, as amended).

Constitutional Act of 23 April 1992 on the Mode of Developing and Passing of the Constitution of the Republic of Poland (Journal of Laws No. 67, item 336).

Council Directive 2006/112/EC of 28 November 2006 on the common system of value added tax.

Act of 26 July 1991 on Personal Income Tax (Journal of Laws 2000 No. 14, item 176, as amended).

Act of 10 January 2014 Amending the Act on Computerisation of Activities of Entities Performing Public Tasks and Certain Other Acts (Journal of Laws, item 183, as amended).

Act of 11 May 1995 on the Supreme Administrative Court (Journal of Laws No. 74, item 368).

Act of 14 May 2020 Amending Certain Acts as Regards Shielding Activities in Connection with the Spread of SARS-CoV-2 Virus (Journal of Laws, item 875, as amended).

Act of 16 November 2006 Amending the Act on Tax Ordinance and Certain Other Acts (Dz.U.2006.217.1590).

Act of 16 November 2016 on the National Tax Administration (Journal of Laws of 2016, item 1947).

Act of 16 November 2016 on the National Tax Administration (Journal of Laws of 2016, item 1947, as amended).

Act of 17 February 2005 on Computerisation of Activities of Public Entities (Journal of Laws No. 64, item 565).

Act of 17 May 1990 on Division of Tasks and Jurisdiction Specified in Special Acts among the Bodies of Gmina and Government Administration and on the Amendments to Some Acts (Journal of Laws No. 34, item 198).

Act of 2 July 2004 on Freedom of Business Activity (Journal of Laws of 2004 No. 173, item 1807, as amended).

Act of 2 March 2020 on Special Solutions Related to the Prevention, Counteracting, and Combating of COVID-19, Other Infectious Diseases and Crisis Situations Caused by Them (Journal of Laws, item 374, as amended).

Act of 2 March 2020 on Special Solutions Related to the Prevention, Counteracting, and Combating of COVID-19, Other Infectious Diseases and Crisis Situations Caused by Them (Journal of Laws of 2021, item 2095, as amended).

Act of 22 March 1990 on Self-Government Officers (Journal of Laws No. 21, item 123).

Act of 22 September 2006 Amending the Act on Tax Audit and Some Other Acts (Journal of Laws No. 191, item 1413).

Act of 23 April 1964 on the Civil Code (Journal of Laws of 2017, item 459). Act of 24 July 1999 on the Customs Service (Journal of Laws of 1999 No. 72, item 802).

Act of 24 July 1999 Amending the Act on the Departments of Government Administration and Some Other Acts (Journal of Laws No. 70, item 778).

Act of 25 July 2002 on the System of Administrative Courts (Journal of Laws of 2002 No. 153, item 1269, as amended).

Act of 27 August 2009 on the Customs Service (Journal of Laws of 2009 No. 168, item 1323).

Act of 28 July 2005 on Court Costs in Civil Cases (Journal of Laws of 2005 No. 167, item 1398).

Act of 28 May 2021 Amending the Act on the Civil Procedure Code and Some Other Acts (Journal of Laws, item 1090).

Act of 29 August 1997 on the Tax Ordinance (Journal of Laws of 1997 No. 137, item 926, as amended).

Act of 30 August 2002 on Law on Proceedings before Administrative Courts (Journal of Laws 2002 No. 153, item 1270, as amended).

Act of 31 January 1980 on the Supreme Administrative Court and Amendment to Code of Administrative Procedure (Journal of Laws No. 4, item 8).

Act of 8 March 1990 on Local Self-Government (Journal of Laws No. 16, item 95). Act of 28 September 1991 on Tax Audit (Dz.U.1991.100.442, as amended).

Act on Local Taxes and Fees (Journal of Laws of 2006 No. 121, item 844, as amended).

Act of 26 July 1991 on Personal Income Tax (consolidated text in Dz.U. of 2000 No. 14, item 176 as amended)

Regulation of the Minister of Health of 20 March 2020 Announcing the Pandemic State of Emergency on the Territory of the Republic of Poland (Journal of Laws, item 491, as amended).

Regulation of the President of the Republic of Poland of 28 September 1995 on the Establishment of the Bylaws and the Organisational Structure of the Supreme Administrative Court (Journal of Laws No. 112, item. 540, as amended).

Regulation of the Council of Ministers of 16 December 2003 on the Amounts of and Detailed Rules for Collecting Court Fees in Proceedings before Administrative Courts (Journal of Laws of 2003 No. 221, item 2193).

Resolution No. 125 of the Council of Ministers of 4 September 2001 Amending the Resolution on the Bylaws of the Council of Ministers (Monitor Polski 2001 No. 33, item 547).

Resolution No. 13 of the Council of Ministers of 25 February 1997 on the Bylaws of the Council of Ministers (Monitor Polski of 1997 No. 15, item 144, as amended).

Resolution No. 190 of the Council of Ministers of 29 October 2013 on the Bylaws of the Council of Ministers (Monitor Polski of 2022, item 348).

Resolution No. 49 of the Council of Ministers of 19 March 2002 on the Bylaws of the Council of Ministers (Monitor Polski of 2002 No. 13, item 221, as amended).

Ordinance No. 14 of the President of the SAC of 6 August 2015 on the Establishment of the Rules of Office at Administrative Courts (not announced).

Case Law

(1) Decision of the Supreme Administrative Court of 6 December 2018, file ref. I FSK 2261/15

(2) Judgment of the CJEU of 15 October 2020, in case, C – 335/19, E. sp. z o.o. sp. k., ECLI:EU:C:2020:829

(3) Judgment of the CJEU of 12 January 2006 in Joined Cases C 354/03, C 355/03 and C 484/03 Optigen and Others, ECLI:EU:C:2006:16

(4) Judgment of the CJEU of 6 July 2006 in Joined Cases C 439/04 and C 440/04 Kittel and Recolta Recycling, ECLI:EU:C:2006:446

(5) Order of the Provincial Administrative Court in Łódź of 12 December 2012, file ref. SA/Łd 1140/12

(6) Decision of the Supreme Administrative Court of 6 March 2014, file ref., I FSK 516/13

(7) Decision of the Supreme Administrative Court of 19 June 2018, file ref. I FSK 126/18

(8) Judgment of the CJEU of 17 October 2019, in case C-653/18 Unitel, ECLI:EU:C:2019:876

(9) Decision of the Provincial Administrative Court (WSA) in Wrocław of 3 October 2007, case number I SA/Wr 971/07

(10) Order of the Supreme Administrative Court of 15 March 2022. II FSK 1602/19

(11) Decision of the Provincial Administrative Court (WSA) in Wrocław of 25 January 2024, file ref. I SA/Wr 4/23

(12) Judgment of the CJEU of 21.03.2018, in case C -533/16, ECLI:EU:C:2018:204

(13) Judgment of the CJEU of 26 April 2018, in case C -81/17, Zabrus Siret, ECLI:EU:C:2018:283

(14) Judgment of the CJEU of 8 September 2015, in Case C -105/14, Ivo Taricco, ECLI:EU:C:2015:555

(15) Judgment of the CJEU of 5 December 2017, in Case C -42/17, M.A.S. and M.B., ECLI:EU:C:2017:936

(16) Order of the Supreme Administrative Court of 19 May 2016, reference I FSK 224/15

(17) Judgment of the CJEU of 20 December 2017, C -500/16, ECLI:EU:C:2017:996

(18) Judgment of the Provincial Administrative Court (WSA) in Poznań of 9 December 2004, act signature I SA/Po 2342/03

(19) Judgment of the Supreme Administrative Court of 14 December 2004, file ref. FSK 826/04

(20) Judgment of the Supreme Administrative Court of 17.12.2009, file ref. I FSK 1382/08

(21) Wyrok WSA w Białymstoku z 25.01.2010 r., sygn. akt. I SA/Bk 556/09

(22) Judgement of the Supreme Administrative Court of 18.03.2010, file ref. II FSK 1838/08

(23) Judgement of the Supreme Administrative Court of 21.04.2011, file ref. I FSK 487/10

(24) Judgement of the Supreme Administrative Court of 21.04.2011, file ref. I FSK 488/10
(25) Judgment of the Provincial Administrative Court (WSA) in Rzeszów of 9.05.2017, I SA/Rz 143/17
(26) Judgment of the Provincial Administrative Court (WSA) in Lublin of 31.01.2018, file ref. I SA/Lu 941/17
(27) Resolution of the Supreme Administrative Court of 25 June 2012, file ref. II FPS 2/12
(28) Judgment of the Provincial Administrative Court (WSA) in Warsaw of 14 April 2023, file ref. III SA/Wa 2017/22
(29) Judgment of the Provincial Administrative Court (WSA) in Kraków of 11 July 2007, file ref. I SA/Kr 1509/06
(30) Resolution of the Supreme Administrative Court of 25 June 2012, file ref. II FPS 2/12
(31) Judgment of the Provincial Administrative Court (WSA) in Warsaw of 3 September 2015, file ref. VIII SA/Wa 1147/14
(32) Judgments of the CJEU of 7 October 2010 in Joined Cases C 53/09 and C 55/09 Loyalty Management UK and Baxi Group, ECLI:EU:C:2010:590
(33) Judgments of the CJEU of 7 October 2010, in Case C 653/11 Paul Newey, ECLI:EU:C:2010:590
(34) Judgment of 22 November 2018, in Case C 295/17 MEO – Serviços de Comunicações e Multimédia, EU:C:2018:942
(35) CJ judgments in Joined Cases C-180/10 and C-181/10, Słaby Kuć, ECLI:EU:C:2011:589
(36) Judgment of the CJ of 20 June 2013, in Case C-219/12, Urfahr, ECLI:EU:C:2013:413
(37) Judgment of the CJ of 9 November 2017, in Case C 499/16, AZ, ECLI:EU:C:2017:846
(38) Judgment of the CJEU of 24 June 1969 in Case 29/68, Milchkontor, ECLI:EU:C:1969:27
(39) Order of the CJEU of 5 March 1986 in Case 69/85, Wünsche Handelsgesellschaft, ECLI:EU:C:1986:104
(40) Judgment of the Supreme Administrative Court of 25 January 2018, file ref. I FSK 1155/15
(41) Judgment of the Supreme Administrative Court of 7 February 2018, file ref. I FSK 1662/15

(42) Judgment of the CJEU of 21 September 2017, in Case C-605/15, Aviva, ECLI:EU:C:2017:718
(43) Judgment of the Supreme Administrative Court of 15 March 2018, file reference I FSK 953/15
(44) Judgment of the Supreme Administrative Court of 18 January 2023; file ref. I FSK 923/19
(45) Decision of the Provincial Administrative Court (WSA) in Wrocław of 28 December 2023, file ref. I Sa/Wr 92/23
(46) Order of the Supreme Administrative Court of 16 June 2023, file ref. I FSK 535/20
(47) Order of the Supreme Administrative Court of 19 April 2023, file ref. III FSK 3/22
(48) Order of the Provincial Administrative Court (WSA) in Wrocław of 28 January 2022, file ref. I SA/Wr 208/21
(49) Order of the Supreme Administrative Court of 23 February 2022, file ref. I FSK 1712/18
(50) Order of the Supreme Administrative Court of 26 May 2022, file ref. I FSK 1212/18
(51) Order of the Supreme Administrative Court of 23 June 2022, file ref. I FSK 1225/18
(52) Decision of the Provincial Administrative Court (WSA) in Wrocław of 22 September 2022, file ref. I SA/Wr 73/22
(53) Order of the Provincial Administrative Court (WSA) in Gliwice of 28 November 2022, file ref. I SA/Gl 942/22
(54) Order of the Supreme Administrative Court of 28 December 2022, file ref. I GSK 380/19
(55) Order of the CJ of 6 March 2007, in case C-168/06, Ceramika Paradyż, ECLI:EU:C:2007:139
(56) Judgment of the CJEU in Case C-255/02 Halifax and Others, ECLI:EU:C:2006:121
(57) Judgment of the CJEU of 8 February 1998, in Case C-320/88 Shipping and Forwarding Enterprise Safe, ECLI:EU:C:1990:61
(58) Judgment of the CJEU of 14 July 2005 in Case C-435/03 British American Tobacco and Newman Shipping, ECLI:EU:C:2005:464
(59) Judgment of the CJEU: of 3 June 2010 in Case C-237/09 De Fruytier, ECLI:EU:C:2010:316

(60) Judgment of the CJEU of 18 July 2013 in Case C-78/12 Evita-K, ECLI:EU:C:2013:486
(61) Judgment of the CJEU of 21 November 2013, in Case C-494/12 Dixons Retail, ECLI:EU:C:2013:758
(62) Judgment in Case C-494/12 Dixons Retail
(63) Judgment of the Supreme Administrative Court of 26.03.2015, I FSK 2174/13
(64) Judgment of the CJEU of 25.02.1999, in Case C-349/96 CPP, ECLI:EU:C:1999:93
(65) Judgment of the CJEU of 27 October 2005, in Case C-41/04 Levob Verzekeringen BV, ECLI:EU:C:2005:649
(66) Judgment of the CJEU of 17 January 2013, in BGŻ Leasing, C 224/11, EU:C:2013:15
(67) Judgment of the CJEU of 16 April 2015, in Wojskowa Agencja Mieszkaniowa w Warszawie, C 42/14, EU:C:2015:229
(68) Judgment of the CJEU of 18 October 2018, Volkswagen Financial Services (UK), C 153/17, EU:C:2018:845
(69) Judgment of the CJEU of 19 November 2009,Don Bosco Onroerend Goed, C 461/08, EU:C:2009:722
(70) Judgment of the CJEU of 28 October 2010, in Axa UK, C 175/09, EU:C:2010:646
(71) Judgment of the CJEU of 27 September 2012, in Field Fisher Waterhouse, C 392/11, EU:C:2012:597
(72) Judgment of the Supreme Administrative Court of 24 October 2023, file ref. I FSK 2201/18
(73) Judgment of the CJEU of 8 May 2019, in EN.SA., C 712/17, EU:C:2019:374
(74) Judgment of the CJEU of 25 May 2023, in Case C – 114/22, ECLI:EU:C:2023:430
(75) Judgment of the CJEU of 6 September 2012, in Mecsek-Gabona, C 273/11, EU:C:2012:547
(76) CJEU order of 9 January 2023, in A.T.S. 2003, C 289/22, EU:C:2023:26
(77) Judgment of the Supreme Administrative Court of 24 March 2020, file ref. I FSK 109/20
(78) Judgment of the Supreme Administrative Court of 17 May 2023, file ref. I FSK 82/23
(79) Judgment of the Supreme Administrative Court of 20 October 2022, file ref. I FSK 1347/18

(80) Judgment of the Supreme Administrative Court of 24 March 2023, file ref. I FSK 110/20

(81) Judgment of the Provincial Administrative Court (WSA) in Warsaw of 30 March 2021, file ref. III SA/Wa 1575/20

(82) Judgment by the Supreme Administrative Court of 7 November 1991, file ref. SA/Po 1198/91

(83) Judgment of the Supreme Administrative Court of 29 May 2002, file ref. III SA 2602/00

(84) Ruling of the Supreme Administrative Court of 23 November 2021, file ref. I FSK 2310/19

(85) Judgment of the Supreme Administrative Court of 7 November 2023, file ref. I FSK 40/20

(86) Judgment of the Supreme Administrative Court of 12 July 2006, file ref. II FSK 995/05

(87) Judgment of the Supreme Administrative Court of 8 February 2013, file ref. I FSK 477/12

(88) Judgment of the Supreme Administrative Court of 13 March 2014, file ref. I FSK 614/13

(89) Judgment of the Provincial Administrative Court (WSA) in Warsaw of 19 December 2011, file ref. III SA/Wa 897/11

(90) Judgment of the Provincial Administrative Court (WSA) in Warsaw of 7 October 2015, file ref. III SA/Wa 4019/14

(91) Wyrok WSA w Poznaniu z 6 listopada 2009r. sygn. akt. I SA/Po 479/09

(92) Judgment of the WSA in Wrocław of 29 May 2015, file ref. I SA/Wr 329/15

(93) Decision of the Supreme Administrative Court of 22 October 2013, I FSK 1389/12

(94) Judgment of the Supreme Administrative Court of 14 March 2023, file ref. I FSK 205/20

(95) Judgment of the CJEU of 2 May 2019, in Case C-224/18 Budimex, ECLI:EU:C:2019:347

(96) Order of the Supreme Administrative Court of 28 November 2017, file ref. I FSK 65/16

(97) Judgment of the Supreme Administrative Court of 18 April 2013, file ref. I FSK 943/12

(98) Judgment of the Supreme Administrative Court of 6 July 2017, file ref. I FSK 2148/15

(99) Judgment of the Supreme Administrative Court of 18 July 2019, file ref. I FSK 65/16

(100) Judgment of the Supreme Administrative Court of 10 October 2019, file ref. I FSK 1455/17

(101) Judgment of the Supreme Administrative Court of 14 May 2021, file ref. I FSK 580/21

(102) Judgment of the NSA of 10 December 2013, file ref. I FSK 311/12

(103) Judgment of the CJEU of 29 September 2015, in case C-276/14, Gmina Wrocław, ECLI:EU:C:2015:431

(104) Judgment of the Supreme Administrative Court of 18 October 2011, file ref. I FSK 1369/10

(105) Resolution of the Supreme Administrative Court of 26 October 2015, file ref. I FPS 4/15

(106) Decision of the Supreme Administrative Court of 22 July 2020, file ref. I FSK 2024/17

(107) Judgment of the Supreme Administrative Court of 29 May 2014, file ref. I FSK 757/13 from 27.10.2015, file ref. I FSK 546-550/14

(108) Judgment of the Supreme Administrative Court of 5 July 2016, file ref. I FSK 181-183/15

(109) Judgment of the CJEU of 22 March 2022, in case C 697/20, W.G., ECLI:EU:C:2022:210

(110) Judgment of the Supreme Administrative Court of 8 September 2022, file ref. I FSK 2024/17

(111) Judgment of the Supreme Administrative Court of 1 July 2022, file ref. I FSK 1006/18

(112) Judgment of the Supreme Administrative Court of 13 July 2022, file ref. I FSK 888/20

(113) Judgment of the Supreme Administrative Court of 7 June 2023, file ref. I FSK 440/19

(114) Judgment by 7 judges of the Supreme Administrative Court of 29 October 2007, file ref. I FPS 3/07

(115) Ruling of the Supreme Administrative Court of 9 March 2010, file ref. I FSK 2039/08

(116) Judgment of the Supreme Administrative Court of 18 October 2011, file ref. I FSK 1536/10

(117) Judgment of the Supreme Administrative Court of 5 April 2017, file ref. I FSK 1423/15

(118) Judgment of the Supreme Administrative Court of 13 November 2012, file ref. I FSK 1805/11

(119) Judgment of the Supreme Administrative Court of 18 December 2014, file ref. I FSK 1991/13

(120) Decision of the Supreme Administrative Court of 18 January 2023, file ref. I FSK 923/19

(121) Decision of 28 December 2023, file ref. I SA/Wr 92/23

Ius, Lex et Res Publica
Studies in Law, Philosophy and Political Cultures

Edited by Barbara Janusz-Pohl
Anna Jaron

Vol. 1 Anna Jaron: Socio-Economic Constitutional Rights in Democratisation Processes. An Account of the Constitutional Dialogue Theory. 2012.

Vol. 2 Stanisław Filipowicz: Democracy – The Power of Illusion. 2013.

Vol. 3 Teresa Dukiet-Nagórska (ed.): The Postulates of Restorative Justice and the Continental Model of Criminal Law. As Illustrated by Polish Criminal Law 2014.

Vol. 4 Agnieszka Kupzok: Enforcement of Patents on Geographically Divisible Inventions. An Inquiry into the Standard of Substantive Patent Law Infringement in Cross-Border Constellations. 2015.

Vol. 5 Alicja Jagielska-Burduk / Wojciech Szafrański: Legal Issues in Cultural Heritage Management. A Polish Perspective. 2016.

Vol. 6 Maciej Mataczyński (ed.): The Takeover of Public Companies as a Mode of Exercising EU Treaty Freedoms. 2017.

Vol. 7 Maciej Barczewski (ed.): Value of Information. Intellectual Property, Privacy and Big Data. 2018.

Vol. 8 Pawel Smoleń, Marcin Burzec: Introduction to Polish Tax Law. 2018.

Vol. 9 Łukasz Pohl, Konrad Burdziak: Judicial Interpretation of the 1997 Criminal Code Provisions on Self-Defence. 2019.

Vol. 10 Adam Szot: Judicial Review of Administrative Discretion. The Influence of Court Decisions on Administrative Actions. 2019.

Vol. 11 Michał Peno / Konrad Burdziak (eds.): The Concept of Modern Law. Polish and Central European Tradition. 2019.

Vol. 12 Leszek Leszczyński / Bartosz Liżewski / Adam Szot (eds.): Potential of Precedent in the Statutory Legal Order. 2019.

Vol. 13 Łukasz Bolesta: In Search of a Model for the Legal Protection of a Whistleblower in the Workplace in Poland. A legal and comparative study. 2020.

Vol. 14 Paweł Chmielnicki / Adam Sulikowski (eds.): New Perspectives on Legislation. A Comparative Approach. 2020.

Vol. 15 Marcin Burzec / Beata Kucia-Guściora / Paweł Smoleń: Agricultural Activity in Poland: A Fiscal and Legal Study. 2020.

Vol. 16 Magdalena Półtorak / Ilona Topa (eds.): Women, Children and (Other) Vulnerable Groups. Standards of Protection and Challenges for International Law. 2021.

Vol. 17 Josef Albert Fox: Die polnische Verfassung vom 3. Mai 1791. Hintergründe der Entstehung und der Außerkraftsetzung. Stellung Polens im Zeitalter der Aufklärung. 2021.

Vol. 18 Barbara Janusz-Pohl (ed.): Juvenile Justice Systems: Poland-Brazil-Portugal. 2021.

Vol. 19 Leszek Leszczyński: General Reference Clauses in the Judicial Process. Context of Legislative Intentions Interpretative Discretion. 2021.

Vol. 20 Francisco J. Campos Zamora: Das Problem der Begründung richterlicher Entscheidungen. Eine Analyse auf der Grundlage der Theorie der juristischen Argumentation. 2021.

Vol. 21 Aneta Skorupa-Wulczyńska: Language Rights of the Citizen of the European Union. 2022.

Vol. 22 Mateusz Osiecki: International Legal Aspects of Aerial Terrorism. Methods of Law Enforcement in Avia-tion. 2022.

Vol. 23 Vladimír Sharp / Gabriela Blahoudková / Jakub Handrlica (eds.): Law, Pandemics and Ownership Restrictions. 2022.

Vol. 24 Piotr Kasprzyk / Anna Konert: Drones – Future of Aviation Law? Interference of Public Law in Private Law. 2023.

Vol. 25 Szymon Pawelec (ed.): Consensual Procedures in Criminal Law – Comparative Perspective. 2023.

Vol. 26 Dorota Pudzianowska: The Statelessness in Public Law. 2023.

Vol. 27 Bogusław Przywora / Aleksander Wróbel: Formalised Access to Pre-jurisdictional Free Legal Aid. Analysis based on Example of Ukraine, Poland, Great Britain and Sweden. 2023.

Vol. 28 Ewa Dawidziuk / Patricia Panero / Anna Tarwacka (eds.): Family, Law, and Society: from Roman Law to the Present Day. 2023.

Vol. 29 Marian Grzybowski / Bogusław Przywora / Aleksandra Syryt (eds.): Free Legal Aid, Theory, Legal Basis and Practice. European Standards. 2023.

Vol. 30 Karolina Gmerek: Trial as a Social Communication Occurrence. Interactions Between Professional and Non-professional Participants of a Trial. 2023.

Vol. 31 Paweł Wiliński (ed.): Effective Legal Remedies in Criminal Justice System. European Perspective. 2024.

Vol. 32 Olga Sitarz / Anna Jaworska-Wieloch / Jakub Hanc : On the (Non)existence of the Right to Religious Freedom of Persons Deprived of Liberty. A Reconstruction of the Normative Standard Based on Polish and German Regulations in Comparison With Empirical Studies. 2024.

Vol. 33 Marian Grzybowski / Bogusław Przywora / Aleksandra Syryt (eds.) : Free Legal Aid – A Comparative Approach. Volume 2. 2024.

Vol. 34 Dominik J. Gajewski (ed.) : Functioning of Administrative Judiciary in the Context of Economic Changes. 2024.

www.peterlang.com

www.ingramcontent.com/pod-product-compliance
Ingram Content Group UK Ltd.
Pitfield, Milton Keynes, MK11 3LW, UK
UKHW021829100926
8556IPUK00004B/242

9 783631 919118